LEADING THE MODERN UNIVERSITY

York University's Presidents on Continuity
and Change, 1974–2014

Leading the Modern University

York University's Presidents on Continuity and Change, 1974–2014

EDITED BY LORNA R. MARSDEN

UNIVERSITY OF TORONTO PRESS
Toronto Buffalo London

ISBN 978-1-4426-4875-3

♾ Printed on acid-free, 100% post-consumer recycled paper with vegetable-based inks.

Library and Archives Canada Cataloguing in Publication

Leading the modern university : York University's presidents on continuity and change, 1974–2014 / edited by Lorna R. Marsden.

Includes bibliographical references and index.
ISBN 978-1-4426-4875-3 (cloth)

1. York University (Toronto, Ont.) – History. 2. York University (Toronto, Ont.) – Presidents. 3. College presidents – Ontario – Toronto – History. 4. Universities and colleges – Ontario – Toronto – History. I. Marsden, Lorna R., 1942–, author, editor

LE3.Y6 L42 2016   378.713′541   C2016-903247-7

University of Toronto Press acknowledges the financial assistance to its publishing program of the Canada Council for the Arts and the Ontario Arts Council, an agency of the Government of Ontario.

Canada Council **Conseil des Arts**
for the Arts **du Canada**

Funded by the   Financé par le
Government   gouvernement
of Canada   du Canada

Canadä

Contents

List of Figures and Tables

Figures

Tables

Acknowledgments

When recollected in tranquility, the challenges of serving as president of York University appeared to me to have much more to do with past plans and events than with innovation. On close examination the majority of the decisions I took with my Board and colleagues modified, updated, or added to the founding principles of the academic programs, the complexities of university funding rooted in the late 1960s in Ontario, or the morale issues accepted as standard practice in the culture of the campuses. To mark the fiftieth anniversary of York University I thought it was imperative to have an institutional history of those years prepared, and Professor Michiel Horn produced a splendid account. Others began to write their memoirs and analyses, and the more I read and discussed, the more important became the years between the late 1960s and the early 1970s. The two presidents in those crucial years – founding president Murray G. Ross and second president David Slater – have both died. Since then five presidents have held office at York University.

Fortunately not only are the presidents from 1974 to the present alive, they are the most congenial and interesting group of individuals, and with one exception are still living in Toronto and regularly present on campus. They had been consistently helpful during my presidency, even when they disagreed with my decisions, because they are all committed to the success of the University. How had they analysed and handled the fallout from the controversies of the early 1970s? A search of the literature on presidencies indicated that few are written from the inside viewpoint of more than one president at a single university. Yet here at York we had the opportunity for five individuals to present their analyses of the same issues.

In 2012 I had lunch with Ian Macdonald to test the idea. He thought it over and then gave it the nod. I approached Harry Arthurs to see if he was interested. He was thinking about writing his memoirs and I hope he still will do so, because this study is much more limited. Susan Mann was most reluctant. But we needed everyone if this idea was to attract a publisher. To my delight, in the end all the presidents, even the sitting president, agreed to write a chapter focused principally on the core issues they faced. I thank them for their commitment, their patience over the intervening years, and for all they have done to make this volume possible. The University of Toronto Press, with Acquisitions Editor Doug Hildebrand, accepted the proposal. In the late spring of 2013, we met in the Murray Ross Room at Glendon campus and made a plan.

After we had prepared the initial drafts of our own chapters and read the other chapters, we adjusted the plan, because some powerful themes emerged around which we focused our analysis. When we gave the first completed manuscript to the publisher, Doug Hildebrand found several excellent readers whose insightful comments have greatly helped, and we are grateful to them. Doug, with his wide knowledge of the post-secondary sector in Canada, has been unfailingly patient and encouraging at all stages. The final version has been significantly improved by our freelance copy editor, Barry Norris, who truly understands the niceties of endnotes and clear sentences.

We drew on the offices of York University's vice-president finance and administration for data and advice, and on those of the York University Development Corporation, the Media and Communications Department, and Alumni and Special Events for pictures and documents. Former York vice-president Sheldon Levy described his history with funding of the University, and Dr Paul Stenton generously gave us access to his 1992 doctoral dissertation, in which he explains and analyses the funding formula in Ontario up to 1986 and which, along with the York University Fact Book and the personal papers of the authors, is the source of much of our data. The work involved a great deal of the time of Suzanne Dubeau, archivist in the Clara Thomas Archives of York University; of the Secretariat, first under the leadership of Harriet Lewis and recently that of Maureen Armstrong; and of assistance recruited by each of the authors, as noted in the appropriate chapters. They and all their staff members have been unfailingly interested and helpful. Some retired during the writing of this volume, but nonetheless continued to help us by reading drafts and searching their own papers and memories. We hired a graduate student, Renée Jackson-Harper, to search out documents, and Caitlin Stewart to help with manuscript preparation. Funding for this support came from my research funds, but we drew heavily on the time and goodwill of many others, and the University as a whole has been most supportive of this project. We sought out the memories and advice of our colleagues, and some of the many individuals are recognized in the chapters that follow. All, including our families, have our deep and sincere gratitude. If we have it wrong, it is despite their best efforts and the fault is mine.

We hope this volume tells an engaging story of the development of York University as viewed by its recent leadership, adds to understanding of the modern university, and allows future presidents to see the roots of the challenges they might face.

Lorna R. Marsden
April 2016

Contributors

H. Ian Macdonald, 1974–84

Ian Macdonald came to the presidency of York University with richly diverse experience. He had earned a Bachelor of Commerce degree with the Governor General's Medal from the University of Toronto, followed by a Rhodes scholarship. At Oxford in the mid-1950s, he earned an MA and then a BPhil before returning to teach Economics at the University of Toronto. While moving up the ranks in Economics, he also served as dean of men at University College, giving him insight into the lives of undergraduates. In 1965 he was appointed chief economist for the government of Ontario and very soon afterward the most senior positions in Treasury. By 1972 he was deputy minister of economics and intergovernmental affairs. His long and distinguished contributions to public administration led to the Vanier Medal in 2000. In 2005 the government of Ontario created the H. Ian Macdonald Visiting Economist position in the Ministry of Finance in recognition of his work. In 2013 he was honoured as one of eight Legends of the Ontario Public Service and as an Alumnus of Influence by University College, University of Toronto.

His ten years as president and vice-chancellor of York University began in 1974, and he is still at York as professor of public policy and economics and president emeritus. Chapter 2 provides his account of his work as president. His contributions to York's reputation internationally have been extraordinary both in community service and in positions such as director of York International (1984–94) and leadership positions in the International Association of Universities, the Inter-American Organization for Higher Education, the Association for Commonwealth Universities, the North-South Institute, the Canadian Executive Service Organization, president of the Canadian Rhodes Scholars' Foundation, and president of the World University Service of Canada.

As an avid and still active hockey player, he was chairman of Hockey Canada and vice-chair of the Canadian Hockey Association. In 2013 York University created the Ian Macdonald Award for the member of the York Lions Men's Hockey team with the best academic record. He has received a great many other distinctions, including a number of honorary degrees from Canadian and international universities, including York University. He has received numerous medals and recognitions, including Officer of the Order of Canada.

When not travelling to international meetings and academic events, he can be found in his office in the Schulich School of Business on the Keele campus of York University.

Harry Arthurs, 1985–92

Harry Arthurs is University Professor Emeritus, former dean of Osgoode Hall Law School (1972–77), and former president of York University (1985–92). He has published extensively in the fields of legal education and the legal profession, legal history and legal theory, labour and administrative law, globalization, and constitutionalism. In addition to serving as an arbitrator and mediator in labour disputes, Arthurs has conducted inquiries and reviews at Canadian, British, and American universities, and has provided advice to governments on issues ranging from higher education policy to the constitution to labour and employment law. Most recently he has chaired reviews of federal labour standards legislation (2004–06), Ontario pension legislation (2006–08), and the funding of Ontario's workplace safety and insurance system (2010–12).

Arthurs' contributions have been recognized by his election as an associate of the Canadian Institute for Advanced Research, a fellow of the Royal Society of Canada, and a corresponding fellow of the British Academy. He has been awarded the Canada Council's Killam Prize for his lifetime contributions to the social sciences (2002), and both the Bora Laskin Prize (2003) and the Labour Law Research Network prize (2013) for his contributions to labour law. He was also co-winner (with Joseph Stiglitz) of the International Labour Organization's Decent Work Research Prize (2008). He has received honorary degrees from a number of Canadian universities.

Susan Mann, 1992–97

Susan Mann was born in Ottawa and raised in a CCF household of teachers that expanded during the parliamentary session to include MP Stanley Knowles, of whom she wrote a biography (*Stanley Knowles, the Man from Winnipeg North Centre*). As a girl and young woman she spent three separate years abroad, in Scotland, Switzerland, and Japan. A graduate in history from the University of Toronto, Western, and Laval, she began her teaching career at l'Université de Montréal. She subsequently taught at the University of Calgary and the

University of Ottawa, where she held administrative posts as department chair and vice-president academic before being headhunted for the York presidency.

One of the early anglophones to study Quebec history (*Action française: French-Canadian Nationalism in the 1920s; Dream of Nation: A Social and Intellectual History of Quebec*), she was also among the pioneers of women's history in Canada (*The Neglected Majority: Essays in Canadian Women's History*, edited with Alison Prentice). The history of military nursing caught her fancy after being president of York (*The War Diary of Clare Gass; Margaret Macdonald, Imperial Daughter*). She now lives bilingually in Montreal, where she is pursuing a life-long interest in the arts (*Historians' Stories from Canada*), as well as an artistic pursuit of her own, ceramic sculpture.

She is a member of the Order of Canada and a fellow of the Royal Society of Canada, and holds honorary degrees from Concordia University, the University of Ottawa, and l'Université de Montréal.

Lorna Marsden, 1997–2007

Lorna Marsden came to York in the late summer of 1997 after five years as president and vice-chancellor of Wilfrid Laurier University. She had spent twenty years on the faculty of the University of Toronto, serving in several administrative positions: graduate director of the Centre for Industrial Relations, chair of the Department of Sociology, associate dean of the Faculty of Graduate Studies, vice-provost, and from 1984 to 1992 as a part-time professor. During the latter period, she was a senator in the Parliament of Canada and taught one graduate course at the University. She experienced leadership positions in the community as president of the National Action Committee on the Status of Women, 1975–77, and as vice-president and national policy chair of the Liberal Party of Canada, 1975–84. She acquired knowledge of the business world through directorships of public and mutual companies. She visited universities in Britain, many continental European countries, China, and Japan, as well as studying in the United States. She received her BA from the University of Toronto in 1968 and her doctorate from Princeton University in 1972. She greatly enjoyed teaching at the University of Toronto, and published articles and books in her field of sociology. She was one of the founders of the Canadian Institute for Advanced Research and a member of its research committee until 2002. She is a member of the Order of Canada, the Order of Ontario, and the Order of Merit (Federal Republic of Germany). She holds honorary degrees from six Canadian universities.

Mamdouh Shoukri, 2007–

Mamdouh Shoukri was appointed the seventh president and vice-chancellor of York University on 1 July 2007. Dr Shoukri began his career in academia at McMaster University, serving in administrative leadership positions at all levels of the academy, including as graduate program director, department chair, dean, and vice-president. During his term as dean of Engineering, the Faculty enjoyed significant growth, leading to McMaster's becoming one of the foremost engineering schools in Canada. Under his leadership as vice-president research & international, McMaster was designated Research University of the Year by Research Infosource Inc. in 2004. Dr Shoukri was also responsible for creating and implementing the vision for the McMaster Innovation Park, which has become a major innovation hub and catalyst for the region's economic recovery. Prior to joining McMaster, he held progressive roles in the Research Division of Ontario Hydro, where he was responsible for industrial research.

A champion of innovation, Dr Shoukri has guided York's transformation into a comprehensive and research-intensive university. Among his achievements as president are the establishment of the Lassonde School of Engineering and major capital development projects, including a new Life Sciences building, Glendon's Centre of Excellence, Osgoode Hall expansion, the CIBC Pan Am/Parapan Am Athletics Stadium, a new home for the Lassonde School, and the extension of the Toronto subway to York's Keele campus. He has also overseen the advancement of York's internationalization and social innovation agendas, as well as plans for future growth in the York Region.

Dr Shoukri serves on the Ministry of Industry's Space Advisory Board, the Board of Directors of Cancer Care Ontario, and the Canadian Merit Scholarship Foundation, and is chair of the Government and Community Relations Committee for the Council of Ontario Universities. He is a member of the Standing Advisory Committee on University Research for the Association of Universities and Colleges of Canada, and was a founding Board Member of the Ontario Centres of Excellence and a member of the Ontario Research and Innovation Council.

For his contributions to the flourishing of Ontario's academic institutions as both an engineer and an administrator, Dr Shoukri was named a member of the Order of Canada and the Order of Ontario in 2013, and awarded the Queen Elizabeth II Diamond Jubilee medal. He is a senior fellow of Massey College and a fellow of both the Canadian Academy of Engineering and the Canadian Society for Mechanical Engineering. Dr Shoukri's scholarly interests are in thermo-fluid science, and he is the author or co-author of more than 120 papers that have appeared in refereed journals and symposia.

LEADING THE MODERN UNIVERSITY

York University's Presidents on Continuity
and Change, 1974–2014

Introduction

LORNA R. MARSDEN

In the early 1970s York University was suffering through multiple crises: a crisis of succession, a financial crisis, and a crisis of academic purpose. Over the years since, the University has been led by five presidents who worked their way out of these crises with strong teams of vice-presidents and deans, along with astute governors and chancellors. In this book we look at the nature of the crises, and each president, in succession, presents his or her recollections and analysis of events during their terms of office.

The first ten years of York University have been well described by the founding president in his memoirs and the detailed report he wrote at the end of each of his five-year terms.[1] Vice-presidents and deans have given their views and recollections on the growth of the institution. In particular, John (Jack) Saywell, Dean of Arts at York from 1964 to 73, who was important to York's academic development, has written a vivid account of the crises identified in this study.[2] An institutional history was commissioned for the fiftieth anniversary of York in 2009, and tells the story through interviews with many faculty, staff, students, governors, alumni, and friends of York. Its author, historian Michiel Horn, brought a lifetime of experiences as a York faculty member to the project.[3] These books and articles have informed this study, and are referred to throughout the chapters that follow.

Here we start after the early founding years with York's third president, and conclude with the seventh president, who is still in office. How did each individual analyse the University and react to the events of prior years? How did each contribute to York's growth academically, organizationally, and in reputation? As time went on the crises of the early 1970s faded away, but they remained a fundamental part of the history and institutional memory. They influenced the University's practices and its reputation in the larger community. As each president succeeded the last, there were points of continuity as well as innovations.

In any large organization, a new leader faces questions linked to past events as much as questions about his or her ideas for change.

The University was about fifty-five years old when these four former presidents and the serving president decided to write about its development after 1974. As each person took up a five-year term as president of York, the threads from the work of all predecessors were picked up and drawn forward or woven into a new pattern. Each president did this in the context of the times, in terms of his or her own ideas and ambitions for the institution, but unavoidably in the light of what had gone before. Each of the five presidents came from a different background: an economist and senior public servant; a lawyer and an academic; an historian; a sociologist; and an engineer. All had administrative experience elsewhere, and all had been involved in depth with university life in Ontario for some time. They saw the institution in different ways while sharing an enthusiasm for the work, a deep feeling for the importance of York University, and a strong desire to see it grow and prosper.

The central "person" in this account is really not the presidents but York University, the complicated but changing institution to which each president has contributed. In fact, the fifth president writes her chapter in the voice of the University. No university turns on a dime; many projects are years in the conceiving and completing. That is part of why universities are so interesting. They are long-term institutions that carry certain values and folkways with them through the generations. As President Lowell of Harvard said when asked what is required to make a university great, "Three hundred years!"

Scholars and students have been organized into universities for centuries, so there is a rich history of these organizations, as part of the larger community and as workplaces. Memoirs abound written by students, professors, and administrators. The constantly changing nature of universities attracts analysis in Canada as elsewhere.[4] Almost all those writing about universities point out the differences in the structure, organization, and governance of these institutions as compared to those of government or public corporations. Reference is made to those differences in these pages. The lines of power and authority, the power of culture and tradition, and the influence of sources of funding – whether from government, student fees, donations, endowment, or founding organizations such as religious groups – are fundamental to understanding how universities operate and are led.

Many presidents of universities, including the founding president of York University, Murray G. Ross, have written their memoirs. Other works analyse the role and behaviour of presidents based on surveys and interviews with presidents.[5] This study is unusual in that the authors are five presidents who took office one after another in the same institution after crises occurred. Each had to work within the context of their predecessor while finding opportunities for their own ideas and mandates. This account shows that, although some issues facing university presidents are constant, others are resolved by focusing on more than one presidency. History matters, too, and although this is not a history of York University, what is written here is part of the institution's history. This is the story of York University over the past forty years.

First, however, we look at York University as it exists today. It was founded in 1959 following the advocacy of a group of North York citizens whose ideas and organizing work are described in more than one history.[6] The founding of a university is crucial in the development of its culture, and has a significant influence on the work of all presidents. Universities share common goals and purposes, but how these are met depends a great deal upon institutional history and leadership. Like other Ontario universities, York University was created through an Act of the provincial legislature, which is its legal foundation. Named in the Act are those with the legal authority to manage and direct the institution: a chancellor with the power to confer degrees on the recommendation of the Senate; a president and vice-chancellor, who is the chief executive officer; and two governing bodies, the Board of Governors, chaired by an independent member of the Board, and a Senate composed of faculty members along with student, alumni, and administrative staff representation.

York University has had seven presidents consecutively in office since its founding, five of whom served from the period of crises until the present. (Three acting presidents are not discussed here.[7]) The issues they faced, the priorities they chose, and the way each dealt with the constant challenges of government policies, funding, governance, academic matters, and organization are the substance of the chapters they have written.

York was the first of several "new" universities created in Ontario during the period. Some were created with existing, usually religious, institutions, such as Laurentian (1960), Windsor (1962), and Guelph (1964 with agricultural colleges). Trent (1963), Brock (1964), and Lakehead (1965) were created anew as secular institutions. These mid-twentieth-century universities have faced many of the same problems as York, and their histories will show similar struggles.

York is a very large and complex organization and a leadership challenge. As this was written in 2015, it had eleven faculties with over 1,500 full-time faculty members, a wide array of support services, and over 270,000 alumni. Since its founding in 1959, it has grown from an entering class of 73 students to over 50,000 undergrad and 6,000 graduate students, some of them part time.[8] It has grown from one borrowed building to two campuses and a third planned. The Glendon campus in mid-town Toronto is the site of York's bilingual Faculty,[9] with 2,800 students set in the beautiful grounds of an old estate on the banks of the Don River occupied by York since 1960. The Keele campus is in northwest Toronto, and holds the other ten Faculties. It occupies the land of five former farms on the border of the City of Toronto and York Region, with several original woodlots, Black Creek on its western border, and views down to the Niagara Escarpment from the upper floors of its many buildings.[10] In addition, the Faculties of business and of law teach some of their programs in the office towers of Toronto's downtown financial district, and there is a third campus being created in Markham, York Region. The first two campuses have student residences for undergraduates and, at the Keele campus, for married students with families. There are sports facilities with field houses, playing fields, and tennis courts, and, on the Keele campus, a hotel designed for the executive development programs of the Schulich School of Business, but that accommodates visitors to the campus, academic and otherwise.

Some of the many academic programs, focused in the fall and winter terms according to Canadian tradition, are also offered in spring and summer terms. The campuses hum all year with research and teaching,[11] so construction, maintenance, cleaning, and upgrading projects have to work around classrooms, laboratories, conferences, and summer camps for neighbourhood children. The vice-president academic, or VPA – currently called the provost, although in earlier years the provost was the vice-president for students – is responsible for all academic matters and their development, and the dean of each Faculty reports through that position. Several vice-provosts also report through the VPA.

A separately incorporated York University Development Corporation (YUDC) oversees planning and development outside the academic core of the Keele campus, and interacts with municipal and other levels of government for land development purposes. It also operates a mall on the Keele campus that contains many stores, restaurants, and services as well as offices used for research centres of the University. There are daycare centres, about two dozen restaurants and cafes, banks, a post office, bookstores, health services, seven libraries, and the Clara Thomas Archives, while the smaller Glendon campus has the Frost Library, cafes, a bookstore, and a Senior Common Room for faculty members and senior staff. Both campuses are served by buses and, soon, a subway to the Keele campus from the south and the north. The buses are operated by the cities of Toronto, York Region, and Brampton, and the GO regional transit service. Tens of thousands of cars are parked on the campuses each day. Security services operate day and night, and in case of need can call upon local police forces. The University operates a power plant with co-generation units that supply much of the Keele campus's electricity and steam requirements. It recycles tons of waste in as efficient a manner as possible, and holds to a high standard of environmental sustainability.

Like many corporations, York manages very large operating and capital budgets. It has a legal department, a corporate secretariat, a centre for human rights, and an internal audit office. The University has large pension and endowment funds. It issues bonds for capital construction purposes and has public-private partnerships. The vice-president, finance and administration, oversees a very major division with expert staff, and is a key officer of the corporation.

When founding president Murray Ross stepped down in 1970, there was a crisis of succession: no traditional practices or rules about presidential searches had been established in the culture of the University; I describe the contentious atmosphere that surrounded this transition in Chapter 1. When the second president, David Slater, attempted to deal with this, he faced an onslaught of changes in Ontario government policy about university planning and funding as well as a financial crisis. He left the position early, and turmoil followed. The question asked in the early 1970s, very publicly, was: Should York University continue to exist?

Although crises in organizations and serious problems are not uncommon when the founder leaves, this situation was particularly complex. The province required the University to completely change its plans, as I describe in the next chapter, and faculty and staff began to realize that the conditions of their employment were changing dramatically. This was no longer to be a small university with gradual growth. It was no longer to have funding on the scale of other universities with a different mix of programs. Its leadership was to be challenged both from within the University and from the wider community. Morale among faculty and staff members dropped to a very low point.

The focus here is on how the next five presidents engaged with these organizational and financial problems, providing leadership in both the academic core and the administrative decisions. Presidents are often in an extremely hot seat. Each person taking that seat has to pick up decisions made by their predecessors, fulfil the mandate set by the Board of Governors to whom he or she reports, and respond to current conditions.

Presidents are selected for many reasons, but they nearly all inherit long-serving faculty and staff members, undergraduates and graduates, campuses and buildings, too little money, and too many ambitions and obligations. All university presidents everywhere face some similar challenges,[12] but the history of a particular institution, the geography, the state of the economy, and the politics of the times are the contexts in which ambitions are achieved or deferred. They are the contexts that explain a great deal about what occurred in the forty years during which these five individuals sat where the buck stopped at York.

As universities in Canada have grown and changed, a president's duties have evolved from largely academic leadership to positions in which both the academic and complex business operations are under presidential authority. Risks abound, and government relations and the collegium place powerful pressures on presidents to fulfil their responsibilities.[13] Ross Paul's recent study of presidential leadership in Canadians universities documents the rapid transformation that has occurred in Canada in the role and duties of a president from moral and pastoral leader to chief executive officer of a complex organization.[14] Forms of authority a president can exercise have shifted greatly from the traditional authority embedded in universities based on religious and scholarly traditions to the bureaucratic authority stemming from legislative and regulatory powers. Presidents came to exercise bureaucratic authority as most university boards of governors became accountable for public and tuition funding. But universities are not predominately either moral communities or rational-legal corporations. Most administrators, including presidents, are faculty members exercising authority on a temporary basis, while long-serving support staff might lead "moral" community building departments, such as student affairs.[15] Presidents also are required to practise symbolic as well as substantive leadership. Each president is selected to embody some quality the university wishes to emphasize at the time of appointment.

The practice of searching for a new president at York University has been through many changes. As some scholars of presidencies said in 1983, "[u]nlike business organizations, which have found it beneficial to identify and groom their future leaders, educational institutions continue to follow a policy of 'natural selection.'"[16] Murray Ross, founding president, was appointed in an arrangement between those selected to lead the new Board of Governors and the University of Toronto's president, with the blessing of the provincial government of the day. The second president was selected through a Board of Governors' committee with the advice of the Senate. It was a very messy process that divided the Board and Senate and alienated some of the University leadership, and it has been documented in more than one book about York University.[17] Because of that crisis, for the search for the third president, the Board and Senate negotiated a new process that included faculty and student representation. Search rules and processes have continued to evolve.

Indeed the waves of energy emanating from the crises of 1970–73 have echoed in academic, governance, and financial developments for the past forty years, growing fainter with the passage of time, but never disappearing from the atmosphere inside the institution in search committees, budget anxieties, and forward planning. Much of this echoes in the accounts that follow.

Chapter 1 provides a context for the entry of the third president into York and lights up some of the key events in the early years and their consequences for all those presidents who write in this volume. It was a particular moment in the history of Ontario, of Canada, and within Canadian universities. By the time the third president was appointed in 1974, the complexities of York University had already become clear.

NOTES

1 Murray G. Ross, *The Way Must Be Tried: Memoirs of a University Man* (Toronto: Stoddart, 1992); idem, *These Five Years 1960–65: The President's Report, York University* (North York, ON: York University, 1965); idem, *Those Ten Years 1960–70: The President's Report on the First Ten Years of York University* (North York, ON: York University, 1970).

2 John Saywell, *Someone to Teach Them: York and the Great University Explosion, 1960–1973* (Toronto: University of Toronto Press, 2008).

3 All these memoirs and studies of York are listed in the bibliography, and when exact references or quotations are selected, end notes are provided.

4 See, for example, George Fallis, *Multiversities, Ideas and Democracy* (Toronto: University of Toronto Press, 2007); and idem, *Rethinking Higher Education: Participation, Research and Differentiation* (Montreal; Kingston, ON: McGill-Queen's University Press, 2013).

5 Examples of such studies include Nicholas J. Demerath, Richard W. Stephens, and R. Robb Taylor, *Power, Presidents, and Professors* (New York: Basic Books, 1967); and Ross Paul, *Leadership Under Fire: The Challenging Role of the Canadian University President* (Montreal; Kingston, ON: McGill-Queen's University Press, 2011).

6 See Ross, *Way Must Be Tried*; or Michiel Horn, *York University: The Way Must Be Tried* (Montreal; Kingston, ON: McGill-Queen's University Press, 2009).

7 York's acting presidents have been Richard J. Storr (1973), John W. Yolton (1973–74), and William C. Found (1984). All were professors at the University. The first two served when President Slater resigned in 1973 before the end of his first term and until a new president was installed; Professor Found served while President-designate Harry Arthurs took research leave.

8 For detailed numbers by year, see the reports of the Office of Institutional Planning and Analysis located at http://oipa.info.yorku.ca/. The Fact Book contains such data. The most recent data are in York University, Office of the President, *Impact: President's Impact Report, 2014* (Toronto: York University, 2015); available online at http://president.yorku.ca/2015/04/annualreport2014/, accessed 24 June 2015).

9 To distinguish between the organizational use of the term and individual members, Faculties are capitalized and faculty refers to the professors who teach in the Faculty.

10 In her memoirs, Jill Ker Conway describes the early days of the Keele campus, where her husband, John Conway, was the first Master of Founders College and

they lived in one of the old farmhouses. See Jill Ker Conway, *True North: A Memoir* (Toronto: Alfred A. Knopf, 1994), chaps 6 and 7.

11   In his excellent analysis of US research universities, John V. Lombardi describes the "academic core composed of a group of faculty guilds that have primary responsibility for the academic content and quality of the enterprise" and the "administrative shell"; see John V. Lombardi, *How Universities Work* (Baltimore: Johns Hopkins University Press, 2013), 2. All of York's presidents have been members of faculty guilds, of course, but this study is primarily of their work in the "administrative shell."

12   Good descriptions are found in Paul, *Leadership Under Fire*; and Rosanna Tamburri, "The Evolving Role of President Takes Its Toll," *University Affairs*, 12 February 2007, available online at http://www.universityaffairs.ca/news/news-article/the-evolving-role-of-president-takes-its-toll.aspx

13   For a particularly contemporary crisis, see the account by Michael Sokolove of the Penn State problems that led to criminal charges against its long-serving president: "The Trials of Graham Spanier, Penn State's Ousted President," *New York Times Magazine*, 16 July 2014.

14   Paul, *Leadership Under Fire*.

15   Roberta Hamilton, *Setting the Agenda: Jean Royce and the Shaping of Queen's University*. Toronto: University of Toronto Press, 2002.

16   Kathryn M. Moore, Ann M. Salimbene, Joyce D. Marlier, and Stephen M. Bragg, "The Structure of Presidents' and Deans' Careers," *Journal of Higher Education* 544, no. 5 (1983): 501.

17   Four accounts of this presidential transition are found: James Gillies, *From Vision to Reality: The Founding of the Faculty of Administrative Studies at York University, 1965–1972* (Toronto: York University, Schulich School of Business, 2010); Saywell, *Someone to Teach Them*; Ross, *Way Must Be Tried*; and Horn, *York University*.

1 Background to the Events of 1973 at York University

LORNA R. MARSDEN

How It All Began

H. Ian Macdonald was an economist and deputy treasurer of the province of Ontario in 1974 when he was persuaded to become York's third president. The University had completed its first ten years under the leadership of Murray G. Ross and a further two and a half years with David Slater as president. But Slater had left the position early under some duress, and the provincial government was worried about York's future. The University was emerging from a period of crisis, the provincial economy was experiencing a downturn, the government had revised its policies towards universities, and the morale of the University was at low ebb. Even the local newspapers were asking: Should York continue to exist?

The historical origins and the values established in the years before Macdonald took up the reins had serious consequences for how the institution was perceived, its systems of governance, its funding, and, importantly, the type of leadership attracted to meet these challenges.[1] As Ross Paul says in his study of university presidents, "[u]ltimately, whatever the individual's leadership style, it is imperative that a president take full account of the university culture – its values, its priorities, its way of doing things ... The position is about more than skills and experience."[2] In the case of York's third president, the culture was in transition and the recent three years had disrupted values and priorities significantly.

Why was there such a crisis? The founding president, Murray G. Ross, with the support of his Board of Governors, had built the new university according to his own ideas and the circumstances of the late 1950s and early 1960s. But, as I describe below, circumstances had changed dramatically. His retirement as president came at a point of changes in government policies, and his successor was selected by the Board from a deanship at a very different type of institution.

Crises of succession from a founder to the next regime are not unusual in organizations,[3] and in itself this crisis would have been a minor episode. It became a serious issue, however, because of a growing mistrust between the Board of Governors and faculty members represented through the Senate. The Act of the Ontario legislature that was York's founding document in 1959 had been drawn from some of the acts that had created earlier universities. The Act, as described in Michiel Horn's history of York,[4] was somewhat vague, and the division of powers among the Board, the Senate, and the president were not clarified. The Board chair thought that the Board's powers should be expanded, and wanted the Act revised. The faculty thought, however, that the powers of the faculty and Senate were too constricted. The struggle over power resulted in a revised Act in 1965, with some lingering sentiment that the Board and Senate were in opposition to each other. Some saw this as a vigorous, democratic campus climate. Others read it as disharmony.

So when it came to the selection of the second president, as Ross completed his ten years in June of 1970, a full-blown crisis of succession emerged in a struggle between those faculty members who felt the Senate had the final say and those who emphasized the wording of the Act that the Senate's powers were to "advise" the Board. Because of the quite public power struggle, several serious candidates for the position, from inside the University and elsewhere, were either dismissed from contention or placed in an impossible situation and withdrew their names. Struggles about student representation and power contributed to the disarray. A great deal of confidential or personal information was leaked to the press. David Slater, a distinguished economist from Queen's University, was selected as the second president, arriving in a tense and difficult situation not all of York's making.

The dramatic policy and financial changes of the Ontario government described below contributed to the tensions. In the end, the succession crisis became part of the public view of York as a venue of conflict, power struggles, and disharmony. It was a very difficult climate in which President Slater had to establish his leadership. As former Dean James Gillies says in his memoirs about the unfortunate departure of the second president, "the University went through a period of instability from which it took years to recover. Indeed, some would say it never did."[5]

The Ontario government's policy and financial shifts helped to make the situation intolerable for David Slater, but to understand the full impact of those changes, it is necessary to understand the academic model that Murray Ross had created and the conditions under which the senior faculty members had been attracted to York – two early decisions that were drastically affected by the government's changes in direction.

Murray Ross was selected as York's founding president from his position as a vice-president at the University of Toronto (all but two of York presidents have graduated from the University of Toronto).[6] He set out to create at York a very different curriculum and atmosphere from the University of Toronto.[7] His memoirs reveal that he was deeply embedded in the values of the University of Toronto and the Ontario business and political elites as they existed in the 1950s. But he was also greatly interested in the university atmosphere in the United States, where a different, more open model existed. He favoured the US three-year degree as compared to the British-Canadian specialized honours degree.[8] He supported professional schools and new subjects such as sociology, psychology, and environmental studies.[9] He opposed elitism and the exclusion of women and minorities. From early days, Ross advocated building a part-time evening college.[10] He believed, as Gillies puts it, "there was no conflict between high standards and the extension of higher educational opportunities to the broadest possible number of qualified people … and that they should schedule programs and classes to meet the needs of the students, rather than those of the professors." Furthermore, "as a result of his ideas, Murray [Ross] was always considered somewhat of an outsider by the traditional university establishment – a characterization of which he was extremely proud."[11]

Ross recounts his early convictions about this new university: it should have a broad general and liberal arts curriculum;[12] it would grow slowly to about 4,000 students by 1970;[13] it would not replicate programs in which other universities already had excellence; it would have a balanced faculty and not raid other universities, but try to recruit young Canadian faculty back to Canada. The nature of the curriculum Murray built required faculty members to teach in broad general courses, rather than in their own worldwide guilds of specialization. For faculty members trained to occupational, rather than organizational, careers in the traditional universities, this was a challenge. Ross had been warned about this difficulty when he applied for a grant from the Ford Foundation to bring in such a program. No doubt he expected to have to persuade some early faculty members to agree to this approach. However, as tensions emerged over the issue of a disciplinary, as opposed to an organizational, approach, it became framed, not as a matter of academic approach, but in the context of the politics of faculty-administrator relations.[14] This early struggle in the Senate of York between the faculty and administrators also divided faculty members between those who came because of the small student body, the broad general curriculum, and the modern approach to university studies, and those who favoured specialization and more traditional curricula. Matters tended to escalate rather quickly into a struggle between the administration and faculty factions. This disagreement about the direction of the academic program was forced to crisis when President Ross was told by the Ontario government that the University must grow, and grow rapidly. The pressure for growth increased throughout the 1960s and beyond.

Why did policies change? Given that the majority of Canada's universities are publicly funded, relations with governments and donors are always important for all university leaders. In his history of Ontario universities from the beginnings to the 1950s, A.B. McKillop describes the ways in which the early universities were funded.[15] He ends his study about the time the Ontario government began to expand and fund universities in new ways initiated during the post-war opportunities for returning veterans. York University was founded in 1959, when financing began to be linked to enrolments as the government realized that post-secondary education was a key to economic growth. As the 1960s and 1970s went on, the extent of the change from the 1950s universities became even more obvious. Higher education was the new form of human capital to stimulate the economic expansion needed in the province, and between 1960 and 1970 seven Acts establishing public universities were passed by the Ontario legislature. As the labour market demands for highly skilled workers increased and post-war immigrants settled into Ontario, their children surged into the schools and eventually universities, dramatically increasing the demand for spaces.

The rapid social change in Ontario was manifest throughout higher education. It was in the period of the founding years of York that the Colleges of Applied Arts and Technology were formed as a highly differentiated form of higher education. Ryerson Institute of Technology was an important technical college. Graduate schools grew in size as the demand for doctoral and other advanced degrees expanded. Governments began to take a more detailed interest in admissions, tuition rates, employment of graduates, and the allocation of resources. The Ontario government began serious efforts to predict enrolment growth and to tie funding to student numbers, a radical departure from earlier funding, which had been negotiated between each university and the government. This new policy included a formula for funding with a number of variables, such as weighting for particular programs of study. Because of the Cold War, the sciences and professions were important in public policy, and weighting them over humanities advantaged some programs and institutions. York was not advantaged. Its founding programs, in humanities and social sciences, were the majority of its offerings, as Ross had planned. Programs in engineering and medicine had been developed by the York Senate and Board, but rebuffed by the provincial bodies overseeing expansion in those fields.[16]

Originally, the president, with the Board of Governors and a dean, created Faculties around a central budget. In the very early stages, there was a clear line of sight for governors and administrators, with deans appointed by the president and Board of Governors. Colleges were created to be residential and the core of student life. As the size of the university increased and deans had to hire faculty members and enrol students rapidly, this changed. Deans had been chosen to be distinguished leaders in their fields, and had now to be given the resources to carry out the expansion, so they acquired considerable independent power and authority in the University. This created tension among the senior leaders.

The administrators of Ontario universities spend a great deal of their time bridging the chasm between the community of scholars and the regulations and requirements of modern-day government. As Murray Ross pointed out at the time, there was rapid and radical change in Ontario, and adjustment to those changes "caused disharmony within York."[17] The pace of social change overwhelmed his careful planning.[18] As Table 1.1 shows, between 1967 and 1968, enrolment at York grew dramatically. The entire University was geared towards continued growth.

Table 1.1. Enrolment History, York University, 1960–74

Year	Undergraduate Students			Graduate Students			Total Students
	Full-time	Part-time	Total	Full-time	Part-time	Total	
1960	73	0	73	0	0	0	73
1961	216	0	216	0	0	0	216
1962	304	267	571	0	0	0	571
1963	506	653	1,159	0	0	0	1,159
1964	781	1,102	1,883	11	0	11	1,894
1965	1,447	1,911	3,358	36	0	36	3,394
1966	2,440	2,819	5,259	119	309	428	5,687
1967	3,493	3,529	7,022	242	414	656	7,678
1968	5,501	6,532	12,033	420	574	994	13,027
1969	7,149	4,422	11,571	585	654	1,239	12,810
1970	9,002	6,299	15,301	785	774	1,559	16,860
1971	10,735	6,885	17,620	871	858	1,729	19,349
1972	10,427	7,523	17,950	913	915	1,828	19,778
1973	10,498	8,874	19,372	1,032	1,005	2,037	21,409
1974	10,720	9,800	20,520	1,158	1,088	2,246	22,766

Source: York University, Management Information Infomart, "York University Factbook: York University's Enrolment History as of November 1st 1960 through 2012" (Toronto: York University, Office of Institutional Planning and Analysis, 2013); available online at http://www.yorku.ca/factbook/factbook/index.php?year=2012%20-%202013.

The student power movement of the late 1960s was an additional pressure. As Horn's history makes clear, the real struggle for power by York students came in 1971–73, during Slater's first years.[19] In Ontario, Saywell attributes the student movements on campus to the 1966 Duff-Berdahl Report on university government.[20] That report, commissioned by the Canadian Association of University Teachers and the Association of Universities and Colleges of Canada, raised in the community the question of the role of students in university government. Student power was a widespread theme internationally, but the pressure for more student power varied. At York the "Americanization" of both faculty hiring and women's rights emerged quite quickly as flashpoints that engaged student leaders. Committees were set up to examine the implications of the Duff-Berdahl Report for York. By 1973, after a series of reports to the Senate, campaigns by the York Student Federation, and responses by the Board and others, students won representation on virtually all governing bodies – most prominently at the Faculty level. In the process there were significant demonstrations and attacks on administrators in *Excalibur*, the student newspaper. There were protests about governance and teaching, and attacks on some faculty members and on Dean Saywell. Much of the colourful protest was written up in the local newspapers and magazines. This added to the pressures on President Slater.

During its rapid growth, several new Faculties, in addition to Glendon and Arts, had been created under Murray Ross and David Slater: the Atkinson College of part-time studies, Graduate Studies, Administrative Studies, Science, Environmental Studies, Fine Arts, Osgoode Hall Law School, and, in 1972, Education. Eventually, in President Slater's administration, there were ten deans, the University librarian, the secretary of the University, and three vice-presidents. As Horn attests, it was the deans who, in 1972, had exerted sufficient pressure on the Board of Governors to cause Slater to resign.[21]

But if governance and administration had developed some clarity, the culture and values of York were still uncertain. There was little history and no tradition to fall back upon in times of trouble. The values – combining not only the traditional values of universities such as the power of scholarship, collegiality, and freedoms in research and speech, but also how decisions are taken and problems dealt with – had not been deeply embedded.

Unlike some of the other new universities that had emerged from long-standing religious colleges, such as the University of Windsor and the University of Ottawa, York was secular, actively rejecting religious influences and deliberately tuned into the values of a new era. Ross had purposefully established York to be very different from the University of Toronto, the city's other university. Indeed by the time Ross left the presidency, there was little love lost between the two institutions.[22] So the culture of leadership at York might be described as developing, rather than resilient. Students, faculty members, and staff were caught up in the issues of the times, and the president was not in a position to appeal to history, traditions, or eminent alumni to restore calm and order.

Universities are not hierarchical in the way bureaucracies are. Faculty members, by virtue of their standing in their fields of scholarship – their "guilds," as scholar John Lombardi calls them – are in many ways more powerful than any administrator. Their careers are dependent upon their standing in their guild, not the organization in which they hold jobs.[23] Faculty members at York University have been heard to say "*We* are the university." In many senses they are correct. Students, both undergraduate and graduate, sometimes also make the same claim. They are conscious of the fact that, without them, there would be no university. Certainly faculty members have power in their scholarship and through their part of governance in the Senate. Presidents are both part of the scholarly community and leaders in the administrative world, and value their membership in both.

Administrators, whether from the ranks of faculty or from quite other backgrounds, must take on the duties of bureaucrats: rational and explained decision-making, record-keeping, accountability, and hierarchy, and ensuring peace and order. They are the "administrative shell" Lombardi describes. In the end, the university is a very large community of faculty members and students along with the administrators and staff who support the institution. The president adds a highly visible symbolic and substantive leadership for all the constituents of the university, including the external governors and, with the regular change of president, the community signals its priorities to fit the times. These characteristics of universities, quite unlike classic bureaucracies or corporations, have been significant in the history of many universities and most certainly were at York.

For David Slater, arriving as York's second president, the times were not propitious. Rapid enrolment growth, but with per student funding at the low end because of government financial restraints and the program mix, meant York was painfully short of funds. Slater faced serious unhappiness as faculty and students realized that the academic plans put in place by Murray Ross were not sustainable. The financing was not there to complete the new Keele campus or to improve their salaries or class sizes. Students were demanding representation on all committees and more "power." When in 1972 enrolment projections – and therefore income – dropped precipitously and Slater's administration had to consider dismissing faculty members for fiscal reasons alone, a serious crisis faced the entire University. The faculty association was alarmed, the administrators had no experience in enrolment decline, and the government's in-year funding allowed no time to sort out a proper plan. The governors finally lost confidence in the president, but it was the Senate that effectively seized control of the issue and created an ad hoc committee that ultimately led to the resignation of President Slater. The details are described in the Horn history of York University in historical context,[24] but at the time the details – including letters highly detrimental to the University – were published in the two main Toronto newspapers. Many factors were involved in this resignation, but the precipitating one was the link between funding based on in-year enrolments and an unanticipated drop in projected enrolments – a drop that, in fact, never occurred.

There had been serious difficulties for York from its first emergence on the provincial scene. The idea of a new university had stemmed from a group of businessmen in North York, and only after several years and many efforts had the provincial government been persuaded to create the new institution and only under certain conditions, such as the aegis of the University of Toronto, Ontario's most powerful university. As A.B. McKillop points out, "[t]he University of Toronto holds a special place in this universe of separate existence but collective understanding. As the 'provincial university,' blessed from the outset by the munificence of the provincial state, it quickly became the benchmark by which other institutions measured themselves and their relationship to provincial administrations."[25]

This is highly significant for York University, which was founded at, and with the consent of, the University of Toronto. In fact, Murray Ross reports in his memoirs that the president of the University of Toronto, Sidney Smith, had spoken frequently in favour of a second university in Toronto, obtained faculty approval for it, and formed a committee to help the men who wanted to create it.[26] A condition of York's creation was that the University of Toronto curriculum and examinations be used at York for four to eight years, and this lasted until 1964. Since it was to inhabit the same city, York could not establish itself as a regional competitor, but had to compete for students, funding, and attention in close quarters with the University of Toronto. The history of universities illustrates the tensions that exist in such an unequal competition in close geographical proximity for resources of all kinds. In Canada, one thinks of McGill and Concordia, UBC and Simon Fraser, University of Saskatchewan and University of Regina, and so on. In the United States and the United Kingdom, it is not dissimilar.

When President Slater resigned and quickly left the University, morale was low, finances a priority for the Board, and long-term academic planning not anyone's priority. There had been several resignations of senior academic administrators. An interim president was drawn from the faculty members while the Board regrouped to search for a successor.

What might have happened at a university with a longer history, a staunch alumni, and a major endowment could not happen at York. The University was just over a decade old and its academic programs had had even fewer years to be established because of the founding requirement that, for the first five years, the courses and examinations were to be set by the University of Toronto. What is described as the first real York graduating class had convocated in 1964. There were generous supporters of York among the governors and other citizens, but only a tiny endowment, and the finances ran year-to-year. Growth in student enrolment, faculty hiring, and campus buildings had been the only story from its founding year. Change in aspects of governance had come rapidly both in changes to the Act and in the addition of students to all the governing boards and committees. Yet, although challenges to the authority of the President had occurred during the decade of Murray Ross, none had been successful.[27]

The departure of President Slater was a low moment, but York did have important strengths to draw upon. It was a new university with innovative ideas. Rules and traditions were yet to be established, and the great opportunity was to be part of a new university, not yet barnacled with traditions. The majority of faculty members regarded teaching their students as a highest priority, and their dedication to teaching was then and remains a strong feature of the York culture at a time when research was beginning its domination in higher education priorities. There was pride in the many accomplishments of this relatively new university and a vibrant sense of colleagueship. The prologue to James Gillies's memoir of his years at York, including founding what is now the Schulich School of Business, attests to the excitement and optimism surrounding York's creation.[28] Anyone who doubts the enthusiasm and happiness of York's early students need only read the third chapter of Horn's history, in which many of those students speak directly to their experiences.[29]

York was welcoming in many ways to women faculty and women's studies long before many other universities.[30] In line with Murray Ross's personal convictions and therefore those of early faculty members he hired, discrimination against minorities, women, and some religious and cultural groups was not found at York. Saywell documents the hiring decisions of some professors considered too controversial to be hired at the University of Toronto at the time, such as Gabriel Kolko and Andreas Papandreou.[31] The commitment to human rights, freedoms, diversity, and support for students from low-income backgrounds was and remains firm. Social commitment characterizes much of the work of faculty and staff, reflected in relations with the surrounding communities and internationally, as well as in their research and teaching programs.

As students, faculty, and administrators attest, unlike many long-established universities, York was prepared for change. There may have been long committee meetings, debates, arguments, and even hard feelings in some quarters, but change occurred frequently with the consent of both governing bodies representing all the constituencies – students, faculty, Board, staff, and alumni. It is equally true that the ideas and values of early planning documents remain alive even now. In short, now over fifty years on, there is continuity and memory, as well as frequent changes in York's culture.[32]

The Structures of Governance

York University is governed by a Board of Governors and a Senate for all internal matters and by the laws and regulations of Ontario and the local municipalities for many other issues.[33] The formal governing structures were established by the time this story starts in 1974, and have been modified ever since, sometimes by the president and Board, and sometimes by students, faculty, or external disruptions, but always through consultation and debate. There has been no dramatic change as the University of Toronto experienced in moving to a unicameral system of governance in 1972. That change led Murray Ross to publish a long article entitled "The Dilution of Academic Power in Canada: The University of Toronto Act,"[34] which, no doubt, contributed to the strength and effectiveness of the Senate of York University. The Board of Governors and the Senate remain as separate but cooperating formal powers.

Students were expected to form their own governments from the founding of the University, but it was only in 1966, according to Saywell, that students came to be viewed as participants in the senior decision-making processes.[35] First, the York University Student Council was created – later the name evolved into the Student Representative Council, the York Student Federation, and, finally, the York Federation of Students. Graduate students formed their own association in 1967, by which time they numbered over 656 in full- and part-time studies.

An important feature of York and other universities formed in that era is the self-perpetuating nature of the Board of Governors. There are no government-appointed representatives, but student, faculty, and staff representatives are elected by their peers to seats on the Board. Beginning with Robert Winters in 1959, the Board has been chaired by a series of very distinguished citizens who have guided it and the administration through successes and some difficult times. The Board approves the annual budget and all capital spending. It oversees the endowment, the pension plans, and campus development. It appoints the chancellor and the president, and oversees the work of the president and executive team. It retains the residual powers. Until recently the Board had no special meeting chamber, but met in various locations. It now has a handsome classic boardroom in the Kaneff Tower on the Keele campus.

Although the offices of chancellor, chair of the Board, president, chair of the Senate, dean, librarian, and University secretary have existed since 1960, vice-presidents and similar administrative offices emerged as the University grew and have changed greatly under various administrations.[36] Over the years, the University has also created semi-autonomous subsidiaries, such as the York University Development Corporation, the York University Foundation, and others, which also have changed with circumstances.

Each of the University's Faculties has a formal Faculty Council to which the dean (or principal, in the case of Glendon) provides leadership. Their proposals for academic changes move up to the Senate committees for debate and approval. Faculty, students, and staff who serve on the committees dedicate many hours to these tasks. Senate committees propose changes in academic programs and policies, faculty appointments (and very rarely dismissal), and the granting of tenure and promotion. They approve lists of students who may graduate and course changes. The annual University budget is taken to the Senate for explanation and discussion, although it is approved by the Board of Governors.

The Senate meets monthly during term, and virtually all issues of any importance to faculty members or students are raised and discussed. For some years, meetings of the Senate and the Board of Governors were held in the Council Chamber on the Glendon campus. At Keele campus, the Senate Chamber is arranged as a theatre and sees much of the drama that occurs in York's governance. The Senate is the point at which the community of scholars intersects most visibly with the accountability of bureaucracy and formal governance. The chair of the Senate faces many difficult and delicate situations, and some highly skilled faculty members have chaired that body.

Over the years, Faculties have increased in number – there are now eleven – and changed. In the early years, Faculties such as Fine Arts and Environmental Studies were created first and faculty members hired later. A Faculty of Graduate Studies was created in 1963, although a dean of graduate studies was not appointed until 1965. Faculties have merged or been formed out of pre-existing departments, such as the Faculty of Health, the Schulich School of Business, and recently the Lassonde School of Engineering. Faculties have disappeared, as in the case of the Joseph E. Atkinson College.[37]

The library, created in 1960 at the Glendon campus, has expanded into a number of specialized libraries, such as law, business, science and engineering, and women's studies. The librarians and archivists are members of faculty.

The archives were formed in 1970 as part of the library but with designated archivists.

The alumni association was formed with the first class of graduates in 1964, and elected the recently graduated Bruce Bryden as its president. In 1982 Bryden became the chair of the Board of Governors, typifying many alumni who have served not only in the alumni association but also on the Board and in many advisory and governance capacities. But the York University Alumni Association is not the only alumni group. Faculties as well as some departments have their own active alumni groups. In addition, there are York alumni associations nationally and internationally, with a particularly active group in Hong Kong, as well as in London, Tokyo, New York, Atlanta, and several Canadian cities. Many alumni contribute as generous supporters of York. As well, some of their sons and daughters have become York's students. The most avid sports alumni turn out for intermural competitions such as the Red-Blue game, played each fall between York and the University of Toronto. Homecoming, begun in 1978, as President Macdonald describes in the next chapter, is now a tradition at York.[38]

Funding: The Great Limitation

A main problem at York was and is poverty relative to many other universities, especially the University of Toronto, with which York has always had to compete for students and faculty members. It started at York's founding and catch-up has never been possible. It is quite understandable that no university wants to see the pot of government funding divided to its disadvantage, but it is curious that successive Ontario governments have never worked out a policy of funding designed to serve the students and the regions in some sort of rational way to maintain competitive quality in higher education. Studies of the funding system seem to show that the drive to coordinate a "system" of higher education, despite the differences of history and ambitions between universities, has led to inequality among institutions and academic programs, a high degree of bureaucratic overlay, and little equality in funding.[39] Having begun with a highly differentiated group of academic institutions until the first half of the twentieth century, the outcome of post-war public funding has resulted in pressure on all universities to become more like one another. They must take students in large numbers to maintain sufficient income, replicate programs to attract the students, and create research priorities to retain faculty members. These pressures push the institutions towards similarity, not differentiation.

Furthermore, the history of Ontario universities tells us that inadequate and inequitable funding has long been the case. McKillop cites the many ways in which the "provincial university" [University of Toronto] received much more in public funds than the other universities in the late 1850s.[40] In these early years, operating grants were distributed annually according to the government of Ontario's decisions. In the post-war period, controversy over funding inequities arose that led eventually to formula funding. In 1963–64, several universities complained to the government that their operating grants were inadequate. Funding expert Paul Stenton, who has examined lobbying by university administrations and their supporters, quotes from letters between Minister of Education William Davis and University of Toronto officials (President Claude Bissell; Chair of the Board of Governors Neil McKinnon; and Governor Lieutenant-Colonel W.E. Phillips). Stenton points out that the University of Toronto lobby was successful in obtaining more funding. But for the other universities, Western and Queen's, which had also requested additional funds, "the Toronto solution did not fit their needs":

> It is interesting, however, to compare the differing institutional reactions and tactics when confronted with a similar problem – that of attracting more funding to cover perceived shortfalls. The University of Toronto's reaction was almost immediate, well-orchestrated, sophisticated and highly political. The University of Western Ontario's reaction was delayed well into the fiscal year when it saw the likely financial consequences of the level of funding provided. Unlike Toronto and Western, Queen's dealt with the operating funding matters as an equity issue, comparing itself with other institutions and taking a longer-term view that in relative terms it was systematically treated unfairly.[41]

In light of this intense lobbying, one can imagine that the Ontario government found a clear statement of policy objectives and a formula for dividing up the provincial pot of money for universities necessary for relief from such pressures.[42] Although formula funding eventually resulted, the lobbying of universities has never ceased, and each minister responsible for universities is bound to endure it.

Notwithstanding the two major policy goals said to be part of the government's plans in the 1960s, and even now – access for every qualified student and equality among institutions – these have not been the outcomes of formula financing. Indeed as Stenton illustrates in his study, funding stability soon became the goal, access funding was modified, and inequality remained.[43] But, as he also points out, from the government's point of view, formula funding was a way of allocating the money available for universities. From the universities' point of view, the funding, which should be sufficient to meet budget needs, is persistently inadequate.

The problem for York University (and not only for York) was that it opened its doors just when formula funding ideas were being developed; furthermore, the basic academic model for York then consisted largely of the least-well-funded academic programs. Under formula funding, three-year programs provided fewer dollars per student than honours programs, the arts provided less than science and engineering, and York's only professional programs – Fine Arts, Law, Education and Administrative Studies – received far less funding than medicine, dentistry, pharmacy, and engineering programs, of which York had none. Added to this was the government's unanticipated demand that York absorb a huge number of students quickly and at discounted funding weights. So, for example, a student in English or History at York would be given less funding than a student in the same academic program at, say, the University of Toronto. *Costs per student* were more or less the same – in terms of faculty salaries and benefits, staff costs, and maintenance – since both universities were drawing from the same labour force and paying the same rates for utilities and other supplies. But their *income* for the same type of students was very different.

Formula funding – the most important type of public support for an Ontario university – has been changed and modified many times over the years. It has not, however, reduced the inequities among universities. At every level, unequal resources show. The results for labour relations, retention of star faculty members, student services, class sizes, and maintenance of buildings and grounds are significant. These funding differences present a challenge to each new administrator, particularly presidents.

Every Ontario university has its own special frustrations with the funding system as well as a strong sense that governments demand more of them with fewer resources. At York, a serious consequence of lower funding quickly became evident in labour relations.

The faculty members had formed the York University Faculty Association in 1962 as a voluntary association to ensure that members were protected in their jobs and compensation. Unhappiness with pay and benefits had already begun to surface in the 1960s, and by 1970 faculty members were contemplating job action.[44] Severe provincial cutbacks in the early 1970s and a proposal to reduce the number of tenured and tenure-stream faculty aroused particularly serious unhappiness. A successful union drive began among faculty and librarians in 1975, leading to a first collective agreement in 1976. There has been consistent pressure in bargaining and threats of job action, but only two strikes of faculty and librarians, in 1985 and 1997. In all strikes money is at the heart of the matter. Faculty, staff, and students point out that they face the same costs of living as their counterparts at other Toronto universities. Since York does not receive the same funding as universities with higher-weighted academic programs and mixes of programs, there is less money to pay those salaries. The downstream consequences of this are not difficult to work out.

Conclusion

By the time the third president was installed in 1974, the basic organization of York University existed in both the formal and informal senses. Both the Board of Governors and the Senate had established procedures. Student organizations and alumni groups were in place. The staff association had formed. The local media had settled into their critical watch on York's affairs. Many of the main buildings were completed, but contracts for more of the much needed infrastructure had been cancelled due to budget cuts.[45] Ten Faculties had been established. The Keele campus had opened, and the Glendon campus had become the intimate, bilingual Faculty it has remained.

Many of those who had joined the University as faculty members, staff, and governors in earlier years remained with the University for their entire career. Those who retired sometimes remained involved with their Faculty, and even continued with their research on campus.

Despite these building blocks of stability, the crises of the early 1970s – succession, governance, academic purpose, power, and finances – all dominated campus conversations, newspaper coverage, and the priorities of the governors. Into this distraught community, this governance structure, and this uncertain culture, Ian Macdonald was installed as the third president on 28 September 1974.

NOTES

1 There have been several accounts of the founding of York University; the reader may wish to consult the writings of, for example, Horn, *York University*; Ross, *Way Must Be Tried*; and Saywell, *Someone to Teach Them*.

2 Paul, *Leadership Under Fire*, 87.

3 See, for example, Edward B. Harvey, *Industrial Society: Structures, Roles and Relations* (Homewood, IL: Dorsey Press, 1975).

4 Horn, *York University*, 58.

5 Gillies, *From Vision to Reality*, 264.

6 Neither David Slater nor Mamdouh Shoukri has a degree from the University of Toronto; all others are graduates of University College, University of Toronto.

7 Murray G. Ross, *The New University* (Toronto: University of Toronto Press, 1961).

8 This seems to have been a strategic error since honours students were always better funded than general students. When, many years later, the University of Toronto

declared all its undergraduates to be in four-year degree programs – more heavily weighted in the funding formula – its income rose accordingly.

9 Sociology had begun at McGill University in the 1920s, but remained controversial. See, for example, Marlene Shore, *The Science of Social Redemption: McGill, the Chicago School, and the Origins of Social Research in Canada* (Toronto: University of Toronto, 1987), who gives an account of the development of the social sciences more generally.

10 This latter was made possible by a generous grant from the Joseph E. Atkinson Charitable Foundation and became Atkinson College.

11 Gillies, *From Vision to Reality*, 20–1.

12 See that conviction from the point of view of the University of Toronto in Robert Craig Brown, *Arts & Science at Toronto: A History, 1827–1990* (Toronto: University of Toronto Press, 2013), 135–6.

13 See Horn, *York University*, 42.

14 Gillies, *From Vision to Reality*, 24–8.

15 A.B. McKillop, *Matters of Mind: The University in Ontario 1791–1951* (Toronto: University of Toronto Press, 1994).

16 For a description of these attempts, see Horn, *York University*, 128–9.

17 Ibid., 21.

18 Even more difficult changes occurred in the 1980s and 1990s; see Paul Axelrod, *Values in Conflict: The University, the Marketplace and the Trials of Liberal Education* (Montreal; Kingston, ON: McGill-Queen's University Press, 2002), chap. 4.

19 Horn, *York University*, 109–11.

20 Saywell, *Someone to Teach Them*, 96–106; see also James Duff and Robert O. Berdahl, *University Government in Canada* (Toronto: University of Toronto Press, 1966).

21 Horn, *York University*, 117.

22 For a richer description of the prevalence of such differences, see Laurence R. Veysey, *The Emergence of the American University* (Chicago: University of Chicago Press, 1965), especially the Preface.

23 Lombardi, *How Universities Work*, describes the faculty members, or the academy, as the "engines of quality," and indeed they are.

24 Horn, *York University*.

25 McKillop, *Matters of Mind*, xix.

26 Ross, *Way Must Be Tried*, 7.

27 John Seeley was a friend whom Ross hired to the faculty in the first years of York. A dispute arose, and while Ross was away during the summer, Seeley led an ultimately unsuccessful campaign to force Ross's resignation. This divided the faculty and caused great tension with the Board of Governors. See Horn, *York University*, 43–7.

28 Gillies, *From Vision to Reality*, iv–v.

29 Horn, *York University*, 61ff.

30 As will be seen later in this volume, President Macdonald created the Office of the Advisor to the University on the Status of Women in 1975, while a Women's Studies program in 1983 led to the establishment of a Centre for Feminist Research in 1991 and a doctoral graduate in 1997. See Gillian Teiman, *Idealism and Accommodation: A History of Human Rights and Employment Equity at York University, 1959–2005* (Toronto: York University, 2007).

31 Saywell, *Someone to Teach Them*, 87.

32 After the years of student upheaval, two sociologists surveyed sixty-eight US universities, ranging from private Ivy League universities to state institutions, over the 1968–71 period to determine if changes had occurred in their organization and power structure. Their first survey occurred before student activism had challenged the authority and power structure of the university, and their last was in 1971, after the majority of challenges were over. The finding that surprised them was how little the organization and power structure had changed in that period despite the fierce challenges. Of interest is their observation that the internal players in the universities (president, administrators, faculty, students) had confirmed their community of interests and drawn further apart from the external players (regents, governments, and outside communities). In addition, the differentiation among universities and other forms of higher education had increased. Universities were withdrawing from community evening classes, for example, and emphasizing their scholarly missions. Whether these findings can be transferred to the Ontario setting is questionable, but their major observations would appear to hold.

33 Parking is a major issue at York, as at other universities, and falls under municipal regulation. Some universities turn their parking issues over to the city. So far York has not done so. At York, all who park pay, from the president to the part-time student.

34 Murray G. Ross, "The Dilution of Academic Power in Canada: The University of Toronto Act," *Minerva* 10, no. 2 (1972): 242–58.

35 Saywell, *Someone to Teach Them*, 112–28.

36 Linda J. Muzzin and George S. Tracz point out that, prior to 1965, there were practically no vice-presidents in Canadian universities; see "Characteristics and Careers of Canadian University Presidents," *Higher Education* 10, no. 3 (1981): 340.

37 Atkinson College was created to offer part-time studies. By the end of the 1990s, it became obvious that part-time studies were being offered in many Faculties, and the constraints on both Atkinson and other Faculties concerning teaching schedules and curriculum were extreme. I describe the results of this in Chapter 5, in this volume.

38 I think here of Western, Laurier, Queen's, McGill, and other universities where alumni gather annually.

39 There are many studies of the funding of Ontario universities; see, for example, Axelrod, *Values in Conflict*; Edward Monahan, *A History of the Council of Ontario Universities, 1962–2000* (Waterloo, ON: Wilfrid Laurier University Press, 2004); and J. Paul Stenton, "The Ontario University Operating Grants Formula: Its Development to 1986" (PhD diss., University of Toronto, 1992). See also the websites of the Council of Ontario Universities, at http://cou.on.ca/; and the Higher Education Quality Council of Ontario, at http://www.heqco.ca/en-CA/Pages/Home.aspx. A clear description is found in Ontario Federation of University Faculty Associations, "Making Sense of the Funding Formula for Ontario Universities," *OCUFA Report* 9, no. 8 (2015), available online at http://us1.campaign-archive2.com/?u=ca9b5c14da 55e36f1328eb0f1&id=03222d971f&e=.

40 McKillop, *Matters of Mind*, 26–50.

41 Stenton, "Ontario University Operating Grants Formula," 78.

42 For a clear description of the formula, see Arthurs, in this volume.

43 Stenton, "Ontario University Operating Grants Formula."

44 Horn, *York University*, 138–40.

45 All of the Glendon campus buildings were completed before 1970 except the new Centre of Excellence, which opened in 2013, and twenty-one buildings on the Keele campus are listed as having been built and occupied by 1970, and several more were occupied in 1970–71, which means they must have been under construction by the time the third president arrived (ibid., appendix D).

2 York University, 1974–84 (as Seen through the Eyes of a President)

H. IAN MACDONALD

I am sitting in my office on the Keele campus of York University looking across at the Pond Road woodlot. Turkey vultures are enjoying an unscripted aerial ballet while jet aircraft pursue their flight path into Pearson Airport. It is the eve of my eighty-fifth birthday. I am looking forward and backward, metaphorically speaking: forward to the completion of this assignment on my years as president of York University, and backward over the forty years since I assumed that office. With my back to the burgeoning campus, I have no trouble imagining it as it appeared on the day I arrived, as president, on 1 July 1974 – the remnants of the Stong farmlands interspersed among tastefully designed academic and college buildings. I had in prior days heard mutterings about the wide-open windy spaces, but I prized this quintessential Canadian landscape. In fact, it was only a few years later that I thought to undertake a duty tour of the tunnel from the Stedman Building to College Complex One – my first and last visit.

Such was the beginning of my long and lasting love affair with York University. My other love affair had resulted in five children, twelve and under when I was appointed in November 1973 to the presidency. As my obligations to York grew far beyond my expectations, so did the challenge of my responsibilities as father and husband. As a result, Dorothy, my wife, is my first thought as I begin these reflections on "My Presidential Years."

I intend to concentrate more on my view of the nature of a university and my approach to administrative leadership in an academic environment. The earlier history of York has been well noted in various reflective works, particularly Michiel Horn's official history of York University.

York University's early years could best be described as an organization in rapid transit, characterized by strenuous debates about its basic purpose and the appropriate style of administrative leadership. For all its travails, however, there is a paradox: the fact of its academic accomplishments in a relatively short

Figure 2.1. Ian Macdonald, 1974

period of time. In 1974 York was a mere institutional adolescent, fourteen years into its classroom life, yet there was so much of which to be proud. That was my first and early impression.

I had been aware of the York story from its early days when close friends – Denis Smith and Don Rickerd – were part of Murray Ross's young team of enthusiastic administrative colleagues. Denis Smith was the first registrar of York University and was succeeded by Don Rickerd. During the 1965–74 period, when I was in the Ontario public service, where I served first as chief economist then as deputy treasurer and deputy minister of treasury, economics and intergovernmental affairs, I met many of the early academic colleagues at York and was a guest at a variety of events on the Glendon and Keele campuses. I had come to know Murray Ross at the University of Toronto, where I had taught for ten years, during our work together on the annual Couchiching Conference – the summer thinkfest on the shores of Lake Couchiching north of Toronto – and later, when he became York's first president. In fact, during that period, I was courted to be a candidate both for the principalship of Glendon College and the deanship of the Faculty of Administrative Studies (now the Schulich School of Business). As well, I had been sounded out about the presidency of the new Brock University, founded in 1962. These recollections are relevant because, while I was fully engaged in my responsibilities at Queen's Park, I was closely in touch with university affairs in Ontario, particularly at York University.

From the beginning, York struggled with the task of defining its basic purpose and organizational format, a topic well covered in the literature about the early days of York, and in the initial chapter in this book. However, the basic dilemma about York as a small, liberal arts college of bilingual character on the idyllic Glendon campus, as opposed to a large metropolitan university, had a continuing impact on the shape of York, particularly its decentralized quasi-federal structure, which I always thought was important to preserve and regarded not as a weakness but as a strength. I will refer to this analogy frequently in view of its subtle influence on the evolution of York and my belief that it is the faculty, albeit encouraged and supported by the central administration, which accounts for a university's character and reputation.

In a sense, to the extent that the dilemma was resolved, it was more by circumstance than by formal agreement, while the building of a strong academic base continued throughout all the organizational heavy weather. When I contemplated the achievements of this young, adolescent institution at the time I was a candidate for president, I realized it was a demonstration of what is so characteristic of the university tradition: academic strength can survive a lot of administrative chaos. Think of the stars in York's constellation at that time:

- the first all-purpose Faculty of Fine Arts in Canada;
- the first comprehensive Faculty of Environmental Studies in Canada;
- the high promise of Glendon College for bilingual education;
- the highly innovative Faculty of Education;
- the much admired Atkinson College as a home of "second chance," providing degree studies for mature students on a part-time basis;
- the instantly successful and respected Faculty of Administrative Studies (still the most accurate description of York's business school);
- the arrival of Osgoode Hall Law School with its superb reputation;
- the initial Faculty of Graduate Studies;
- the small but powerful Faculty of Science;
- a large and eclectic Faculty of Arts with a variety of novel programs in humanities and social sciences and pioneering ventures in interdisciplinary studies.

Curiously, these strengths were often most noted in other parts of the international academic community, as too often York was like the Biblical prophet: not without honour, save in his own country, and in his own house.

Notwithstanding those accomplishments, the search for York's third president was conducted in a somewhat apocalyptic atmosphere. "Was it all a mistake?" "Should it continue?" Those were observations that I heard too often in influential places. It seemed that York's critics far outnumbered its friends, not the least in media circles. Indeed, there were real problems. What was the circumstantial reality?

- There was lingering ill will over the pre- and post-appointment of the second president following Murray Ross, with President Slater resigning after thirty-one months, a situation that was conducted under a media spotlight.
- The evolving funding formula was highly unfavourable to York, allowing lower per-student weight to the York student base, compared with some of the older universities.
- This compounded York's problem in terms of the growth of enrolment, since York was still in the early stages of development but was not rewarded proportionately for taking such a high number of new students.
- The Ontario government announced a freeze on capital spending for university buildings in 1973 at a time when York was already short of space for academic and recreational activities.
- It was evident to me that strenuous efforts would be required to bring the deans together in a concentrated focus on University-wide leadership, since academic developments had evolved within the ten Faculties in a strongly decentralized fashion.

In the midst of this situation, a search for a new president was launched under the chairmanship of the late Mavor Moore, the distinguished Canadian actor, playwright, and founding chair of the Theatre Department in the Faculty of Fine Arts at York. The guiding principle was that the search should be open, highly democratic, and participatory. The conventional wisdom about such procedures is that no one will sign on to play that game. Quite the contrary: a number of well-known and highly qualified candidates were nominated and allowed their names to stand. This process involved a willingness to come to the campus to meet with a variety of York groups – faculty, staff, and students – in completely open discussion. I well recall a question from a professor of philosophy. At that time, as I indicated, I was deputy minister of Treasury, Economics and Intergovernmental Affairs in the Ontario government and highly involved in all of the government's central decisions. The question was: "Why would a pillar in the corridors of government with access to power, money, and influence be interested in a position with no power, no money, and constant criticism and scrutinizing?" My answer was: "I have been on the fringes of politics for so long that I thought it was time to turn pro!"

The answer was only partly facetious. A successful university president must come equipped with a value system about the purpose and operation of the university. His or her objectives and awareness of the characteristics of the institution must be clear and realistic. At the same time the candidate must perceive at the outset the needs, concerns, and expectations of the community. The successful leader of a symphony must have an ear, not just for the harmonious tones, but also for the discordant notes. Likewise, the university president must be aware that its strength is derived from its academic members, with the president, like the conductor, drawing the whole performance together. These sessions were immensely helpful in enabling me to understand York and in making the community aware of the prospect of a successful partnership. The presidency involves difficult decisions, and they will not please everyone. In fact, sometimes they will even disappoint many. However, an advance sense of common values, identified in open discussion, contributes to an environment of trust, and that is a prerequisite for harmony. We must never forget that a university is a collegial institution, not a corporation. In business, not all members of the Fortune 500 survive and flourish – nor do we expect them to. In September 2013, I attended the 750th anniversary of my Oxford college, Balliol. It has survived all that time because the college is its members and vice-versa.

One day, following a meeting of the York Board of Governors, a governor who had been an undergraduate classmate and was now president and CEO of a major corporation approached me with a question. There had been a story that morning in the *Globe and Mail* about a York faculty member who had criticized the University about some issue (I cannot even recall what it was). He said to me: "If that happened in my corporation, his office would be locked, his key taken away, and he would be marched out the front door." My reply was: "Do you remember what I have been telling you all these years about the difference between a university and corporation?"

Of course, the president is not just working with colleagues and the formality of the Senate. Ultimately, the president is appointed by and responsible to the Board of Governors. In this bicameral system, the role of interpreter and communicator between the two sides is a major part of presidential responsibility. It distinguishes the position from that of a corporate CEO. For that reason, I thought it essential never to miss a Board meeting or a Senate meeting. One factor that some might regard as an idiosyncrasy was my decision to serve as my own vice-president (academic) throughout my first five-year term and as chair of the Senate Academic Policy and Planning Committee (APPC) throughout my ten years. Since I was coming from outside and since the institution was so young (in institutional terms), this seemed not only the best way to know chapter and verse about the academy but also to influence and support it. As I will describe later, that exercise was extremely helpful in dealing with the arrival of formal unionism on the campus: the best way to deal with a somewhat contradictory situation is unorthodox administrative procedure. The remarkable thing to me was how readily it was accepted and even welcomed. The world of negotiation involves two parties: labour and management, but, in a university, there is a third party – the collegium, to which both unions and management belong. This unique organizational characteristic would become a defining point for so much of York's subsequent history. It could be a challenge or a catastrophe. In later comments on negotiation, I will try to explain why accepting the challenge was the only real alternative.

It also seemed to be important to have a daily reminder of the University's basic purpose. For that reason, I taught a graduate course throughout most of my ten years, often a welcome antidote to the rigours of the administrative life and an opportunity to see our students at their best. That experience, combined with participation in ninety-nine convocations, provided a sense of the University's continuity. I never had enough of seeing the proud faces of relatives as our graduates received their degrees. As Ontario's former premier and York chancellor John Robarts was fond of saying, this was one of those rare occasions where everyone was a winner.

1974: The Road Ahead

In my Installation Address of 28 September 1974, as part of the Atkinson College Autumn convocation, I sought to link the success of the past and the problems of the present with two high priorities for the future: the need to establish clear goals and objectives; and the importance of putting in place an organizational structure to achieve those goals and objectives. In addressing those priorities and what they entailed, I described the environment within which we were to function:

I have always thought it inappropriate for the installation of the President to focus unduly on the individual, and I would suggest that we should be thinking more of the meaning of the Office and its functions in the governance of the University. Whereas the word President has a republican ring, these affairs have tended to resemble a coronation. If then, the President is really a constitutional monarch, we can begin to understand why beheading is more commonplace than impeachment, and a Waterloo a greater likelihood than a Watergate!

I have suggested that the true York University community is represented here today in all its constituent parts. Any one part might survive without every other but it cannot flourish. But all can flourish from a recognition that our constituent parts form more of a Copernican universe than a corporate pyramid. We have a founding deity at Queen's Park which determines the outer limits of our universe, a Board of Governors overseeing the movement of our planets – the Faculties, stars of the Senate to illuminate our way, meteoric students occasionally streaking across the horizon, and of course, our own solar hot-seat – the Office of the President. Hopefully, elements of lunacy occur only at infrequent intervals. Would that our finances were as astronomical as my metaphor! But we also have an interested group which is not only affected by this universe, but is also entitled to participate in its operations. I refer to the general citizenry and, particularly, the community that supports this University. Many friends of the University from the so-called "public at large" are here today, and I hope you will always feel as welcome at York as, you may be certain, you are today.

This University along with most public institutions in Canada today faces tough decisions, and the battle for a higher place on the public scale of priorities will be arduous and demanding. Much has been written recently about the bloom being off the educational rose in Canada, with the universities in particular showing signs of frost-bite. I do not believe that the prevailing sentiments of the people of this province are anti-education. During the past few years, my responsibilities have taken me to numerous corners and various crossroads in Ontario, and I believe that the essential respect for education is as strong as ever. This is particularly characteristic of so many families who are newly arrived in this province in recent years. These new arrivals have increased the number seeking university education, and enhanced the cultural diversity of this university in particular. What the public is seeking, however, is reassurance that the universities have clear goals and objectives, and that they have equipped themselves to perform effectively and responsibly in meeting those objectives.

In this province, at this time, the cost of existing services is multiplying, while countless new claims and overriding priorities are being pressed upon the public purse. I do not see those conditions moderating in the remainder of this decade. The universities face a severe problem in maintaining their position on the ladder of public priorities and in competing for public funds. Therefore, I see three major and overriding priorities at York.

1) to plan our long-term goals and objectives and to present them clearly and forcefully to both the public and governments;
2) to develop a long-run financial plan for the University to ensure adequate support for our goals and objectives;
3) to provide the capacity for qualitative enrichment and creative development of our programs, particularly in the case of those relevant to our social goals in Canada.

For these reasons, the University can take great satisfaction from the willingness of the members of the Board of Governors to embark on our current $10 million Endowment Fund Campaign.

In reviewing those passages, it is interesting to note that nothing has changed and everything has changed. The basic task of deciding on goals and objectives is necessary again at York University under the current prioritization exercise, aimed at deciding which programs will be the York banners of the future. On the other hand, the playing field has expanded exponentially. I noted the 1974 Endowment Fund Campaign, under way that year for $10 million. In 1981 York embarked on a second campaign to raise $15 million, and I recall the extensive debate within the Board of Governors as to whether that was overly ambitious. By 2009 the 50th Anniversary Campaign was designed to achieve $200 million. In 1981, while we struggled to agree on $15 million, during the week it was announced, both Yale University and the University of Chicago went public with $500-million campaigns, of which substantial amounts had been pre-pledged. And the University of Toronto is currently seeking $2 billion, the largest target by far in its long history.

This reflects a major change of attitude with a variety of associated problems and consequences. As a result of the change in government funding, universities like York, without an endowment history, were obliged to pursue this route to complement public finances. Nor were donors alone called to step into the breach. In my years, although student fees accounted for approximately 15 per cent of University revenue compared with over 50 per cent today, that still had huge consequences for equity and accessibility, particularly at York, with so much of its enrolment, at that time, from families in which neither parent (as in my own case) had attended university. Meanwhile, dependence on private and corporate donors required an intensified watchful eye to ensure that the situation did not court interference with academic plans or programs. It also raised the spectre of the University's shaping itself in the corporate mode. Other than by anecdotal reference to my conversation with a former Board member, that was not an issue for university presidents during my period of office, certainly not where I was concerned, and if it should occur, it was readily addressed. When a substantial and well-to-do business figure proposed making a major donation to York University in exchange for an invitation to become York's chancellor, the conversation was abruptly concluded.

As far as goals and objectives were concerned, I will describe later the story of the President's Commission on Goals and Objectives (1976–77), its organizational consequences, and what I believe to be its longer-term impact on York University.

1974: Pot Holes on the Road

The troubles described in Chapter One concerning the period between President Ross's retirement and my beginning in office were not without consequence for my own early years. Indeed, such was the frenzied pace of York's first fourteen academic years that much of the basic administrative infrastructure remained to be assembled. Fairly early on, I recall noticing that we lacked a basic personnel policy to address grievances. Very quickly, with the arrival of the trade unions (I use the formal legislative term under the Ontario Labour Relations Act), even more administrative process was required. In the face of our funding shortcomings, this posed a major problem. I was determined, however, to preserve discretionary dollars for much-needed academic nourishment, and I probably overdid constraint of administrative and staff support. As a result, that is now a part of the University organization that I can scarcely recognize forty years later.

Partly, this was the product of my experience as a deputy minister in the Ontario government. Bureaucracies always find good reason to grow, revision is difficult to accomplish, and self-preservation is often a barrier to good communication. The administrative organization at York, while often more the product of available talent than of organizational planning, had the great merits of openness, adaptability, and inventiveness. To build upon this basis without losing its merits was a challenge that became increasingly apparent over ten years in the President's Office.

On the academic front, however, there were even greater challenges. There were unfulfilled promises, real or imagined instances of a perceived lack of appreciation, unease over the system of tenure and promotion, and a particular problem of finding a justifiable employment practice for so-called pre-69ers – those who had joined the academic community prior to 1969 and for whom special tenure and promotion procedures had been established.

The Issues

Every president arrives with a list of objectives and quickly discovers a group of imperatives. Each incumbent feels confident about tackling some of those issues; in other cases, you hope for the best. However, there was no school for university presidents of which I was aware, and no manual of operations. One of my children remarked to me: "When you get to the office on the first day, how will you know what to do?" Learning quickly is a prerequisite to survival. In turn, any president's style of operation is a composite of what comes naturally and easily, and what is necessary for the good of the institution.

In York at that time, among other characteristics were the following:

- a sense that a new direction was urgently required;
- a high degree of uncertainty about the appropriate direction of the University and its organization;
- a belief that strong leadership was necessary from the centre without challenging the importance of the highly decentralized tradition in the Faculties;
- an apparent lack of institutional self-confidence as a still young university in a world of giants;
- doubts about the college system within a large metropolitan university, along with a passionate allegiance on the part of its supporters;
- a sense of pride in the campus community, along with the desire for a stronger linkage to the wider community;
- as in most institutions, a willingness to see change while preserving the most cherished characteristics;
- above all, a need for complete "openness" and "transparency" as products of a strong belief that every member of the community was entitled to a voice in its direction.

Of course, all of that existed in an overall environment of chronic underfunding, questions about enrolment prospects, the prospect of unionization lurking in the shadows, the cloudy public perception of the University, and the continuing desire to reconcile its small, liberal arts college beginning with the reality of a large metropolitan university in the making.

In the light of those characteristics, I believed that the president of York University faced three overriding administrative tasks, apart from normal managerial and ceremonial responsibilities: the University needed to be approached as a political constituency; a clarification of institutional goals and objectives was essential; and there needed to be a lean, clear administrative structure that combined central leadership while respecting decentralized operations. Beyond that, as I suggested, every new president arrives with a list of pet projects for which the University seems an ideal setting and as a reflector of his or her own values and interests. In my case there were three organized research areas that I hoped to see established, building on existing academic strengths and capacities already apparent at York: a Centre for Research on Latin America and the Caribbean (CERLAC); a Centre for Canadian Studies; and a Centre for the Study of Violence. That these are now acknowledged strengths of the University is a source of great satisfaction. However, each contains a story about the way in which academic operations are often created in the most unusual circumstances; some further comment will help to clarify this assertion.

For years, I had attended conferences, meetings, and business sessions at which noble sentiments were expressed about building greater ties with Latin America, yet very little happened. The discovery that York was replete with academic resources, keen to focus on this relationship, led to the creation of CERLAC. Similarly, our strength in History, English, and other disciplines made York a natural setting for a formalized Canadian Studies program, notwithstanding some academic resistance to the concept. The untimely death of our chancellor, John Robarts, provided the impetus to realize that objective. Subsequently, having persuaded the late Judy LaMarsh to donate her papers and files from her commission on the study of violence to our Archives, I asked for her permission to lend her name to a centre for research on violence. Shortly before her death she agreed, although I still hear her resonant voice: "But it has to be called violence – no euphemisms allowed!" As someone deeply concerned about violence in society, this was one of my happiest moments at York.

The Topics

Any checklist of topics addressed over a ten-year period will be both arbitrary and incomplete. However, these ten areas encompass most of the issues confronting the University and its president (1974–84) and the manner of dealing with them. It is difficult, if not impossible, to provide any chronological order because most of them were in motion at the same time, but by careful cross-referencing, it should be possible to describe them with reasonable clarity:

- the decentralized tradition at York;
- York in the international community;
- York in the local community;
- the York challenge: self-confidence;
- Women's issues at York;
- the academic environment;
- administrative challenges;
- unionization;
- funding, the ongoing albatross; and
- the President's Commission on Goals and Objectives.

Each president could produce a similar, even identical list. The interesting consideration is to examine their linkages and interconnections, and to note how any particular president would approach these circumstances.

The York Decentralized Tradition

One of the most compelling issues of governance and administration in the public sector is the centralization of power. The temptation to control the direction of a government, a university, even a religious institution from the centre is understandable, if not always advisable. Anyone who has been a student of the great Canadian economic historian H.A. Innis has been sensitized to the dangers of centralized power supported by forceful and substantial bureaucracies.

In the case of Canada, it always seemed to me that the model of a decentralized state was, unquestionably, the appropriate form of government in recognition of the fact that Canada was a "community of communities." Indeed, regional differentiation made it an imperative. That firm conviction preceded my entry into the public service of the government of Ontario on 1 January 1965. The nature of my responsibilities at that time for economics and intergovernmental affairs required me to contemplate on a daily basis the requirements and consequences of Canadian federalism. Nowhere was that more apparent or exciting than during the negotiations leading to national medical insurance in the late 1960s. Here the issue was to reconcile the role of the federal government to provide leadership on an issue of national importance with the reality that the responsibility for the health care delivery system reposed in the provincial governments. Watching how leadership played out through a tough and arduous process of negotiations provided a significant background for my new responsibilities as president of York University.

In terms of history, structure, and responsibility, the university is a very different institution from government. However, York University seemed to me to be the academic equivalent of a federal state. The reasons for this were deeply rooted in its background and evolution, from the foundation at Glendon to the establishment of the large campus in Downsview. There was a need to reconcile the original direction of a small, liberal studies campus and the emerging metropolitan university. Of course, the university is a collegial institution, and the faculty members bear a large responsibility for its governance and evolution. In the case of York, this took the form of strong faculty self-determination and residential colleges. In both instances, my strong belief in decentralization was tested, as I will describe in recalling the story of the President's Commission on Goals and Objectives.

A strong collegial system, responsible for academic policy, need not diminish the role and the contribution of the Board of Governors. It is essential, however, that there be a strong symbiosis between the Senate and the Board, a connection which the president is responsible for maintaining. York University has been fortunate to have a strong and supportive Board of Governors from the outset. In the early years it demonstrated an innovative and creative style that brought outstanding faculty members to York and established novel and original Faculties, an adaptability that was the envy of some of the more established universities.

It was exciting and challenging to steer that relationship in order to combine the strengths of the bicameral model with the advantages of the unicameral system. There were times when the Board had some unease over the system, notably the procedure for selecting deans. A majority of the Board came from the corporate world and were accustomed to top-down appointments in senior administrative positions. Deans at York were the product of a Faculty search committee, with a short list recommended to the president and a final choice proposed by the president to the Board. Along the way there was a continuing process of consultation among the president, the outgoing dean, and the search committee. Interestingly, every selection process had its own characteristic flavour, but the norm was to be presented with two final names – often that of an insider and an outsider, often a reflection of the degree to which some in the Faculty wanted a change from the current leadership. Frequently, the ultimate choice required calming the waters among those who clearly had supported the runner-up.

I faced two quite different challenges in appointing approximately fifteen deans during my term as president. In the case of the Faculty of Administrative

Studies, there had been a strong push to find a new leader from the corporate community – certainly, the whole search process was strongly steered in that direction. And so it appeared that the ideal candidate had emerged, and I was prepared to take the recommendation to the Board of Governors on the following Monday. On Friday afternoon I received a call from the candidate, who had changed his mind, even though there had been no signs of hesitation during the courtship. As a result, the incumbent dean graciously agreed to stay put, while the whole process resumed *de novo*.

The second example was even more unorthodox and even more stressful. The controversial dean of Atkinson College, Harry Crowe, had completed his term at the same time my presidency began. His successor, Margaret Knittl, concluded her five-year term, and Professor Crowe entered the lists to return as dean. Although Atkinson College limited any first term to five years, no provision prevented a former dean from being considered after an interval, and he was the unanimous recommendation of the faculty. Although I had a good relationship with Professor Crowe, some members of the Board of Governors were not enthusiastic. The recommendation was accepted, however, but, sadly, Dean Crowe died in the early years of his second term. Associate Dean, Ron Bordessa, who stepped into the breach, subsequently was appointed dean and, some years later, became president of the University of Ontario Institute of Technology. One remarkable and disappointing characteristic of deans in that period was that, with the exception of Dean Knittl, they were all men, notwithstanding all our efforts at gender equality (a subsequent section of this narrative), but there were never any candidates. Happily, that situation appears to have rectified itself, to a degree, over subsequent years.

York in the International Community

A university can thrive best as a member of the wider universe of universities; this has always been the case, but has become increasingly so. Although individual academics have always found their own external networks, promoting institutional linkages requires careful nurturing and support.

York embarked along that path early in its institutional existence, a process that came naturally with so many of its faculty members coming from outside Canada. The bellwether of that orientation was the York-Kenya Project, a CIDA-funded development initiative that began in 1969 and continued until 1984. The project spilled over many of our Faculties and involved a significant number of faculty members and their research. Notably, it brought some 120 young civil servants from the government of Kenya to pursue an MBA, an MES, or an MA in Economics. Some years later, in 1987, on a visit to Nairobi,

I invited those graduates to a reception where I learned that all except three had returned to the public service and were well launched on significant careers. At the same time, many senior ministers and officials in the Kenyan government encouraged their daughters and sons to study at York in a network that exists to this day.

Other ventures are too numerous to mention. Among them, however, were the popular and fulfilling exchange agreements with York University in the United Kingdom, the Hebrew University of Jerusalem, the University of Bordeaux, and the University of Thessalonica.

Not surprisingly, when the Ontario government introduced a differential foreign student fee in 1982, many of my colleagues and I regarded this policy as highly unfortunate as applied to York University. Many of my public presentations were directed at describing the unsuitability of such a practice. And yet it was often a lonely vigil, particularly where my fellow Ontario presidents were concerned. In preparing for a meeting of presidents with the premier, treasurer, and minister of education, we agreed that each of us would take the lead in presenting a particular topic and the rest would add their support. Naturally, the foreign differential student fee fell to me. After the presentation, I turned to my colleagues to be met with dead silence. It could be, of course, that, after I had spoken, there was nothing further to be said!

York in the Community

Of even greater importance than membership in the international community is the role that the university can play in the local community. The enhancement of that role was a large task in 1974. Not only was York struggling to display a positive image (as described earlier), but it had managed to be known more for its warts than for its remarkable successes. In part this was the product of its relative isolation, certainly in the minds of the many Torontonians who regarded Eglinton Avenue as the northern limits of the city. York was seen as adrift on the windswept Stong farm in the foothills of the neighbouring oil tanks. On the one hand, this was an advantage, as York was free to create its own community; on the other hand, these tasks were often performed in an unsupportive environment. It was important to develop allies and champions in every possible way. The York University Alumni Association began in 1964, but was a relatively quiescent organization. However, my discussions with several chapters of the Association, across the country and as far away as Hong Kong, convinced me how important it could be to create a body of instant ambassadors. Some of my administrative colleagues were doubtful, but our first Homecoming Weekend in 1978 provided the impetus for a reinvigorated Alumni Association, which is

Figure 2.2. York's Keele campus, 1970. Courtesy of York University

now a vital partner in the enlarged York community. Part of the objective was to provide a new source of fundraising. I made a joke on myself that became the source of much amusement in its retelling. At the suggestion of Alumni Director Steve Dranitsaris, we offered donors of $500 or more a luncheon with the president. The invented story was about a call from an alumnus who asked: "Is Ian Macdonald still president of York?" When told yes, he then said: "In that case, I would like to give $499!"

At that time the issue was not just one of being an acceptable partner and neighbour in the local community, but also of drawing our academic quality to public attention and indicating why York was a desirable place to which potential students should aspire. The attraction to a particular university, or even a Faculty within, is often the result of teacher-mentor encouragement. In 1974 York was not yet old enough to have many graduates as teachers in high school classrooms as advocates. These circumstances persuaded me that I needed to be out speaking for York at every possible opportunity; I was told that I spoke at nearly five hundred events over the period of ten years. Several lessons were impressed upon me in that peripatetic journey. First, listeners readily came to believe that York would provide a welcoming atmosphere for so many students whose parents had never been to university. Second, so many of those parents had an idealized vision of the university that we had a responsibility to nourish and sustain. I recall speaking to a meeting of the Purchasing Agents Association of Ontario and none of those present had ever attended or even been near a university. One might have expected that they would be primarily concerned with the prospects of "occupational preparation" for their sons and daughters. However, I decided to take a chance on giving a "Cardinal Newman" talk, in the sense of his idealized concept of the classical "ivory tower." That led to an experience that I have never had before or since. Audience members lined up afterwards to shake my hand and remark, some with tears in their eyes, what a wonderful privilege it must be to attend a university. People expect a university to be a special place, and so it should be, although, with so many students obliged to combine paid employment with studies, that is not always easy to achieve. Yet recently – forty years after I came to York as president – one of my students thanked me at the end of term and remarked: "You look exactly like what I visualized a professor to be." I took it as a compliment without further inquiry.

There were other situations in which we worked very hard to put the York name before the public – and not just in conventional ways. The first was the securing of the National Tennis Centre to provide a home for the Canadian Open Championships (1976–78); the second was to offer a place for the Metropolitan Toronto Track and Field Centre along with the highly modern Sports Injury Clinic in 1978. Such projects brought young people and their parents to the campus, and thereafter led them to look further at what we had to offer. Nor was it always easy to convince our academic colleagues that these were acceptable components of an academic institution. However, more people learned the location of York University (and even its existence) in a single week when the Canadian tennis championships were played at the National Tennis Centre than in a whole year, and not just locally, as I discovered when watching on one occasion from my hotel room in South Africa.

Often, York University was ahead of the pack, not just in such initiatives, but also in academic organization of significance to the public. In two important cases, York led the way: the establishment of the joint York-Seneca program in Early Childhood Education, and the first course for credit on local radio through Atkinson College. Neither venture enjoyed an easy passage through the

Senate. There was considerable concern about York's compromising academic standards in participating with a community college. However, agreement was reached to combine York's academic knowledge with Seneca's practitioner experience. From there, the rest is history in the province of Ontario.

The radio course for credit was delivered by Atkinson College in collaboration with CJRT-FM. I was always quite unapologetic about a possible conflict of interest as a Board member of CJRT-FM. It was a pioneering effort, however, as we contemplate the intervening history of distance education. In later years, when I was chairman of the Commonwealth of Learning (1993–2003), it was much on my mind. The Commonwealth of Learning has provided distance education throughout the fifty-four countries of the Commonwealth at all levels of education and in all forms – print, audio, video, and electronic. Once again, York University was the pacesetter. Although I am not an exponent of "branding," if I were pressed that would be my slogan for York: "the pacesetters."

The York Challenge: Self Confidence

York University has suffered badly from a chronic affliction that, although now modified, is far from cured. I refer to a lack of self-confidence. When I came to York in 1974, I was startled to realize how strongly it prevailed. As a result, a pressing priority for me was to find ways of assuring the York community that we were alive and well and living at Glendon and in North York. It is an affliction that I became aware of when I went to Oxford University as a young Canadian Rhodes Scholar in 1952, and found that so many of my fellow Canadians seemed overwhelmed by the perceived superiority of the British students. It quickly became apparent, however, that the yardsticks were all British. The answer was surely to respect them for what they had accomplished, but to acknowledge our totally different experience for its own intrinsic worth.

Similarly, the long shadow of the University of Toronto extended far over the York domain. The answer was to stress the extraordinary York accomplishments and the firm foundation we possessed and on which we could build an even greater future. Although I still see signs of that attitude, it is clear that York need not apologize for not being like other universities in its composition, its emphasis on interdisciplinary studies, its age, and the backgrounds of its students. That is the reason I have always felt that journalistic survey comparisons are inappropriate. Memorial University is unique to the culture and lifestyle of Newfoundland and Labrador. The University of Saskatchewan is deeply imbedded in the agricultural economy of that province, with all its distinctive characteristics. Laurentian University could not have developed in the direction that it has without being reflective of the special characteristics of Northern Ontario. This is a point that any so-called rationalization and prioritization process must address with great care. There were numerous debates about that process of rationalization during my tenure as president. The exercise is only valid if based on the development of the institution's own strengths, rather than becoming a carbon copy of an older institution. Such was part of the problem for the college system at York, which could never emulate the Oxbridge model but faced the challenge of providing a campus port of call for commuter students.

During the years 1984–86, I was involved in a parallel situation when chairing the Commission on the Academic Future of the University of Regina. Like York and Toronto, Regina measured itself against the much older, well-funded University of Saskatchewan. The whole burden of our message in Regina was: be yourself, be proud of your accomplishments, and travel your own path in the future. How interesting it was to be travelling along a similar road in Regina as I had ten years previously at York.

Women's Issues at York

As I noted, there was only one female dean during my presidency at York, and this was not surprising or unusual for Canadian universities at the time. When I assumed the presidency of York, Pauline Jewett at Simon Fraser became the first woman president of one of the newer Canadian universities. By the time I concluded my term, Margaret Fulton had become the first lay person to be appointed president of Mount St. Vincent in Halifax. The history of women in Canadian universities was much on my mind when I came to York, largely as the result of my observations over ten years as a faculty member at the University of Toronto. Women faculty members could be found in junior positions and were relatively underpaid, it was understood that some departments simply did not have women, and staff members were mainly women working in the shadows and in the back offices, notwithstanding the fact that the institution could not have functioned without them. Of course, there were outstanding women such as Professor Kathleen Coburn in the English Department at Victoria College and Professor Mabel Timlin at the University of Saskatchewan, but those were rare exceptions.

It was not so very different during my ten years in the Ontario public service. Whereas the Ontario government was noted for having some outstanding women in a variety of positions, they were not at the senior level. Only at the end of my period of service in 1974 was the first woman deputy minister appointed – Yvonne Crittenden in the Ministry of Social and Family Services. Of course, the face of Ontario was changing rapidly as people of very different backgrounds joined the service. Whenever we met in later years at York, Board member Naline (Goel) Stewart would remind me that, when I hired her in 1966, she was the first woman of Indian background to be hired in the Ontario public service, and "in a sari no less."

To address this issue was a top priority for me at York. Fortunately, I had a windfall to build upon. The Senate had commissioned a study on the status of women faculty members, tabled early in my first year (autumn 1974), that was largely the product of the initiative of Professor Joanna Stuckey, whose perseverance in the earning of a PhD in the Graduate Department of English at the University of Toronto in the era that I described made her a natural for the task. The report revealed that women faculty members, in comparable positions to those of men, were earning about two-thirds the corresponding salary levels of men. To tackle this issue and push through the recommendation, implementation would require the support and determination of a respected faculty member. That was the background to creating the position of advisor to the president on the status of women, not simply as a watchdog but also as a leader. Professor Jane Banfield Haynes was that person. She became the role model for a succession of outstanding York women to occupy that position during my ten years in the President's Office. From that beginning followed the York Women's Centre; the Women's Resource Centre, the first degree course in Women's Studies, and other initiatives, most of which are described in Professor Horn's history of York. Over the years, my colleagues from Canadian universities have remarked to me how important this was to their institutions and to the role of women. As in so many areas of university life, York led the way.

The case of women staff members was similar, but of a different flavour. Wisely or unwisely, I wanted to establish recognition of the staff fairly soon after my arrival at York. Ill funded as we were, I introduced a voluntary across-the-board salary increase for staff. This, I hoped, would remind everyone that staff were part of the collegium, not to be neglected. However, no sooner had we completed that task when one of the vice-presidents came to my office to inform me that a certification notice had just been posted to start the process of unionizing the York University Staff Association (YUSA). "You might well have saved yourself the trouble," he remarked and, by implication, the money. I will return to this subject in the commentary on unionization.

There comes a time, on all social issues, when an appropriate administrative action must be taken. Such was the case, in my second presidential term, when I received a complaint about an alleged situation of sexual harassment. Although the problem was resolved to the satisfaction of all parties, it was strictly on an ad hoc basis. There was no due process, nor any administrative procedure to deal with such matters. As well, the environment of the day was

strictly reactive, rather than providing the necessary education about unacceptable behaviour. To that end, I established a Presidential Advisory Committee
on Sexual Harassment, chaired by Professor Ann B. Shteir, which issued a thorough report in January 1982. This led to the creation of the Sexual Harassment
Education and Complaint Centre, demonstrating once again the leadership of
York University in establishing the first such centre in any Canadian university.

The Academic Environment

How does an academic environment grow in terms of its scope and content?
The first time that I recall contemplating that subject was sitting in the quad-
rangle of Balliol College in 1953 and watching one of my tutors strolling by. In
my estimation, he was a great teacher, a successful researcher, and well-known
public figure. Yet he did not succeed in being appointed a Fellow of the College. Universities are places of dissent, criticism, ideology, and creativity – but
not of uniformity. As a result, the academic path of change and development
is more often random than planned, evolving rather than preordained, and
from the ground up rather than from the top down. It was fascinating how
often the academic landscape developed from the initiative of faculty members
who perceived that the addition of faculty member X or Y would change the
whole future of a department or even a Faculty – for better or worse. By the
same token, the exclusion of someone from the Faculty could leave it much
diminished.

On the positive side, I was always intrigued by playing with the York "raiders"
to bring in a star from a different planet. To "recruit" Professor Ken Davey in
Biology, Professor Don Smiley in Political Science, or Professor Frank Cosen-
tino in Physical Education would have instant impact and did so. That was my
definition of successful "branding."

On the other side, danger could lurk in the tenure and promotions system
unless a remarkable degree of objectivity existed. This was readily apparent
to me since, at York, the president by the constitution of the University was
responsible for the final recommendation to the Board of Governors. In my
first year alone, I recall receiving 155 files, nor did that number decline greatly
in subsequent years. I confess that I spent many hours agonizing over those
decisions, particularly in the case of split judgment among department, Faculty,
and Senate Committees. With unanimity, it was easier to proceed with confidence. Otherwise, I recall making positive recommendations on my own initiative. Discretion prevents me from listing the distinguished faculty members
and academic administrators whose tenure was owed to a presidential decision.
Nevertheless, I found a partial solution to my lingering unease through the

creation of a Senate Tenure and Promotions Appeals Committee, which the Senate adopted. That process introduced a final degree of fairness, at least by the yardstick of consistency with my own judgment in subsequent cases.

The Administrative Challenge

A new executive head of a university (or most organizations) faces two choices in terms of the senior administrative structure: to retain the existing structure or to transform it. I chose to do both. Although I was appointed by the Board of Governors in November 1973, I was unable to leave my duties in the Ontario government and join York until 1 July 1974. That was a mixed blessing. The interval provided an opportunity to meet a variety of people at York, learn more about it, and be involved in "looking in" at the current administrative process. In that period, I owed much to the inestimable Professor John Yolton, who assumed the role of acting president. He involved me in every step along the way, including the appointment of one or two deans. I joined him on many occasions at the University, and he briefed me regularly. It is interesting that I detected in John a hidden flair for administration, and I have no doubt that he could have been a successful president, notwithstanding or even because of his studied and quintessential professorial style. At the conclusion of the period, the Chairman of the Board asked if I would join in a recommendation for an honorary degree for John, and I was delighted to do so. Even without his administrative contribution, he was worthy on grounds of his substantial academic career.

In 1974 there were two York vice-presidents: William Small as VP administration and William Farr as VP (everything else). Like most things at York, however, there was an unorthodox flavour. William Small essentially looked after Physical Resources, and William Farr Finance, Labour Relations, and Student Affairs. The President's Office consisted of the executive officer, Yvonne Aziz, the font of wisdom (and knowledge of buried bodies); Ron Kent, driver, messenger, and jack-of-all trades; and Barbara Goodman, a new young secretary. Shortly we were joined by Michael Scott, who had been my executive assistant at Queen's Park; as special assistant, he assisted with my schedule, speeches, and community involvement. When Scott left, we replaced him and hired one additional officer.

As well, the Office of the Secretary of the University, under Malcolm Ransom, supported my office as an emanation of its responsibility for the business of the Board of Governors and the Senate. As the University grew and became more complicated, particularly with the advent of unionization, I decided to appoint an executive vice-president as *primus inter pares* among the non-academic vice-presidents. Brigadier General George Bell had been an assistant deputy minister in my final ministry days at Queen's Park. He also had a remarkable academic background, and was largely responsible for the establishment of our Centre for Strategic Studies in 1976 (subsequently known as the Centre for International and Security Studies). His role was to support the central administrative structure, to be responsible for finance, to help link academic policy (the Senate) and finance and property (the Board), and to assist in outreach initiatives such as the Metropolitan Track and Field Centre.

In later years, two interesting new offices emerged: the associate vice-president for institutional affairs (Sheldon Levy) and the provost, responsible for student affairs (Tom Meininger). Then, as noted earlier, the office of vice-president academic (William Found) was re-established in 1979. The great challenge was to find the resources to maintain responsible administration and staff support throughout the University in a time of severe fiscal restraint, while pursuing a policy that every discretionary dollar should find its way to the classroom, the library, and the laboratory. I always thought our colleagues performed heroically in the face of that challenge. One new approach to budgeting was the product of my experience at the Ontario government. As the end of a fiscal year approached, I observed the departments spending furiously to preserve the level of their budgetary entitlement for the following year. We introduced the practice at York that deans would keep 50 per cent of unspent funds from their budgetary allocation for the following year while returning 50 per cent to the centre. This proved popular and successful. The metaphor that comes to mind is that of a large crab looking over the University, with one claw representing underfunding and the other representing the growing appetite of the growing institution. That was the reality and the environment that characterized those ten years.

Unionization

Unionization was a fact of life and an ever-challenging feature of the new university as opposed to the traditional collegium. Could those models be reconciled? There was no choice, but it was substantially uncharted territory, and required subtle navigation lest the whole administrative system implode.

It is interesting that I had an early inkling of this prior to York. Although universities were not part of my parish, my ministry extended throughout the government in terms of finance and intergovernmental affairs. I recall discussions with colleagues in the Ministry of Colleges and Universities about the impending arrival of unions in the universities, which led me to study the Ontario Labour Relations Act and its responsibilities. Because of my interest in

occupational health and safety and involvement in the work leading to mandatory seat-belt legislation, the whole philosophical issue of institutional responsibility for employees, as compared to self-determination by employees, became
a fascinating subject. Thus, I was amused by a passage in the regulations under
the Ontario Labour Relations Act to the effect that "notice of certification must
be posted wherever workers gather, including the boiler room" – an interesting image for the academic members of a university. I recall suggesting that a
new statute was surely necessary for the university world, the old statute having
been forged in the assembly lines and the mineshafts of the Ontario industrial
economy.

That issue stared me in the face very quickly at York. YUSA had become a
reality as a union in 1975. The faculty followed suit, forming the York University Faculty Association (YUFA), which developed quickly and became certified in 1976. At that point, labour relations at York existed in a world of six
separate unions. All of these situations were totally the product of their times. It
seems almost unimaginable today that, around 1978, we temporarily broke off
a bargaining session with YUFA when the University (management) refused to
budge beyond a 14 per cent across-the-board salary increase.

The most intellectually exciting event in the whole process was the court
challenge, led by some members of the Faculty of Science and others, to the
legality of the application of the Ontario Labour Relations Act to the University,
whereas, in my previous years at Queen's Park, as noted, I had suggested that
we needed a different kind of statute to apply to universities. This was a highly
delicate matter because it threatened to divide the collegium. And there was
strong pressure on the Board of Governors and the administration to support
the challenge. The danger in not doing so was the possibility of the president's
losing the confidence of that particular group and throwing the University back
to the fragile days of 1972–73 to which I have alluded. That was a lonely time
because there was really no one to consult; partisans were on one side or the
other. I recall sitting up very late and writing in long hand a lengthy address
that the Senate granted me approval to deliver in the Senate Chamber. My position was that we had to begin from respect for the law and, whether we liked
it or not, the Act applied to the University and we were obliged to follow its
dictates. It was now the job of the court to validate that position or not, and to
proceed from the basis of its judgment. The court determined that the law did
so apply. I believe it was a great demonstration of the new maturity of York University that the decision was accepted, because the second part of my address
was to urge that all colleagues unite and accept the challenge of finding a way
to reconcile the contradictory collegium and labour-management models. This
has never been easy, and it has continued to be vexatious, but then universities

are supposed to be creative. We certainly were then, and we have been often in days since that time.

In the final two sections of this chapter, I will comment more briefly on funding and the President's Commission on Goals and Objectives. In the first case, this is a common denominator that has confronted all presidents of York and continues to do so. In the second case, the objective of the Commission was to encourage the York community to continue with the process of innovation and change that had been the hallmark of its early years.

Funding

It remains a paradox of Canadian public policy that, for decades, it has been argued that the future of the Canadian economy depends upon the creation of a knowledge society, on the development of human capital, and the broadening of educational opportunity, while at the same time funding has become even more constrained. Nowhere has that been more true than in Ontario. Therefore, there is little to add, other than to describe the special characteristics of the 1974–84 period, when the rate of increase in York's revenue was less than the rate of inflation in each of these ten years.

The growth of student numbers at York, particularly between 1979 and 1984, combined with limited financial resources, was truly challenging to the faculty: how to maintain teaching standards while enlarging research potential. I recall pointing out to the Board of Governors that we had experienced a 40 per cent increase in undergraduate enrolment with only a modest increase in the number of full-time faculty. Borrowing a phrase from the vocabulary of the private sector, I challenged the corporate Board members: "Show me a comparable increase in productivity in your own businesses."

On the other hand, the boom in enrolment that began in the 1960s was continuing apace, and the more so in the newer universities that were created for the very purpose of accommodating that increase. In those circumstances, teaching was a priority, a necessity, yet even more supportive funding was required to facilitate the strengthening of research. The funding formula was skewed against universities such as York and Trent in favour of the older universities of the province. Some of those universities argued that the newer universities deserved a lower level of funding because they were not heavily research based, when, in fact, they were lagging in the development of research because of underfunding.

This sense of entitlement on the part of the older universities compounded the difficulties the newer universities experienced as the result of the Ontario government's encouragement of "rationalization" on a variety of occasions.

This was interpreted by the older universities in the Council of Ontario Universities to mean the rationalization of the newer universities. I shall never forget a telephone call from the president of one of Ontario's most distinguished institutions that went like this: "We believe that we should demonstrate a seriousness of purpose about rationalization. The Faculties of Education would be a good place to begin with the closure of York's Faculty of Education." Of course, "we" meant the cabal of older universities, with no regard for the highly innovative success story that characterized York's Faculty of Education. That suggestion was so preposterous that I have often pressed myself to wonder if I imagined it. However, having made clear that I did not want to hear that suggestion again, it never became a public issue, nor did I ever need to smooth ruffled feathers at York. Senate vigilance seemed preferable to ringing the alarm bells. In organizational and administrative matters, it is preferable to have everyone directed in a positive direction, as indicated by the continued prominence of our Faculty of Education. The president's task is to protect colleagues from any unnecessary threat to morale. In the jargon of today, there may be times when "less transparency" is preferable to more.

The President's Commission on Goals and Objectives

Of all the events of those ten years, the President's Commission on Goals and Objectives was perhaps the most controversial. It is important to note that the purpose of the Commission was not to establish a blueprint for the University to follow slavishly. Rather, it was to engage the whole community to reflect on where we had been, where we were now, and where we might consider going in the future. The intention was to debate the overriding issues while employing a number of task forces to consider the enhancement of various areas of University life. To that end, I want to include a portion of the Introduction to the Commission's Report.

> The Commission on Goals and Objectives of York University was created in response to a number of pressures from within and outside the University. Short- and long-term financial prospects and demographic projections, combined with changing public and governmental attitudes toward institutions of higher learning, have stimulated universities to define publicly their future goals and set a course toward them; in fact, studies similar to this one have already been undertaken in many other Canadian universities. Charges from the public, on the one hand, of irresponsible use of taxpayers' money and from the universities, on the other hand, of unwarranted government interference in their affairs, are irreconcilable positions. It seems clear that in order to live in an atmosphere of continuing

financial constraint and at the same time respond to the need for new initiatives, the University will not only have to identify its own priorities, but to seek a less dependent status for itself and assume a role of advocacy in the larger community.

Within the Senate, interest in future planning was aroused as early as the fall of 1974, and in May, 1975, the Senate's Academic Policy and Planning Committee (APPC) was requested to prepare a draft statement of the University's priorities and academic goals and the process by which they could be realized. APPC made note of the fact that academic goals cannot be framed or achieved in isolation from other important goals such as social goals – both in the broader sense of the University's future role in society and in the sense of the nature of the society within the University – nor in isolation from economic and administrative factors. It was that Committee's view that a draft statement of priorities written solely from the academic point of view would fail to serve the desired purpose unless administrative structures were subjected to a re-evaluation at least as intensive as academic issues were to receive. Furthermore, if the administration were not a partner to the debate on priorities and committed to the same objectives favoured by academic bodies, realization of these aims could be problematic. Because it was apparent that many, if not most, of the issues requiring debate would fall outside of APPC's terms of reference, the Committee came to the conclusion that a smaller body having broader terms of reference would be needed to conduct a thorough-going exercise. After discussing various alternative structures for a commission, APPC and its Steering Sub-Committee accepted a model proposed by the President: a five-member University Commission to be headed by the President and to include two faculty members nominated and elected by the Senate. It was anticipated that APPC would have a major participatory role to play in bringing forward many of the Commission's recommendations for Senate discussion and assisting with the process of implementation.

A motion proposing that Senate lend its full co-operation to the establishment of the Commission on Goals and Objectives was approved by Senate at its meeting of September 25, 1975. Professors Robert Haynes and John Yolton were elected by Senate to the Commission, and shortly afterward Mrs. Naomi Wagschal, representing the alumni, and Mr John Bankes, representing the students, were elected. Mr Michael Scott served as Executive Secretary until September 1, 1976, at which time that position was assumed by Mrs. Barbara Abercrombie. The Commission's secretarial work was ably performed by Mrs. Peggy Cowley of the President's Office.

The first meeting was held on January 16, 1976[,] and terms of reference were established. At that time the Commission adopted as its overriding aim an examination of "the fundamental question of the structure of York, its academic programmes and priorities, and how the University is equipped to deal with them."

It was our hope that this process would not result only in generalized statements on familiar themes, but also in concrete courses of action for the University which could be projected over at least the next decade. The University's traditional goals of excellence in teaching, research, and public service were to be re-evaluated in the light of best estimates of the realities of life in the seventies and eighties.

The Commission began work by soliciting briefs from a wide cross-section of academic bodies, associations, and individuals. Letters were sent out to, among others, the Senate, the Faculties, the Council of the York Students Federation, YUFA, and YUSA asking for their views on York's future and a frank evaluation of its strengths and weaknesses in the present. We held conversations with almost all of the groups responsible for making submissions, during which an attempt was made to explore the issues raised by the briefs in an informal manner by sounding out the participants on changes in the structure or environment of York that might enhance the quality of our intellectual and cultural life on campus. In addition to meeting with such groups as the Faculties, the libraries, the Women's Centre, and the Council of College Masters, we held three dinner meetings with members of the surrounding communities in which York is located and from which it draws the bulk of its student population; some enlightening perceptions of the role York plays, and is asked to play, emerged from these sessions. After discussing matters brought out in the sessions with the Faculties, we invited each of the deans and the principal of Glendon College for an interview concerning his or her Faculty and University affairs in general. In all, the Commission held eighty meetings between 16 January 1976 and 3 April 1977, forty-eight of them in consultation with others who had a stake in the University's future.

Throughout these meetings, mindful of the danger of forming precipitate judgments about specific components of York, we sought chiefly to be instructed and informed, particularly on questions related to quality: the quality of life on campus, the quality of our teaching and research, the quality of the academic programs, of the student body, and so on. Divergent or opposing points of view were thoroughly investigated. Financial questions were put to one side until we had determined what seemed to us to be the proper objectives for the future. In no instance did Commission members come to a hearing with a plan in mind, or with any predetermined opinions.

The Commission's recommendations were then taken by APPC through the Senate in detailed fashion. Some were accepted, others were rejected, and others were left to be absorbed into the University by osmosis. The most controversial involved the future of the Faculty of Arts, which accounted for about half of the total students in the University. The suggestion was that breaking up the Faculty into smaller, college-based organizations could provide better institutional balance in the University and an academic *raison d'être* for the colleges. It did not happen, but in recent years some of its staunchest opponents have suggested that they might have been wrong to oppose the idea of making the colleges academic bodies in terms of responsibility for the departments of the Faculty of Arts.

However, many of the ideas and recommendations have become part of the York development over the years, which is what I hoped and expected. As I remember it, I was astonished at how much was accomplished between June 1976 and February 1977, and how many members of the York community played an active part in the process. That process, in turn, continues to be instructive for other such exercises, not the least today. In keeping with the decentralized nature of York, it was not a highly centralized activity, but a basically democratic and participatory exercise. We also learned much about how to operate a young university in its evolution. One of the most interesting debates in the Senate revolved around the resolution: "This university should build on its areas of academic strength." Thereupon, a senior faculty member from Glendon College proposed an amendment: "And upon its areas of weakness." I have thought of that often, notwithstanding the extent to which the idea seemed ridiculous. Were the present strengths necessarily the best future prospects? Were the weaker areas the result of less support and fewer resources? Certainly, some of York's most conspicuous successes today were not even contemplated forty years ago. Perhaps Yogi Berra, the former New York Yankees baseball legend and master of malapropisms, was right after all when he remarked: "Planning is very difficult, particularly when it involves the future." And so is academic work if we are – as Tennyson urged us in "Ulysses" – "to follow knowledge like a sinking star, beyond the utmost bounds of human thought."

Now I conclude as I began, in my office on the Keele campus. Last night Dorothy and I enjoyed a lovely evening of theatre and music at the Berkeley Theatre in Toronto – a performance of the music of the singer Charles Aznavour called "What Makes a Man?" In my lyrical meditation, that metamorphosed into "What Makes a University"? My objective in writing this chapter, as it was in coming to York University, was to help answer that question. As a result of both ventures, I have a clearer idea.

NOTE

I wish to thank Margaret Lawrence for her generous assistance in typing numerous drafts of this chapter over many months.

Figure 3.1. Harry Arthurs, 1985

3 "The economy is the secret police of our desires": York University, 1985–92

HARRY ARTHURS

No York president has ever had too much money or too few ambitions. I had better reason to know this than any of my predecessors or successors. I was York's first (and still only) internally appointed president, having been a faculty member for sixteen years – half of that in decanal positions – before taking office. Moreover, during six months of research leave after being appointed, but prior to taking office, I had ample time to contemplate the challenge of matching my expansive dreams with York's limited budget.[1] I spent that leave in London, where I encountered this graffito: "the economy is the secret police of our desires." From that moment on, I knew that my presidency would be about eluding the "secret police" and doing my best to remedy the damage they had visited on my University.

Of course, presidents cannot elude "police" or remedy damage, much less pursue dreams, on their own. That is why I said in my installation address that my first priority would be to "re-establish a sense of what we have in common as members of the York community." This would be no easy task given our chronic financial difficulties, the stunting effect they had on our development, and the disputes and reputational damage they engendered. Nonetheless, I said, I would try to organize a broad consensus around three themes: "excellence, social justice and a concern for the quality of our communal life."[2] In this chapter I will focus on how York attempted, during my presidency, to build that consensus and to address the themes I identified. Whether or not we succeeded is for others to say.[3]

The Struggle for Resources

York's plight

Why did York suffer so severely at the hands of the "secret police"? From the mid-1960s onwards, all Ontario universities were supposed to enjoy access to public support on the same terms. This was to be accomplished by a system with four principal features: an "operating grants formula" that provided a standard per capita subsidy for each student enrolled in a particular discipline at a particular level of study; province-wide tuition fees fixed by government regulation (again with some variation based on field and level of study); a "space formula" that established each institution's entitlement to capital grants, based on enrolments, program mix, and other objective factors; and a "buffer body," the Ontario Council on University Affairs (OCUA), that was mandated to provide independent and objective advice to the government on grants, tuition fees, and other aspects of higher education policy. These arrangements were complemented by the activities of the Council of Ontario Universities (COU), which provided a variety of services to member institutions, mediated their diverse interests, and acted as their collective advocate in discussions with OCUA and the government.[4]

Of course, from the outset it was clear that, notwithstanding the policy of providing equitable access to public funds, Ontario universities would enjoy significantly different levels of financial support. Depending on their mix of programs, some institutions would be entitled to much higher grant and fee revenues than others; those with science, engineering, medical, and graduate Faculties generated more and larger research grants and contracts than those without; older universities were able to attract greater support from their more affluent and numerous alumni than newer ones; and the University of Toronto, in particular, exercised unique, often clandestine, influence over public policies and the expenditure of public funds.

Nonetheless, all the elements of an equitable system were still in place in the mid-1980s when I became president – but only formally. In practice, the funding formula had been suspended, amended, and manipulated from the mid-1970s onwards so as to discount the grants provided to new, expanding universities such as York; the space formula had been consistently ignored in the distribution of capital grants; significant pressures were mounting to deregulate student fees, especially in professional programs; and OCUA's status as an independent advisory body had been eroded by the appointment of several ad hoc advisory commissions with overlapping mandates,[5] by ministerial indifference to its advice, and especially by the willingness of individual universities, or groups of universities, to lobby OCUA and the government for policies that would favour themselves and beggar their neighbours. As a result, COU's ability to perform its traditional brokerage functions and to speak for a united university community was significantly impaired.[6]

York was poorly situated to deal with this turbulent situation. True, it had achieved much for a university then just twenty-five years old: it was Canada's third-largest university; its student body reflected the new demographics of Toronto and Ontario; senior professors as well as junior faculty were strongly committed to undergraduate teaching; its academic culture valued innovation and encouraged interdisciplinarity; strong professional schools had been established in Business, Law, and Fine Arts; and some individual scholars and research groups in both the natural and social sciences enjoyed international reputations.[7] However, York's trajectory of growth and achievement was interrupted by two crises in quick succession: a highly publicized dispute over the appointment of a new president in 1969–70 and a serious financial and governance crisis in 1972–73.[8] These crises earned the University – quite fairly – a degree of public notoriety and impaired its capacity to respond to the increasingly hostile provincial policy and funding environment, described above, that prevailed during the decade prior to my appointment.

Because it had few friends and little influence in government, OCUA, and COU policy debates, York fared poorly in the competition for resources. By 1984–85, it was receiving only 79 cents for each dollar in operating grants provided to the average Ontario university (some institutions received as much as $1.10), and had less than two-thirds of the academic space it was entitled to under the provincial formula. Nor could York make up the deficiency from grants or gifts: it generated derisory amounts of research funding and few research contracts, and its then-60,000 alumni/ae donated a risible $57,000 annually – less than the costs of solicitation. Desperate for funds, and under pressure from government and the communities it served, York accepted more and more students, with lower and lower entering grades. But while these students paid standard fees, they earned York only heavily discounted per capita grants (and, by the mid-1980s, none at all). All aspects of the University's activities suffered as a result: student-faculty ratios were among the least favourable in the province; more and more teaching was done by less highly paid and, sometimes, less qualified part-time and contract faculty; little support could be provided to graduate programs or research centres; libraries were unable to keep collections current or properly serve student and faculty users. And because virtually no capital funds had been provided during an entire decade despite York's rapid growth, classrooms had to be used more hours each day than at any other university; no offices were available for new faculty hires;

laboratories were becoming obsolete; and there was little space on campus for community events or student amenities.[9]

Understandably, faculty and support staff became restive. Although salary levels at York remained roughly comparable to those at other provincial institutions, workloads and working conditions did not. Although some elements of the support staff had been unionized since the 1960s, the principal staff and faculty associations and a union of part-time and contract teachers and researchers (many of them graduate students) were all certified as bargaining agents in the mid-1970s. However, although collective bargaining presented obvious challenges for a university radically short of resources, the effect of underfunding on attitudes and behaviour across the campus community was ultimately more significant. Elements of the faculty became dispirited and/or disputatious; students, taught in increasingly large classes and with few of the usual distractions of campus life, often failed to bond with their University; and the undersized, overworked professional, white- and blue-collar staff, overwhelmed with the difficulty of keeping York afloat, was sometimes unable to rise to the challenge of moving it forward. These reactions to York's impoverishment further damaged its reputation in government and academic circles, among current and prospective staff, students, and faculty, and with prospective donors and the general public.

It was clear to me from the outset of my presidency, then, that unless I could devise a strategy to remedy York's underfunding, unless I could elude "the secret police of our desires," or at least demonstrate that I was not in league with them, I would never be able to build the consensus I had committed to in my installation address.

Analysis and advocacy

York's faculty and staff, students, and governors all understood in a general sense that their University lacked resources that were available to other institutions, but seldom understood why or to what extent. Conversely, although most of my presidential counterparts at other Ontario universities and my interlocutors in government fully understood the causes and consequences of York's relative impoverishment, many of them were inclined either to deny the facts or to blame York for its own misfortunes, rather than to acknowledge that they had brought about and/or benefited from our underfunding. My first task, therefore, was one of advocacy. I had to establish the facts beyond question and with clarity, to put them on the public record, and to force everyone to face up to them. In this difficult task, my "secret weapon" was Sheldon Levy, associate vice-president (later vice-president) for institutional affairs. Working with a small team of analysts, Levy and I found new ways to explain how York had been disadvantaged over a decade or more of formula "adjustments," to rebut the argument that York's wounds were self-inflicted, to call into question policy proposals that would further injure York, and to take full advantage of existing rules to ensure that we received the resources we were entitled to.

By a happy coincidence, in June 1985, the Liberal government of David Peterson took office, and committed itself to improving Ontario's system of post-secondary education. Gregory Sorbara, the newly appointed minister of colleges and universities – a graduate of York's Glendon College and Osgoode Hall Law School (and a recent student of mine) – publicly acknowledged in 1986 the need to address problems caused by chronic underfunding,[10] provided $50 million in annual funding to "fix the formula," and asked OCUA to make recommendations as to how those funds should be distributed. Vigorous representations from the so-called MacTwit group[11] of self-styled "research-intensive" universities led to an early decision by OCUA to divide the $50 million equally between universities such as York, which had expanded enrolments without receiving proper recompense for doing so, and those whose financial problems were due to the province's failure to fund their research infrastructure. Based on its share of the system's overall underfunding, York ought to have received $16 million – over 30 per cent of the original $50 million provided by the Ministry of Colleges and Universities (MCU). In the end, OCUA recommended that York receive about $10.6 million – over 40 per cent of the $25 million set aside for universities that had not received operating funds to support their increased enrolments. Then, after back-channel pressures from the MacTwit group, which opposed even this partial relief for York, OCUA revised its recommendation and reduced our share to under $10 million.[12] This was much less than we were entitled to, but did represent both a significant increase in our base budget and explicit acknowledgment that we had suffered a decade of unfair treatment. Through annual presentations to OCUA and MCU, through other advocacy efforts, and through skilful navigation of the funding formula as it evolved over the next few years, we had managed by 1992 to increase York's funding from 79 cents to 94 cents for each dollar received by the average Ontario university. (Subsequent efforts by President Lorna Marsden finally resulted in 1998 in York's receiving "fair funding" – full, nondiscounted per capita grants.)[13]

Having experienced the power and influence of the self-identified elite universities (led by the University of Toronto), we learned our lesson: York needed allies if it was to protect its interests in future public policy debates. We began to take a leadership role at COU (I was elected chair in 1987), entered into an informal coalition with other universities either disadvantaged by the funding formula or appalled by it (or both),[14] and, thanks to Levy, became a major contributor to system-wide technical discussions surrounding the funding formula, enrolment pressures, and other policy issues. We also formed a cross-party "York caucus" of members of the provincial legislature who were York graduates or had some other close connection with us; we cultivated ethnic communities that had a strong interest in York's success (students from an Italo-Canadian background, for example, comprised roughly 25 per cent of our undergraduate population); we reached out to municipalities and business communities across York Region, just north of our campus; and we ensured that York's contribution to the economic development of the Greater Toronto Area was well documented and understood. Through these tactics, we were largely able to counter efforts to create a two-tiered university system in which institutions would be "differentiated" on the basis of their research intensity (measured by peer-adjudicated grants from the three federal research councils), with the upper tier receiving higher per capita operating grants than York and other lower-tier universities. However, we were careful not to oppose funding for research per se, a stance that would have been indefensible on the merits and contrary to our own interests as a university intent on enhancing its research culture.

A little help from our friends

As a young university, York had few affluent or influential alumni to turn to for help with its financial problems. For this reason, perhaps, its advancement office was radically underdeveloped and the returns it generated were meagre indeed. I was fortunate early in my term in being able to recruit Ian Lithgow, an experienced fundraiser, as York's first vice-president (advancement). He did much to professionalize our approach to fundraising and to relations with alumni, public, media, and the government. With his agreement, I decided that we ought not to launch a major appeal for funds until we could demonstrate that we had done everything we could to improve ourselves with the resources we already had. Our new approach to academic planning and the redevelopment of the campus (both described below) would bring us favourable attention, I felt, and assure donors and government agencies that we were a cause worth supporting. As things turned out, however, Ontario's economy went into steep decline in 1990, forcing us to postpone what would have been our first major campaign. Consequently I never had an opportunity to properly test my mettle as a fundraiser – somewhat to my relief, if not Lithgow's.

Nonetheless, we did make some progress in securing private support. A particularly generous gift enabled us to build what amounted to a new "front door" for York (see below) as the centrepiece of our redesigned campus; improved organization of our "annual giving" approach to alumni produced a modest but useful sum each year; and gifts from donors with specific interests – in business, law or fine arts, for example – helped to fund new bursaries, buildings, and academic initiatives.

One of those gifts generated significant controversy. We received an unsolicited donation of $1 million from the Tokyo-based Sasakawa Foundation, whose founder had allegedly committed war crimes in China. This led to dire warnings from some faculty members that accepting the gift would imperil our relations with Asian universities and damage our reputation for social responsibility more generally. However, since contributions from the Foundation had been accepted by scores of leading universities around the world, including several in China, I decided to accept the gift. The Foundation for its part obligingly refrained from insisting that the graduate fellowships it funded be named after its founder. The controversy evaporated, no negative consequences ensued, and numbers of very able students have benefited from the funds in the intervening years. The University has benefited as well: the controversy nudged us into developing a protocol to guide us in our future dealings with donors.

Excellence: York as an Intellectual Community

My primary goal and personal passion as president was to enhance York's performance and reputation as an academic community. This would not be easy. As Lorna Marsden's introduction reminds us, York had (and still has) a very odd intellectual profile. Unusually for a large, urban university, it had neither an Engineering nor a Medical Faculty, its Science Faculty was a fraction of what might be expected, and its graduate programs were seriously underdeveloped. However, it enjoyed an embarrassment of riches in the social sciences and humanities, where teaching was distributed among no less than three Faculties with overlapping mandates: the Faculty of Arts, located on the Keele campus, Atkinson College for mature and part-time students, and Glendon College, a small, bilingual liberal arts college some 15 kilometres away.

This profile created many difficulties. First, numbers of able applicants who wanted to study science-based subjects at York were turned away because those subjects were offered only to a small cohort of students, or not at all. Second, the formal and informal cross-disciplinary exchanges that enliven most campuses could take place at York only on a much-reduced scale, even though we prided ourselves on our interdisciplinarity. Third, the heavy predominance of social scientists and humanists influenced the development of our political culture, while the disproportionate size and budget of the Faculty of Arts relative to other faculties (over 40 per cent of all of York's students at that time) complicated our governance arrangements. Fourth, York attracted far fewer research grants and contracts, and far fewer donor dollars, than it would have done if it had possessed a normal distribution of disciplines. And fifth, York's failure to provide the full spectrum of research and teaching left it (however unfairly) vulnerable to the ever-present threat of relegation to the ranks of second-tier institutions, and prejudiced its struggle to revise the funding formula.

Finally, York – with its roots in the 1960s – was committed to social justice and impatient with convention, authority, and especially hierarchy. This impatience contributed positively to York's hospitable treatment of nontraditional student constituencies and to its energetic, engaged, and innovative academic culture. However, it had a dark side as well: a suspicion of excellence, a disinclination to reward achievement, and a reluctance to undertake collective or institutional initiatives that might generate opportunities for some scholars and not others. Although by no means universal, these tendencies had a number of negative effects: a reluctance to hire established or potential professorial "superstars"; laxity in promotion and tenure decisions; the abstention of some very able scholars from competition for grants or honours; intra-Faculty conflicts over resource allocation, leadership roles, and symbolic behaviour; and formal or informal norms that gave primacy to undergraduate teaching over graduate studies and research activity. Predictably, too, York's reluctance to honour or support its own, or to "normalize" its intellectual profile, resulted in an underestimation of its considerable intellectual strengths and achievements not only by potential students, faculty recruits, and grant-givers, but also by the York community itself.

The obvious response to these problems was to launch an academic planning process that would document them, propose ways of resolving them, and allow the administration to allocate resources so as to nudge the University towards excellence without abandoning social justice. I was reluctant, however, to initiate discussions on a University academic plan because previous attempts to do so had produced more rancour than results. Documenting our weaknesses risked embarrassment for those found wanting; proposals for new initiatives threatened vested interests; and resource allocation decisions invited jurisdictional boundary disputes among the Board, the Senate, and the administration. Nonetheless, I overcame my initial reluctance and proposed a new framework for Academic Planning at York (APAY), which was endorsed by both the Senate and the Board.[15] Its key elements were: the identification of basic goals for the University; wide consultation with all University constituencies; adoption of a rolling three- to five-year academic plan; responsibility for academic policies to reside with the Senate; ultimate responsibility for budgeting and other matters within its jurisdiction (such as the establishment of new Faculties) to reside with the Board; and a commitment from the administration to use its best efforts to execute the plan by budgeting in accordance with academic priorities.

As it turned out, in the early years, the planning process was at least as useful as the plan itself. APAY launched all academic units on a regular cycle of self-study, led us to evaluate the state of our libraries and other academic support units, and prompted deep reflection on University-wide practices and policies that affected hiring, resource allocation, and other determinants of academic scope and quality. Then, in 1986, the Senate adopted the first University Academic Plan (UAP), after what was arguably the most extensive and intensive scrutiny it had ever accorded any matter on its agenda.[16] As to substance, the UAP was not tightly prescriptive; rather, it scrutinized York's current academic profile and proposed a series of goals, achievement of which would represent tangible improvement. Actual implementation would have to take place, of course, largely at the level of Faculties and departments.[17]

In addition the central administration, under the leadership of Vice-President (Academic) Ken Davey,[18] acted independently to improve the quality of teaching and research. He and I began to carefully scrutinize recommendations for appointments and promotions, as well as tenure decisions (all of which required presidential and Board approval),[19] to ensure that searches were open, directed to fulfilling academic priorities, and met quality standards. We also actively promoted research initiatives by discussing their achievements, problems, and ambitions with academic units, and by providing seed funding, space, and other support for worthy projects. Finally, in all our interactions with the University community, we sought to reinforce the UAP's commitment to promoting academic excellence.[20]

Our initiatives did not go unchallenged. Ironically, my first conflict over excellence was with the Senate Tenure and Promotion Committee, whose members had refused full professorships to several highly qualified candidates by setting the bar so high that virtually no one would be able to clear it. Convinced that this represented a misreading of the Senate legislation, if not score-settling by some disgruntled Committee members with less-than-distinguished records, I overruled the Committee (as I was entitled to do) and provided an extensive (and I believe persuasive) explanation of my action to the Senate.[21] On another occasion, the York University Faculty Association (YUFA) brought a grievance alleging that the administration had improperly rejected a candidate for appointment proffered by a departmental search committee; an arbitrator dismissed the grievance, and upheld our right to insist on both proper search procedures and the application of quality standards. But although we gradually won the war, we clearly did not prevail in every battle. The University's tradition of bottom-up decision-making, subject to limited presidential veto, was enshrined in the YUFA collective agreement; chairs and deans were reluctant to second-guess departmental and Faculty committees; and, as a practical matter, members of those committees almost always knew more about the field than anyone else, and their opinions deserved deference, assuming they were formed in good faith and with due regard for the criteria set out in the collective agreement, Senate legislation, or the Committee's mandate.

That said, the coordination of Senate, Board, and administrative policy-making proved somewhat less contentious than I feared. All three were represented on a new Budget Planning Sub-Committee charged with ensuring that academic planning priorities were reflected in the University's financial decision-making. The administration, in turn, undertook to provide an annual accounting to the Senate of its adherence to the UAP.[22] Perhaps most important, Davey and I were both *ex officio* members of the Senate Academic Policy and Planning Committee (APPC), and decided to become active members. Since we had access to background information and time to prepare drafts of what ultimately would become proposals for Senate approval, we soon became influential members as well. Of course, we neither sought nor exercised a veto over proposals, nor were our own suggestions always adopted as Committee or Senate policies. Nonetheless, our intensive and extensive participation in APPC's deliberations generally ensured that planning documents enjoyed the backing of both the administration and the professoriate. Once APPC proposals were adopted by the Senate (as they usually were), the Board seldom if ever exercised the power of the purse to block them; on the contrary, Board members generally welcomed this new activist approach to reinforcing York as an intellectual community.

Over the years, the APAY framework agreement gradually faded into the background, the UAP became more detailed and prescriptive, and jurisdictional disputes occasionally did come to the fore. But in general, academic planning at York proved to be an indispensable strategy for its improvement as an intellectual community, a process by which the University community came to take the pursuit of excellence and other academic reforms quite seriously. This, in turn, improved York's reputation among other universities, and enabled it to respond more effectively to the increasingly frequent attempts by the provincial government to steer the university system towards goals it deemed to be in the public interest. From my point of view, the process proved its worth in two documents adopted in 1992, my last year in office. In *2020*

Vision – a long-term planning document endorsed by both the Senate and the Board – York committed itself to diversifying its academic programs so that they covered the full range of disciplines offered at other major universities.[23] And in that year's UAP, the Senate affirmed that "the University's *highest* priority must be the promotion of *quality* in our dual and inter-related missions of teaching and research and in the recruitment of students and faculty."[24] Both documents properly acknowledged the looming presence of the "secret police"; both accepted that progress towards these goals depended on the availability of resources. But both accorded academic excellence and its necessary corollary, diversification, the high priority they deserved.

Improving the Quality of Communal Life

Reinventing the campus

As mentioned, having increased enrolment by 50 per cent over the previous decade while adding no new buildings,[25] York had by 1985 become dramatically short of space of every sort: classrooms and offices, libraries and laboratories, social space and residences. But this was by no means the only problem with York's campus.

York had spent its first year in borrowed accommodation on the main campus of the University of Toronto, and then moved to what is now the Glendon campus. This property (the former Woods estate) had been bequeathed to the University of Toronto, and subsequently made available to York, on condition that it be used exclusively for educational purposes. However, Glendon could accommodate at most two to three thousand students, whereas it soon became clear that York's destiny was to grow to some multiple of that number.[26] Ultimately, the main body of the University was relocated to a much larger greenfield site on the northern edge of Toronto, which is now York's Keele campus.[27] Unfortunately, the site was remote from housing, shopping, recreational facilities, and adequate public transport. Worse, like other new universities established around the world during the 1950s and 1960s – and despite the protestations of its original designers to the contrary[28] – York was built in accordance with then-prevailing notions of the suburban ideal. The University itself was isolated from the city and nearby neighbourhoods by a ring road and vacant land; individual buildings were located in park-like settings, isolated from one another; the campus plan – developed by UPACE, a consortium of architects, planners, and civil engineers – was rigidly prescriptive, rather than allowing for organic growth as opportunities presented;[29] and visual coherence was to be achieved by adherence to detailed design standards and a very limited palette of materials.[30] Worse yet, those design standards reflected the then-dominant influence of twentieth-century brutalist architecture.[31] And worst of all, the UPACE plan was never realized. The central mall of the campus was meant to house a medical school and an engineering faculty, but these were never established.[32] In their place – in the heart of the campus – emerged predictably but unpleasantly a series of giant parking lots. The UPACE design, which supposedly would have enabled students to walk from class to class in under ten minutes (including time to light a cigarette),[33] failed to take account of the strong winds and inclement weather that prevail for much of the academic year. Impressive student dining halls – intended to animate an Oxbridge-type college system – stood empty, testimony to the failure of the college system itself and to changing student lifestyles.[34] In sum, York's Keele campus not only lacked facilities of all kinds; it was isolated, ugly, windswept, and inefficient – all of which sapped the morale of faculty and staff and deterred prospective students from enrolling, if they had the choice to study in more pleasant surroundings.

What to do about the campus? For once the "secret police" – the economy – worked to advance our desires rather than suppress them. The Keele campus comprised some 300 hectares of land – far in excess of what the University was ever likely to need for academic and related purposes. In fact, York was one of the largest owners of undeveloped land within the city boundaries. Fortunately for us, in the twenty years between 1965, when construction of the Keele campus began, and 1985, when I took office, Toronto had expanded to the north and west, in York's direction. A strategic location in a growing metropolis, with a real estate market that was "hot" and seemed likely to remain so, opened up the possibility that commercial development of our lands would generate the funds we needed to reinvent our campus. I had given this matter considerable thought prior to becoming president, and I arrived in office with a memo setting out the main elements of a development strategy. By coincidence, some months earlier the Board of Governors had struck a committee to examine our development prospects, chaired by Phil Lapp, a visionary engineer and Board member. Lapp and I compared notes in January 1985, discovered that our ideas were remarkably similar, and immediately got to work to translate them into practical reality.

Our strategy involved several elements. Capital generated by land sales would be used to leverage funds from government and donors, which in turn would enable us to build the new buildings York so desperately needed. These buildings, and their associated infrastructure, would be constructed in accordance with a new plan that would greatly improve the convenience and attractiveness of the campus. And, finally, lands surplus to foreseeable academic

Figure 3.2. York's Keele campus, 2003

requirements would be leased (or sold, if necessary) to businesses that were complementary to York's academic activities or that responded to "ancillary needs" of the campus community. Thus, we hoped to attract commercial R&D partners that would collaborate with leading academic units at York, such as Space Science and Fine Arts, as well as housing, retail, and recreational facilities that would enable York staff, students, and faculty to live comfortably on or adjacent to the campus, rather than commute over long distances by car or inconvenient public transport.

Clearly, a long-term project of this magnitude and complexity could not be handled within York's existing governance structures or by York's administration, at least as then constituted. The solution – which we had put in place by May 1985 – was to create the York University Development Corporation (YUDC) to act on behalf of the University in all matters related to land use development. A free-standing development corporation solved several problems: it allowed the University to recruit development professionals with the requisite skill and at appropriate salaries without encumbering the University's academic budget; it ensured that development decisions would result in financial, as well as less tangible, benefits for the University;[35] it permitted us to organize our finances on the basis of a multiyear development cycle, rather than around the annual budget process to which academic institutions must normally adhere; and it protected York's status as a tax-free charitable institution. In general, then, YUDC was able to operate in a developer-like fashion, at arm's length from the University, but as its agent, in its interests, and under its close supervision.

To ensure that it did its job well, YUDC's first Board of Directors included several York-affiliated leaders of the Toronto development community, including Ephriam Diamond, William Dimma, and Joseph Sorbara, as well as Lapp, myself, and several University officials and governors. An experienced developer, Greg Spearn, was hired as its president, along with a few core employees, and YUDC purchased other technical services from the University or third-party providers. And, crucially, YUDC retained experienced, well-reputed, and hard-nosed consultants – the IBI Group – to help it prepare and implement a new campus master plan and to advise it on development strategies; IBI, in turn, engaged architectural, transportation, and other specialists as required.

The formation of YUDC, unsurprisingly, failed to win immediate or universal support. Many professors and students were suspicious of developers, some of whom - it must be said – deserved their unsavoury reputation for poor land use practices and for improperly influencing municipal officials and councils. YUFA, the faculty union, was particularly disgruntled because the Board of Governors had recently rejected its proposal to establish a faculty housing co-op on campus. Some members of York's Board and administration were, not without reason, nervous about parting with University lands – our only significant endowment, sceptical about whether YUDC could achieve its financial objectives, or troubled about locating YUDC outside the University's established governance structures. Municipal officials and city councillors were fearful that development at York would cause traffic problems and otherwise subvert the city's development plans for its northwest quadrant. And residents of neighbouring communities, especially the social housing projects in the so-called Jane-Finch corridor to our west, complained that their needs should be attended to before ours.

For our development strategy to succeed, YUDC had at least to engage with, and it was hoped, win over these critics and sceptics. In May 1985 it met informally with a broad array of stakeholders, and in June formally established the YUDC Advisory Council, on which all stakeholder groups would be represented; it also gave a hostage to fortune by making that body's chair an *ex officio* member of the YUDC Board. In addition, YUDC circulated its plans widely for comment from the community at large, took on board stakeholder concerns, and, at a two-day off-campus charrette in 1987, gained support for the fundamental elements of a new campus plan from most stakeholder representatives.

Those fundamental elements were captured in a new York Campus Master Plan,[36] which replaced the rigid developmental prescriptions of the UPACE plan with more flexible planning principles; reconfigured the road system so as to better integrate the campus with the surrounding community; established protected pedestrian routes through the campus by siting new buildings as buffers against wind and weather; provided much-needed academic space; established clearly defined green spaces and other indoor and outdoor public spaces for formal and informal gatherings; introduced shopping and other amenities so as to encourage the growth of a residential community both within and adjacent to the academic precinct; improved public transit to the campus – initially buses, ultimately a subway – so as to enhance its accessibility for students and faculty, reduce the amount of space devoted to parking (10,000 cars a day!), and respond to concerns about York's environmental footprint; and created a framework for our nonacademic, ancillary and complementary initiatives.

One more major hurdle remained. The proposed development strategy could not be achieved without the support of both municipal and provincial governments. Our status as a provincial institution meant that questions about our development activity ultimately would have to be resolved as a matter of government policy; capital grants to support the construction of new academic buildings depended on ministerial approval; the proposed intensification of development on York's lands raised legitimate concerns about traffic flows, public transit, sewers, and soft services in Toronto's northwest quadrant and the adjacent York Region; and the tax status of both the University and YUDC would have to be negotiated. Intense efforts by YUDC and University officials ultimately resolved these issues, mostly in ways that facilitated our strategy, and we were finally in a position to proceed.

Our first (and only) major commercial development involved the sale in 1989 of 22 acres of land for a condominium complex. Payment was to take the form of a significant up-front payment plus a share of the proceeds when the units were sold. Alas, the "secret police" reverted to form: the economy fell into recession in 1990, land prices tumbled, our development partner became insolvent, the condominiums were never built, and we never received our share of the proceeds.[37] Nonetheless, the up-front payment we did receive enabled us to launch an ambitious building program and to radically reconstruct the campus core and pedestrian system. That program included a new University common – some 10 acres of green space – around which many academic buildings were clustered, bounded by a sheltered pedestrian "street"; several new academic buildings; a student centre; an attractive graduate student townhouse complex; a college residence; a housing co-op and daycare for York employees; and new working space for several administrative departments. YUDC also built and operated York Lanes, a new shopping complex adjoining the common, which contained a bookstore, retail shops, restaurants, a bank, and a health services centre on its ground floor, and a number of University research centres on its upper floors. Over the years, York Lanes has proved to be an important hub of campus social and academic life, as well as providing a significant financial return to the University.

In all, York spent some $190 million between 1985 and 1992 to enhance the convenience, amenity, and efficiency of the campus and to improve its inventory of academic space from about 65 per cent to 73 per cent of its ever-growing requirements. Funds raised by YUDC were used to match or supplement funds provided by the provincial government, by York's students (who voted to tax themselves to pay for the student centre), and by donors – notably George and Helen Vari, after whom the University's formal entry pavilion and adjacent academic facilities are named.

Although not all buildings were equally successful from a functional or aesthetic point of view, the overall reinvention of the campus was regarded even by sceptics as a significant step forward for York. Our formerly "bleak," "windswept," and "ugly" campus was praised by architectural critics, and several of our new buildings won design awards.[38] As a reviewer remarked in a Toronto newspaper, "It's hard to believe that this used to be a windswept wasteland … It's even harder to believe what it is now and how attractive."[39]

These advances, I believe, were achievable only because we had put in place appropriate structures to drive development forward. Although the Senate, Board, and administration retained an ultimate veto over strategic decisions that fell within their respective jurisdictions and were represented in all the forums where discussions occurred (along with alumni, unions, and community and student groups), they were not involved in operational decisions. Instead YUDC, as mentioned, managed the planning process, negotiated with potential development partners, maintained relations with municipal authorities and community groups, and oversaw the work of our consultants. To avoid duplication, competition, or conflict between YUDC and the administration, I established a new Land Use Coordinating Group (LUCG) comprising myself, YUDC's president, and the senior administrators responsible for the University's finances, physical plant, and government relations. Moreover, I was personally involved on a daily basis in many aspects of the process – partly because of the importance of campus development for York's future, partly because I notionally voted on behalf of the University as YUDC's only shareholder, and partly (to be honest) because of my own long-standing interest in architecture and urban design.

My objective was to ensure that development was driven by – and did, in fact, advance – academic values, but also that it was executed with the necessary tough-mindedness and professionalism. This was no easy task. Campus groups lobbied – quite legitimately – for priority attention to their particular concerns: teaching and research space for their programs, faculty and student housing, respect for the environment, a football stadium, parking, "eyes on the street" security, and bicycle racks. The winners of our architectural competitions – almost without exception – designed excellent buildings, but often chaffed under inadequate budgets and the restrictions of our new design guidelines that, although less stringent than the original UPACE requirements, were still meant to ensure a degree of visual coherence in the look of the campus. Attractive projects whose costs had been carefully estimated had to be stripped down to bare essentials as the price of labour and materials in Toronto's "hot" market increased unexpectedly by as much as 1 per cent per month. And York's physical resources department, after a decade of relative inactivity, had suddenly to gear up to handle simultaneously a number of complex building and infrastructure projects, as well as the ripple effects of those projects as space vacated by units assigned to new buildings became available to other users.

My point about values and interests, tough-mindedness and professionalism warrants amplification. When I became president in January 1985, construction was under way on the only academic building that York had built since 1975. When I enquired why it was being built in an inconvenient location on the periphery of the academic precinct, some distance from its nearest neighbour, I was told that the site had been chosen because of its proximity to an existing sewer line. This led me to announce a guiding principle of our new campus development: "never spend a dollar once if you can spend it twice." By this, I meant to convey that new facilities were intended not only to provide space for faculty and students, but also to achieve long-term planning objectives – in this case, infill between existing buildings to facilitate pedestrian movement.

As it turned out, the spending of dollars even once in connection with this particular building was problematic: no one had budgeted for the cost of equipping and furnishing it after construction was completed. This revealed a lack of coordination and oversight in the relevant department, deficiencies soon corrected by the arrival of Peter Struk, an energetic new associate vice-president with both private and public sector construction experience, and of a cadre of engineers, planners, and other professionals working under him. And of course, the new coordinating body, LUCG, contributed greatly to the avoidance of similar mistakes in the future. Not that mistakes were avoided altogether. On one occasion, we decided to invite design proposals for a college residence from young local architects who had won competitions, but whose buildings had not been built. An excellent design was duly selected, but the winning firm was so small that it was incapable of actually carrying the project forward. A larger firm was engaged to finish the job, but it lacked sympathy for the original design, and introduced highly undesirable modifications. On another occasion, vociferous – but misguided – concerns about security in a new building led to the introduction of design modifications that cost several million dollars and negated some of its more attractive features.

Obviously, I accept full responsibility for these mistakes – although, as it happened, both occurred while I was on my summer vacation. But I also accept my fair share of credit for what turned out to be an innovative, highly popular, and largely successful response to the shortcomings of York's campus. My presidential successors and their colleagues in York's administration and board and in YUDC have continued the work, as their chapters will reveal.

York as corporation and community

Like all universities – and for that matter, churches, municipalities, cultural institutions, and trade unions – York is a corporation as well as an intellectual and social community. It earns revenue, incurs expenses, and is disciplined by a bottom line – a balanced budget. It owns land and financial assets; it sells food, shelter, and parking spaces; it has its own security force, heating plant, and waste disposal system; it is constantly involved in legal transactions and disputes;[40] and it is one of the largest employers in metropolitan Toronto. Unlike business corporations, however, the measure of a university's "corporate success" is not the size of bonuses it awards to its executives or the dividends it pays to its shareholders, but the extent to which the quality of campus intellectual and social life is enriched.

Achieving this kind of success is not easy, given the sometimes conflicting expectations of the University's "relevant others": campus constituencies, other universities, donors and supporters, the media, politicians, and the broader community. Moreover, corporate activity has symbolic as well as economic significance – a matter of some sensitivity in a community that is more politically, socially, and culturally aware than most. To take an obvious case, providing a high level of campus security might require a system of video surveillance, ID checks, and restrictions on access to campus facilities that would be inconsistent with the notion of the University as an open and somewhat anarchic community. Or to take another, "the secret police" can become the arbiters of community values. If the University's residences and catering facilities lose money by providing high-quality services at low prices, the quality of student life will be enhanced, but there will be less to spend on academic needs. Conversely, if they turn a profit by increasing prices or diminishing quality, these funds can be used to buy library books or laboratory equipment, but the quality of life of impecunious students will suffer.

As executor of York's corporate functions and custodian of its corporate conscience, I was fortunate indeed to inherit William Farr as my vice-president (administration). A York graduate and long-serving member of its administration, Farr was brilliant, tough-minded, amusingly cynical, articulate, and fully committed to the primacy of academic over business values – so long as the former were authentic, the latter were overridden for good reason and the University was not thereby exposed to legal liability or long-term harm. He defined his job as making it possible for me to do mine. Farr worked closely with Levy and Struk, both mentioned above, and with other officials – most importantly the vice-president (academic) and the deans. He was responsible for ensuring that our budgets were balanced, for the management of our pension plan, for the purchase and sale of all goods and services, for the construction and maintenance of our buildings, and (occasionally, as formal head of security services) for declaring that the University had to close because of a snowstorm. Under Farr, the University's corporate business got done with as much efficiency and as little trouble as could be expected in an underfunded institution. And better yet, it got done in such a way that life on campus gradually became more convenient and congenial. To cite but two very different examples: research accounting procedures were simplified and expedited, so that expenses could be reimbursed with less wear and tear on claimants; and housekeeping improved so that classrooms and faculty offices became more worthy of the high purposes to which they were devoted.

However, York was not only a corporation; it was a community as well. Like any community, it contained some eccentrics and malcontents. One faculty member wrote to ask whether, like the captain of a ship at sea, I could perform marriages; another claimed that he and his son were being persecuted by York's security services; a third wrote dozens of letters instructing me on how to run the University (and sometimes made telling points).[41] At the same time, it offered inspiring examples of good citizenship, of individuals who were deeply concerned about the quality of life of York's students, staff, and faculty. For example, during the presidential selection process, a well-respected faculty member told me that, because York had no faculty club, he and his colleagues brought their lunches to campus in brown bags and ate alone in their offices. His concern for faculty collegiality and morale was palpable, and I was determined to respond to it if I could. Happily, we were able to find some underutilized space in a central location, which I appropriated for a new dining facility; YUFA agreed to join the administration in co-sponsoring a "faculty club"; and we contracted with a trendy young catering team to provide tasty food at reasonable prices in a congenial setting. No membership fee, no crystal chandeliers, no decanters of sherry, and no presidents' portraits on the walls, but York at last had a place where faculty could gather comfortably for lunch, to entertain visitors, and to host special events.

Academic governance

The way in which decisions are made obviously affects the quality of campus life, not only because substantive outcomes matter, but also because the manner of making them produces satisfaction or irritation, depending on how things are done.

As Lorna Marsden's introduction recounts, York – like most Ontario universities – has a bicameral system of governance comprising a Board of Governors and a Senate. However, neither seemed to be functioning optimally when I became president, nor were relations between the two as cordial and productive as they ought to have been. In part this was a hangover from the crises of 1969–70 and 1972–73; in part it reflected the accumulated stress of dealing with years of underfunding; but in part it had to do with the composition and mandates of the two bodies. The Senate, with some two hundred members, was too large for serious debates. Moreover, it lacked the means of gathering, analysing, and evaluating the information it needed to make important academic policy decisions. And it could not ensure that the decisions it did make were carried out by the administration or by the Faculties, departments, and programs to which those decisions were addressed. The Board, while relatively compact and led by individuals passionately committed to York,[42] had a significant contingent of members who were neither familiar with nor closely connected to York, but who were serving out of a sense of civic responsibility. It was also charged by statute with making decisions that the Senate might consider to be within its purview: academic and senior administrative appointments, promotions and tenure decisions, the approval of new programs and Faculties, and, of course, budget decisions that ultimately determined the quality of academic life. The administration – the president in particular – provided each body with information and advice, mediated between the two, and ultimately implemented their decisions, usually exercising considerable discretion at the margins. This exposed the president to potential criticism from both sides, but it also placed him or her in a position of influence, if not always control. I tried to function in policy debates in both bodies as a prime minister, as the leading proponent or indispensable supporter of all important proposals, and to retain practical control over the allocation of University resources.

My ultimate objective, of course, was to help the Board and Senate to make better substantive decisions and to avoid conflict between them. Ideally, this would also have involved some adjustment of their membership and mandates, but I knew that no such change was likely to happen. Instead, I opted to help them to reinvigorate their decision-making processes by presenting them with worthy challenges (academic planning and campus development, for example), by providing them with solid briefings on matters both within and beyond their jurisdiction, by offering them well-defined alternatives, by warning them if they were overstepping their jurisdiction or stirring up trouble with other stakeholders, and by reporting on how matters had unfolded after the fact.

In general, this approach worked. The quality of decision-making improved somewhat; the administration exercised influence, if not control, over their agendas; and relations between the two bodies proceeded relatively smoothly.

On the other hand, this anodyne description glosses over the many day-to-day tensions that exist in any complex organization. For example, reference to "the administration" masks the fact that its senior ranks were subject to centrifugal forces generated especially by the deans. Although most deans were very able, and a few exceptional, all saw themselves primarily as advocates for their Faculty's interests. Those interests were often aligned with general University objectives, but the deans sometimes adopted positions that set them at odds with one another and/or the central administration. Understandably, deans differed over substantive issues: some complained that their Faculty cross-subsidized others, because they generated a larger share of the University's overall revenues than they received by way of annual budget allocations; disagreements occasionally arose over whether new resources should be used to sustain existing activities or to launch new initiatives; and opinions were sometimes divided over whether to resolve problems pragmatically or in accordance with University policies or the collective agreement. Moreover, on rare occasions, deans might fairly be accused of political posturing – of taking stands to establish themselves as vigorous defenders of their Faculty's interests, rather than as compliant members of the central management team.

I attempted to ensure a commitment to common goals by members of the central administration through two bodies. Vice-presidents, deans, and a few other senior officials, meeting as the President's Policy Committee, were asked to develop a consensus approach to budgeting, labour relations, academic policy, and other matters. However, to be truthful, the group functioned more often as a sounding board and mediator among divergent interests than as the originator or executor of substantive policies. I also met weekly with my vice-presidents in a forum that was deliberately loosely structured and mischievously named: the Most Important Things (MITh) Committee. MITh was particularly successful in identifying and resolving matters that straddled the boundaries between vice-presidential mandates, and in giving me speedy and expert advice on significant emerging issues.

Social Justice

Serving communities, causes, and students

Universities have long provided opportunities for young people from disadvantaged communities to rise up in the world. In this regard, York's record was in many ways exemplary: over 80 per cent of York undergraduates were the first in their family ever to attend university; over 40 per cent came from homes where English was not the first language; significant numbers came from recently arrived immigrant communities; the academic, physical, and social needs of mature and part-time students and students with disabilities were accommodated to an unusual (if not yet sufficient) extent; francophone students were able to study in their own language at Glendon; and the law school was the first in Canada to introduce an equity factor in its admissions policies. But York did more than democratize access to higher education; it put social justice on its academic agenda. Professional Faculties such as Law and Education designed courses and programs with social justice themes; research conducted by York's humanities scholars and social scientists was often politically engaged and explicitly aligned with social movements; and many of our research centres – on Women's Studies, Refugee Studies, the Study of Violence, the African Diaspora, Latin America and the Caribbean, and others – made important contributions to emancipatory discourse in those fields. Moreover York regularly preached what it tried to practise through the stances it took in public policy debates, and through symbolic action such as the voluntary divestment of holdings in firms that did business in apartheid-era South Africa and the granting of honorary degrees to prisoners of conscience and other prominent advocates of social causes.

However, York paid a price for these actions and gestures. Progressive York scholars were sometimes disparaged by more conservative colleagues in their own disciplines; York's hiring policies and symbolic actions were dismissed in some circles as "political correctness"; and York had to divert scarce resources from other important objectives in order to assist academically marginal students from disadvantaged communities. But the biggest price York paid for its commitment to social justice was that it exposed itself to the rebuke that it failed to act in accordance with its principles.

During my presidency, at least, such rebukes were infrequent, muted, and largely related to employment issues. However, social justice concerns were implicated in several major decisions that York had to make, such as whether to expand our enrolment. The beneficiaries of any such expansion were likely to be the marginalized communities whose young people we served; conversely, those communities would be prejudiced if we were to hold our enrolment constant, reduce it, or shift it to science-based, graduate, or professional programs with high admissions standards. Still, York could no longer continue to take large numbers of students for whom we received discounted grants or none at all. In effect, we had to threaten to "go on strike" in order to force the government to pay the University properly for complying with the declared provincial policy of broad accessibility to higher education.[43] Nonetheless we renewed our commitment "to ensure that the underserviced communities in our local catchment area are not further disadvantaged in respect to access to higher education,"[44] especially in light of the inability of students from those communities, for financial and cultural reasons, to study elsewhere.[45] We asked only that we be allowed to expand in disciplines identified by our academic planning process and that we be properly compensated for doing so.

Raising student tuition fees was an even more difficult issue. Other institutions pressed for the deregulation of fees, across-the-board or in high-demand professional programs, so that they could recover the actual costs of instruction or at least charge what the market would bear. While we acknowledged that this would provide universities and/or their professional faculties with much-needed revenue, social justice concerns for some time prevented us from endorsing this approach. In internal debates at COU and in public forums, we argued strongly that Ontario instead should adopt a contingent repayment scheme whereby students would be charged higher fees, but excused from repaying loans needed to finance their education if their post-graduation income left them unable to do so. This argument did not prevail, however, and in the end the "secret police" forced us to support COU's position, which endorsed tuition increases so long as they were offset by improvements to the Ontario Student Assistance Program.

Of course, students made legitimate claims on the University that were not directly connected to their formal education. They wanted to govern their own affairs, to be heard in academic and institutional decision-making that affected their interests, to be treated with respect and dignity, and to exercise the same or greater freedoms on campus that they were entitled to off campus. My vice-presidents (student affairs) – initially historian Tom Meininger, subsequently English scholar Elizabeth Hopkins – managed the administration's relationship with our students in a fair and friendly fashion. Among their important achievements were the restructuring of student government, the introduction of financial accountability mechanisms, the promulgation of a new code of student conduct administered by a new disciplinary tribunal, and the building of an impressive student centre (funded by a self-imposed levy) to house student services, organizations, and activities. If these initiatives only partly compensated for the shortcomings of student life in a large, urban commuter university, at least they were generally understood to represent a good faith effort by the administration to create an open, democratic, and supportive campus community.

I did experience two incidents of student radicalism. On one occasion, students seeking divestment of University investments in apartheid South Africa were massing to occupy my office. I intercepted them, told them that they were too late – that the office was already occupied by someone who favoured divestment (myself) – and then we all joined hands and sang "We Shall Overcome." On another occasion, students en route to occupy my office were intercepted at the front door by security officers; the ensuing stand-off revealed some attitudinal difficulties with our security force that we were then able to address. I never believed that demonstrations created an optimal setting for sensible policy discussions. However, I did feel that, as a matter of principle, the University should accept some degree of disruption in the interests of free speech, so long as the participants stopped short of intimidation or violence. Fortunately, my dedication to this principle was seldom tested during my time in office.

Employment relations: Governance, collective bargaining, human rights, and individual concerns

Employment relations inevitably engage social justice as well as economic concerns.[46] Those relations have several dimensions.

First, the University's employees – especially its professors – are important stakeholders in the institution: the University cannot function without their active and enthusiastic involvement. For that reason, employee groups were invited to participate in the University's governance. Faculty and staff were represented on both the Board of Governors and the Senate – and in the latter body, as well as in Faculty and departmental councils, the professoriate properly constituted a controlling majority. However, employee involvement extended beyond these bodies. For example, employee groups were represented on YUDC's Advisory Council and invited to work with YUDC to build a faculty-staff housing co-op. They were asked to participate in the annual budgeting and priority-setting process (see below), and were included in "town hall" meetings to discuss important policy developments affecting the University. Of course, York involved its employees in various aspects of governance in order to secure their cooperation and heighten their loyalty to the institution, but also because it believed that doing so was consistent with its commitment to social justice. At the same time, we were very much aware of the need to respect the law and the logic governing the second dimension of our relationship: the collective bargaining dimension.

Labour laws prohibit employers from interfering in the representation of employees by a trade union – a prohibition that extends to reaching around the union to deal directly with employees with regard to "terms and conditions of employment," which must be settled through good-faith negotiations with their union. Unlike employees in most contexts, however, professors in particular make important employment-related decisions. As members of hiring, tenure, curriculum, and other committees, they greatly influence their own "terms and conditions"; as members of decanal and presidential search committees, they have a significant role in selecting key members of the management team; and because academic administrators are almost always drawn from the ranks of the professoriate and often return there after completing their term, management and rank-and-file employees often retain close personal and professional ties. The arm's-length relationship between employers and employed envisaged by labour relations legislation is therefore difficult to maintain in a university setting.

Moreover, the line between matters to be dealt with through collective negotiations and those to be resolved in some other manner is not easy to define. For example, the aggregate effect of the University's wage settlements with employee groups effectively determines how much (if any) of its marginal resources would be left over for new hires or library purchases.[47] Tenure is a critical issue for faculty members: should it be regarded as an aspect of the University's academic practices governed by Senate legislation or as a "term and condition of employment" to be negotiated with the faculty union?[48] Financial support for graduate students is often provided in the form of teaching or research assistantships that enable them both to earn a salary and to learn their future craft: should the terms of those assistantships be determined by the academic administrators responsible for their programs or negotiated with the Canadian Union of Public Employees, the union that represents teaching assistants and research assistants?[49]

Farr assumed primary responsibility for collective bargaining, while I focused on the governance aspects of York's employee relations. Early in my term, however, I was drawn into a controversy that coloured my relations with YUFA for some time to come. Along with other Ontario faculty unions, YUFA demanded an end to mandatory retirement at York. Reassured by data that suggested that a wave of retirements would occur in the early 1990s, after which we would confront a professorial "sellers' market," and that adoption of flexible retirement policies would cost the University very little, York's administration responded positively to YUFA's demand.[50] However, replacing mandatory retirement with a more flexible approach left a host of problems unresolved: the restructuring of the University's pension and benefit plans, ensuring the periodic renewal of the faculty, how to deal with older faculty members who could no longer perform at an acceptable standard, and other matters. We therefore proposed to YUFA that mandatory retirement should end in principle immediately on the execution of a collective agreement, but end in practice only when the ensuing problems had been resolved by a joint committee. YUFA rejected this proposal, claiming that mandatory retirement was contrary to the Canadian Charter of Rights and Freedoms and should end immediately.[51] When the administration refused to agree, YUFA called a strike on the issue. As things turned out, its members gave only lukewarm support to the strike, which ended less than two days after it began, with only cosmetic changes in the position of both parties. Unfortunately, in its wake, relations with YUFA became difficult, as it attempted to resolve its internal tensions and install a new and more credible leadership cadre. Fortunately, despite hard bargaining and a few strikes and near-strikes, relations with the other campus unions were about as positive as one could reasonably expect in a university that was experiencing ongoing financial difficulties.

A second feature of employment relations during my term was an increased attention to human rights issues. York had a reputation for nondiscriminatory hiring of faculty and staff and, relative to many institutions, it deserved that reputation. As of 1985, however, women and people of colour were still seriously underrepresented in the professorial complement of most academic units and in the senior administration. Early in my term, we established a system of modest financial incentives to encourage Faculties to improve their gender ratio, and I appointed several women to the senior administration as deans or associate vice-presidents (and later as a vice-president). More important – partly as a matter of principle, partly in response to government requirements,[52] and partly in response to pressure from YUFA – York instituted more proactive and transparent professorial search processes, which ensured that all qualified candidates would be identified and fairly considered and that, *ceteris paribus*, female candidates would receive preference. The University also maintained a vigilant stance against sexual harassment, supported the development of Women's Studies as an academic discipline, and took other steps to make York a more hospitable workplace for women and (to a lesser extent, unfortunately) for members of visible minorities.

Nonetheless, York and I were the targets of a well-publicized human rights complaint resulting from a search committee's failure to recommend (and mine to appoint) a woman as dean of Law. The complaint, however, was brought by women at other universities – not a single York faculty member signed it. An investigator appointed by the Human Rights Commission did not recommend further action, and the matter was settled more or less amicably with the establishment at the law school of a Centre for Feminist Legal Studies. In general, however, although human rights were very much on York's agenda during my presidency, they tended to produce positive initiatives, rather than bitter controversies. Some of my successors were not so fortunate.

Conclusion

To the extent that this chapter is part of a larger institutional narrative, it cannot have a "conclusion" – certainly not one that coincides with the end of the author's term as president. Many of York's crucial struggles – for resources, over the form and substance of academic planning, around the role of unions in University governance – began before I became president, continued after my departure, and, indeed, are likely to last indefinitely into the future. In lieu of a conclusion, I therefore propose a few "lessons learned" that might (or might not) be helpful both to future presidents and to other university stakeholders at York and elsewhere.

Universities are complex organisms into which concepts and processes cannot easily be transplanted from other contexts. This is both a strength and a weakness. It has enabled them to survive as institutions longer than almost all states, longer than any business corporation, longer than any organized profession (other than the clergy, who, after all, founded most ancient universities). Indeed, their longevity puts universities in a position to teach businesses a good

deal about how to organize their affairs: how to mobilize the skills and pas-
sions of knowledge workers, how to decentralize authority, how to add value
through the production of ideas, rather than things.[53] But complexity also frus-
trates efforts by universities themselves to change their values, their constitu-
tions, the kinds of knowledge they conserve and disseminate, and, not least,
their relationships with their "relevant others." As a consequence, change in
universities is most likely to be achieved when it is proposed in an academic
vernacular, pursued through established academic decision-making structures,
and plausibly linked to academic values. Change-minded university administrations, therefore, ought not only to think, talk, and act like academics, but
also to *believe* like academics. This implies that, as in academic life itself, it is
the creation, control, and deployment of information and ideas that empowers
university administrations, not their formal authority. It is far easier – and ultimately more effective – to carry the day through convincing arguments than to
prevail through the exercise of presidential powers.

I also learned that no university is an island. Universities feed at the same
trough (to mix a metaphor), whether that trough contains government grants,
student fees, private largesse, or public respect and goodwill. They therefore
inevitably compete with one another for scarce resources. However, they do
more than compete: they influence one another's behaviour by generating
coercive comparisons of good and bad practice that others must then address.
For example, a problem of campus safety on one campus poses a challenge to
security officials at all; a new approach to teaching technology or to monitor-
ing research ethics will soon attract imitators; concerns about deferred maintenance or underfunded pensions in some institutions will force their way onto
the agenda of others that have not yet encountered such problems. And, most
important – as my experience at COU taught me – if universities can be persuaded to act in concert, their collective power to shape public policy adds up
to far more than the sum of their individual influence.

One final insight: the "secret police of our desires" are indeed ubiquitous,
and their power to frustrate the ambitions of universities and their presidents
should never be underestimated. But the "secret police" are neither invincible
nor unrelenting. It is possible to elude, outwit, even co-opt them. Attempting
to do so might demean principled presidents imbued with academic values;
excessive preoccupation with repairing the university's economy might lead
one to give short shrift to other challenges; and the making of Faustian bar-
gains with public funders and private donors might become habit-forming. But
despite these risks, university presidents must take on the job of ensuring that
faculty and students have the resources they need and the support they deserve.
If presidents do not do so, no one else will.

Table 3.1. Selected Statistics, York University, 1985–86 and 1991–92

	1985–86	1991–92	% Increase
Total full-time equivalent students	26,134	31,840	21.8
Undergraduate applications	21,081	30,598	45.1
Minimum entering grade *(%)*	62.0	70.0	
Average entering grade *(%)*	71.2	75.3	
Ontario Scholars *(%)*	12.4	28.0	
Graduate applications	3,864	4,718	22.1
A class masters *(%)*	23.0	28.0	
A class doctors *(%)*	59.0	59.0	
Degrees granted	5,467	6,653	21.7
Full-time faculty	1,134	1,249	10.1
Female faculty *(%)*	21.3	29.2	37.5
Ratio of full-time equivalent students to full-time faculty	23:1	25.5:1	
Ratio of students to staff	24.56:1	25.39:1	
Operating budget *($ millions)*	152.5	269.9	77.0
Average grants / basic income units *(%)*	79.0	93.0	
Space *(millions of square feet)*	1.77	2.06	16.8
Space entitlement *(incr. to 1994) (%)*	65.53	73.15	
Library, volumes *(millions)*	1.53	1.90	23.9
Library acquisitions budget *($ millions)*	2.48	3.89	56.3
Social Sciences and Humanities Research Council awards *($ millions)*	0.66	1.50	137.8
Natural Sciences and Engineering Research Council awards *($ millions)*	3.27	4.94	51.2
All external research funding *($ millions)*	11.93	27.14	127.4
Fellows of the Royal Society of Canada	32	46	
Organized Research Units	9	16	

Source: Harry Arthurs, *The President's Report to the Board of Governors, May 1992* (North York, ON: York University, 1992).

NOTES

1 I had been a leading proponent of the affiliation of Osgoode Hall Law School with York University (1965–68); became the Law School's associate dean (1968–70) and dean (1972–77); was closely involved in the University's financial crisis under President Slater (1972–73); and served for many years as a member of the Senate and various university committees. My appointment as president was announced in late June 1984, but the Board of Governors permitted me to take six months of a previously arranged research leave. Consequently, I assumed office only on 1 January 1985.

2 York University, Clara Thomas Archives and Special Collections, Office of the President fonds, CTASC 2011-040/003(05), Installation Address, 9 May 1985, 8ff.

3 For a numerical summation of some successes and failures, see Table 3.1, at the end of this chapter.

4 For an account of the origins and perturbations of the funding arrangements and of COU, see Monahan, *History of the Council of Ontario Universities*. See also Diana M. Royce, "University System Coordination and Planning in Ontario 1945 to 1996" (PhD diss., University of Toronto, Ontario Institute for Studies in Education, 1998), available online at http://www.collectionscanada.gc.ca/obj/s4/f2/dsk2/ftp02/NQ35418.pdf; and Ontario, Ministry of Training, Colleges and Universities, *The Ontario Operating Funds Distribution Manual*, (Toronto, October 2009), available online at http://www.uoguelph.ca/analysis_planning/images/pdfs/2009-10-Operating-Manual-Sept09.pdf.

5 The Commission on the Future Development of the Universities of Ontario (Bovey Commission) reported in late 1984, just before I took office. It was one of three such commissions appointed during a three-year period. It recommended a series of measures designed to promote excellence in teaching and research, as well as increased student tuition fees and differentiation among universities.

6 Monahan, *History of the Council of Ontario Universities*.

7 See Ross, *Way Must Be Tried*; Saywell, *Someone to Teach Them*.

8 See Horn, *York University*, chap. 4; Saywell, *Someone to Teach Them*, 13–14.

9 These deficiencies were documented in a series of York briefs to OCUA.

10 Ontario Legislature, 21 October 1985 (Gregory Sorbara), S587.

11 Properly, "McTwwq": McMaster, Toronto, Western, Waterloo, and Queen's universities.

12 The chronology is set out in York University, *York's Appeal to OCUA and MCU concerning Advisory Memorandum 86-VII, Modifications in the Operating Grants Formula* (North York, ON: York University, 30 March 1987).

13 "York to receive $12.5 million more each year through funding change," *York University Gazette Online* 29, no. 14 (9 December 1998); available online at http://www.yorku.ca/yul/gazette/past/archive/120998/index.html, accessed 29 October 2013.

14 In the 1986–87 "formula fix" exercise, York's position was supported by Trent, Brock, Laurentian, Lakehead and Ryerson, all new institutions disadvantaged by the formula, as well as by Ottawa and Windsor, institutions that enjoyed relatively favourable treatment under the old formula. See York University, *York's Appeal*.

15 York University, Clara Thomas Archives and Special Collections, Office of the President fonds, "Report of the Presidential Task Force on Academic Planning at York," 18 November 1985, approved by the Senate of York University Minutes at a Special Meeting on 12 December 1985. (F73) Accession 2000-44 / 024 (16) and by the Board of Governors on 9 December 1985. York University, Clara Thomas

Archives and Special Collections, Office of the President fonds, 2000-44 / 011 (9). The Task Force was reconstituted and produced APAY II, an elaboration of the original planning process, which was approved by the Senate in May 1987 and (the record is unclear) apparently acquiesced in by the Board in September 1987.

16 The Senate's deliberations were preceded by extensive consultation. A series of sub-committees developed position papers; the Senate's Academic Policy and Planning Committee used these papers to prepare an initial draft of the plan; the draft was circulated as a "green paper"; comments were solicited from across the University; and two further days of consultation were attended by all deans, chairs of Faculty councils, chairs of Senate committees, senior members of the administration, and the chair of the Board of Governors. See York University, Senate, *University Academic Plan 1986-87*, 1, appendix I. York University, Scott Library LE3 Y6792 S452 1986.

17 *University Academic Plan 1986–87*, approved by the Senate as amended, 13 May 1986.

18 Davey, a biologist and former dean of the Faculty of Science, served as vice-president (academic) for six years of my term; for the first six months, the position was held by Bill Found, a geographer, and during the final twelve months by Stephen Fienberg, a statistician. All were distinguished scholars with strong academic values.

19 York University Act, 1965, ss. 10 (c), 13 (2)(d).

20 The first UAP (1986–87) declared: "The first General Objective of all academic decision-making at York over the next five years should be to enhance the quality of all of its activities" (10). All subsequent UAPs contained similar language.

21 York University, Clara Thomas Archives and Special Collections, Office of the President fonds, (F124 Secretariat), 2000-044/024 (13), Minutes of Senate, 27 June 1985.

22 APAY II recommendation 11, 10.

23 *2020 Vision: The Future Development of York University*, 12ff. Scott Special Collections, YPC 0003. Diversification was also endorsed by the sixth UAP, 8 (emphasis added).

24 York University Libraries, Clara Thomas Archives and Special Collections, Office of the President fonds, 2008-008/019(07) (F124), *The Sixth University Academic Plan*, 1992, 47.

25 In 1984 York did receive funding for a new building to house its Faculty of Environmental Studies, and some related disciplines in the Faculty of Science. This building – the Lumbers Building – was under construction when I became president in 1985 and was completed in 1986.

26 A 1963 report projected a main campus student population of about 16,000 by 1980 and an ultimate maximum of about 25,000. See York University, Department of Campus Planning, "York University Campus – 1980," in University Planners, Architects and Consulting Engineers [hereafter UPACE], *Master Plan for the York University Campus* (Toronto: UPACE, 1963), 40ff.

27 See Saywell, *Someone to Teach Them*, chap. 2; Horn, *York University*, chap. 3.

28 UPACE, *Master Plan for the York University Campus*, 20, suggests that "York will become a great urban university" and rejects the notion of "a pastoral or suburban campus."

29 Ibid., 25, identifies specific sites for the full range of faculties associated with a comprehensive university

30 Ibid., 18.

31 The Wikipedia article on brutalist architecture lists York's Scott Library as an example of the genre. See "Brutalist Architecture," *Wikipedia*, available online at https://en.wikipedia.org/wiki/List_of_brutalist_structures, accessed 12 April 2016.

32 A free-standing faculty of engineering – the Lassonde School of Engineering – was finally established in 2012.

33 UPACE, *Master Plan for the York University Campus*, 17.

34 See Saywell, *Someone to Teach Them*, chap. 3. As Saywell recounts (46), I attempted to resuscitate the college system by assigning each college an academic identity and aligning it with relevant teaching units (Fine Arts, Science, Public Policy, and so on); my attempt was at best only modestly successful.

35 York's Board had granted several outside organizations the right to locate on campus lands in the hope of enhancing the University's "brand" in the wider community. Possibly these arrangements did indeed provide York with goodwill or other intangible benefits, but it was clear by 1985 that they were financially improvident.

36 IBI Group, *York Campus Master Plan* (1987) approved in principle by the Board of Governors on 14 September 1987; see York University Libraries, Clara Thomas Archives and Special Collections, Office of the President fonds, 2000-044/024 (01) F124 – Secretariat, Minutes of York University secretariat, 1987.

37 In 1997, however, we repurchased the land for a small fraction of the original sale price, and resold it in 2004 to another developer.

38 Notably the Student Centre (Diamond, Schmidt architects, completed 1991), which won the 1996 Governor General's Award for Architecture.

39 Christopher Hume, "Vari Hall gives York University a new image," *Toronto Star*, 19 September 1992, G8.

40 When I became president, all of our legal work was undertaken by a distinguished but expensive firm of solicitors. In 1988 I appointed Harriet Lewis, a York graduate and early-career litigator, as York's first in-house counsel. For over twenty-five years, she not only provided the University with expert legal and strategic advice; she also considerably reduced the University's exposure to high legal bills. She held the title of university secretary until her retirement in July 2014.

41 My dedicated, sensible, and hard-working office staff, led by Dorothy Moore, did much to ensure that I enjoyed amicable personal relations with most members of the York community.

42 For most of my presidency, the chair of the Board was Bruce Bryden, a member of York's first graduating class, former chair of York's alumni association, and an

indefatigable worker on behalf of the University. He died unexpectedly in January 1992 and was succeeded by William Dimma, a distinguished businessman, York MBA graduate, and sometime dean of its Faculty of Administrative Studies.

43 This position was set out during OCUA's protracted "enrolment corridor negotiations" (1989).

44 York Brief to OCUA, October 1989, 3.

45 York Brief to OCUA, November 1989, 1ff.

46 As a labour law scholar, mediator, and arbitrator, perhaps I was unduly sensitive to this fact.

47 This no doubt explains YUFA's refusal to engage in budget consultations as contemplated by APAY, our academic planning document.

48 Tenure rules were adopted at York under Senate legislation many years prior to the unionization of the faculty. Attempts by the Senate to amend those rules subsequent to YUFA's certification as the bargaining agent were challenged by the union, leading to frustrating tripartite negotiations among the administration, YUFA, and the Senate that lasted for over fifteen years.

49 Over time, an increasingly percentage of undergraduate teaching at York (and many universities) has been assigned to teaching assistants and part-time or contractually limited faculty. This has reduced the University's reliance on full-time and more highly paid professors, which has helped to ease its financial difficulties. However, the shortage of full-time academic jobs, in turn, has generated demands for a form of job security by teaching assistants and contractually limited faculty, and for access to tenure-stream employment.

50 As things turned out, this was an unduly optimistic assessment of the costs of ending mandatory retirement.

51 The Supreme Court of Canada, in *McKinney v University of Guelph* [1990] 3 SCR 229, ultimately held that the need of universities to renew their faculty complement justified what might otherwise be a violation of the Charter's prohibitions against discrimination on grounds of age. On my instructions, York – alone of all the universities participating in the litigation – did not object to ending mandatory retirement in principle, but argued that because of its implications for faculty renewal, this should be accomplished through negotiations between the faculty association and the University.

52 The Federal Contractors Program, established in 1986, requires all recipients of government contracts (including universities) to take active steps to achieve employment equity. See http://www.labour.gc.ca/eng/standards_equity/eq/emp/fcp/index.shtml, accessed 19 October 2013.

53 One of my most well-received public speeches was an address to the Empire Club of Canada on 22 March 1990; see Harry Arthurs, "Why Businesses Should Be More University-like," *Canadian Speeches* 4, no. 51 (1990).

Figure 4.1. Susan Mann, 1992

4 Tales of York, 1992–97

SUSAN MANN

In 1992, when Susan Mann became my fifth president, I was no longer the wind-swept campus of early days. But I was still called a lot of names: York, "they" said, was upstart, radical, feisty, pinko, beyond the fringe, that latter referring to more than my geographic location. Twenty years on, those names have lost their sting (I trust I am still feisty) as I have become much more established, bigger, weightier, more solid, a force to be reckoned with on the Canadian university scene and, increasingly, well beyond. I'm in it for the long run now, thanks to the people over the years who believed in me, many quite passionately. I'll outlive all of them and their descendants, too. Back in the early 1990s, however, those names could in fact hurt, for they could affect all those people beyond my boundaries who might otherwise look favourably upon the University: the press and parents and donors and government.

In the midst of that, along came someone who tossed the name Ulysses at me. Not Ulysses the warrior or Ulysses the wanderer, but Ulysses the seeker of knowledge "beyond the utmost bound of human thought."[1] I rather liked that, even if it could be said of most of my companions (and rivals) around the world. It was said of me. And it was said by a stranger to our midst, a candidate for the presidency – a woman at that – who came from an older, smaller, and more established place, but one that had grown out of its earlier reputation to become quite high class indeed. Flattered, I pricked up my ninety thousand ears. Might poetry do something for me after all the plans and property and politics?

On that same occasion, someone asked this stranger a question, and you could hear a pin drop. What did she think of compulsory retirement at age sixty-five? That seems an innocuous question today; Ontario has long since legislated an end to compulsory retirement. But then, oh my! Was she aware of the minefield opening before her? If so, she chose to call things as she saw them:

retirement at sixty-five was a way of ensuring access to University positions for the bright young scholars of tomorrow. Five years later, I was flattened, torn apart, by a faculty strike over this very issue.

A few months later, at an autumn graduation ceremony, I officially installed this poetry-quoting, blunt-spoken historian as my fifth president. She used the occasion to trace the historical, geographic, and cultural origins of my name, the real one – "York" – and to show how those origins shaped my character as a "meeting place for wondering about meaning."[2] I hope the graduating students recognized in her words just where they had been over the previous few years. Certainly they were being treated to the best I had to offer: a warm and elegant celebration of accomplishment and anticipation and hope. Four years later I was dismayed to see students occupying my president's office and the police being called in after a week.

Well, that doesn't happen often. Instead, over that presidential term, I gradually enhanced my place in the academic sun, as I had been doing and would go on doing during the terms of previous and subsequent presidents. The difference in those years was that at the same time I weathered one of the worst financial storms to come my way, then or since. But more of that anon. After five years, my Board of Governors was presented by this president with a document that placed me "on the map" internationally, nationally, locally, politically, financially, and in terms of academic reputation.[3] I was, as she frequently boasted, "Canada's higher education success story of the late twentieth century."[4] She believed it; I began to believe it myself. The Board, so very supportive in making that happen over the years, and responding to the president's bidding, set themselves future tasks to ensure the momentum. But their immediate attention was already focused on the selection of the next president, Lorna Marsden. Another woman – two in a row!

The coming and going of presidents with fixed terms, *chez moi* as at all universities, is one of the ways we have change built right into us. Nothing gets too carved in stone, and nobody has to be ousted for overstaying a welcome. Every change of *chef* is the occasion for soul-searching, dreaming, reorienting priorities and activities. All manner of expressed and unexpressed ambitions are vested in the president, each one of whom brings an alteration of style and purpose. In some ways the president is charged with change: please do something different or at least differently. And given my youth, there is always much to be put in place: the sense of building something new is constant at York. At the same time, every new president draws on the work of the one before and leaves traces for the next. If this president likened my work to that of Ulysses ever seeking knowledge, she began to see that the work of the president is more like that of Ulysses' wife, Penelope, steadfastly shaping the future by adjusting the past, altering the pattern to fit the situation, changing colours, dropping stitches, picking threads, tying and untying knots. And then passing the handiwork on to the next president/Penelope to do the same, differently.

So this one came along with ambitions for me. She wanted my academic stature to match my size, which had been so greatly increased, both in terms of numbers and physical presence, by her predecessor. And she wanted everybody – inside and out – to know about it, to work at it, to believe it. She wanted to keep alive my sense of myself as a community, a sense grounded in my beginnings as a small, liberal arts college on the Glendon campus and a sense sorely tried as I became the giant that I am. She wanted financial stability for me as I went on growing, as I was sure to do, given the size and location of my Keele campus at the very centre of the Greater Toronto Area. As students flocked from the four corners of that area (many of them family-firsts for higher education) and, she hoped, increasingly from beyond Ontario and beyond Canada, she wanted them all to have an unforgettable experience at York exploring the life of the mind. She wanted her own academic compass to be mine. She believed in me.

One of her ways of showing that consistent belief was through letters addressed to the York community, sent out a few times per year, on paper no less, and distributed to everyone's mailbox. She even drafted the letters by hand. Nowadays that would be considered very old-fashioned indeed, but I wasn't as technologically advanced at that time: there was no YorkLine or YFile or York-Space that could ensure everyone had access to the same information or heard the same presidential voice trying to connect with some forty-five thousand people (students, faculty, and staff). I suppose she could have used a list-serve and done it all via e-mail (we *did* have that at the time), but she chose not to. Just as she chose not to collapse the annual fourteen graduation ceremonies into one (we couldn't have managed that physically anyway) in order to maintain a personal touch with students and their families.

Let me quote from some of her letters:[5]

1 September 1992

[W]hat we are supposed to be doing: providing the best of higher education to members of our community and exploring the frontiers of scholarship to the best of our ability. I would like to hope that we can do all that in a mutually supportive way, with much intellectual sensitivity to the diversity among us and with much interdisciplinary and inter-faculty co-operation. In times of financial restraint (likely to be lengthy) these may be the only means of ensuring scholarly vitality and innovation.

6 October 1992

I am also concerned about the torrential stream of government initiatives, requests for information and demands for "consultation" that threaten to encroach upon the autonomy of the university. In that connection I have written to the Minister of Colleges and Universities pointing out that York already performs many of the functions he seems now to be demanding via his "restructuring" exercise.

19 April 1993

About a year ago, some of you heard me speak about Tennyson's poem Ulysses. I must say even I did not think the "deep" would "moan round with many voices" quite so soon.[6] Nor did I expect the main source of the voices to be the government. If one were into plots (and I'm not) one might even suppose that the anti-university sentiment voiced so frequently over the past year, and primarily by government officials, was a carefully orchestrated prelude to the proposed "social contract" (that's code for cuts).

1 September 1993

York's fascination with process – one of the big surprises revealed to me this past year – sits sometimes uneasily alongside our equal insistence on innovation ... Faculty are still pushing themselves and their students to intellectual limits, in spite of class sizes. Our professors obtain research grants in ever-increasing number and size; they produce books, articles, conferences and symposia; their talents are solicited far and wide, in Canada and abroad. They win prizes and awards and recognition, for their teaching, for their research. And they keep on encouraging themselves to do better: they ponder the curriculum and they assess teaching methods; they explore computer use and collaborate on research design.

24 November 1993

[T]here are few issues now under consideration that are not motivated by budget considerations.

4 March 1994

I imagine most of us have come to the university to work because we have a respect for and love of learning, a boundless curiosity about people and about ideas and a desire to share those enthusiasms with others, whether through teaching or working in the York community. We should not lose sight of those motives, not even as we collect the paper clips from incoming mail to make up for our shrinking budgets.

6 September 1994

The message in OCUA's discussion paper[7] is clear, and I doubt the message will change no matter what we say: there will be less money, more students and more demands.

10 January 1995

We warned [OCUA] that access and equity are meaningful objectives only if they ensure accessibility to, and equitable treatment within, quality university programmes ... The York arguments [to OCUA] were well presented, well received and, it seems, particularly notable for our team approach.

27 March 1995

With no subway (yet), no clarity on the implications of the recent federal budget (yet), no end in sight (yet) to cuts and their personal and organizational consequences, we are justified in being a bit sombre.

8 January 1996

[I]n order to make the required cuts, we are going to have to go on exercising York's renowned ingenuity and imagination to continue redesigning what we do, how we do it and how to ensure the best possible education for our students ... We need only remember York's very great strengths: its youth, its energy, its innovative programs of both a disciplinary and interdisciplinary nature, its strong faculty (there are shining stars among those becoming full professors this year, and our new faculty are gems), its strong student demand which will be augmented by our location in the fastest growing area of the province, and its reputation for quality and relevance. York is Canada's higher education success story. We have to keep it that way.

25 June 1997

This will be the last of my letters to the York community. Until this letter, I always had a distinct sense of the real entity, the linked group of people that we all referred to as the York Community. People who shared the sense of adventure that has been the mark of York University. People who delighted together in the success of our students. People committed to building a great university. People rejoicing in the public recognition of that greatness. In short, people linked by a common purpose across the structural divisions of Faculty or discipline or occupation or status ... Now I am less sure, not of our individual commitment to York, but rather of our shared sense of that commitment, our shared sense of each other as part of a community. Perhaps York has become too large for that particular sense of community. Perhaps the changing complexities of the world around us exercise irresistible centrifugal forces. Perhaps York, the most modern of Canadian universities, is prey to the very post-modernism that artists and literary specialists and social scientists analyse in late twentieth century culture.

There, you get the idea. She was clearly trying to keep the focus on academic matters and keep everyone's spirits up during a time when finances became the primary concern. You can trace that increasing concern in these excerpts alone. Well, it was a far cry from the financial stability she had wished for. Between 1992 and 1996 three different governments, two provincial (the major source of my funding), and one federal, took turns beating up on me. Of course I wasn't alone: all my Ontario colleagues were being hit – and my Canadian ones, too, once the federal government got in on the act in 1996. There is always something unexpected awaiting every new president, and this was the one she encountered. Not that all presidents don't worry about money. As one of her predecessors has been known to say, "No York president has ever had too much money or too few ambitions."[8] But this time it was different. Money was taken away in unprecedented amounts. Over those five years I was subjected to cuts of close to $50 million, at a time when my annual operating budget was just under $300 million.[9] If mathematically that might not appear so bad – take out a mere(!) $10 million every year for five years – you need to bear in mind that the cuts were not evenly distributed over time and that by far the largest expenditure in a university budget is a fixed one, for salaries. There wasn't much room for manoeuvre.

It all began early in 1993 while my new president was just getting her feet wet. The NDP provincial government, faced with an economy in recession and a huge deficit that it blamed in part on its Liberal predecessors, legislated a "social contract" covering the entire public service in order to eliminate $9 billion in government expenditures. As part of the "contract," an "Expenditure Control Plan" set specific targets for reducing nonsalary costs in each sector of the public service, of which the universities are one. The other part, the "social contract" itself, was to reduce salary costs. The two together, along with some other bits of arcane university funding, meant that York faced cuts of just under $20 million. We were in for a rough ride. Oh, there was an attempt to make it look less rough: we could determine internally what cuts would have to be made to meet "Expenditure Control" targets, and we were invited to come to a "sectoral table" where all the universities and colleges, their employee groups, and the government would negotiate the "social contract" – not the overall amount of the reduction, but merely the means for meeting that amount. And if, by chance, we couldn't come to an agreement, well then, the government would simply impose one. But if we could agree by a certain date, the cut might be marginally smaller. Imagine the circus! Out of those "sectoral negotiations" and the ones that followed within York itself with each of my eleven unionized employee groups came the three-year salary freeze for all University personnel and the postponing for the same period of all contract negotiations.

Before those three years even came to an end, the Ontario electorate put an end to the NDP government in favour of a "common sense revolution."[10] The "social contract," however, remained in place – both parts of it – and the new Conservative government added even larger cuts in the name of "common sense." For York this meant another $28 million to be cut out of my budget. If that were not bad enough, the federal government muddied the waters by reducing transfer payments to the provinces, eliminating a Canada-wide scholarship program for undergraduate science students, and reducing the funding of the research granting councils in the Sciences and the Humanities. It was not a happy time for universities.

But in recounting all this gloom so many years later, let me do what my president at the time did, always balancing the gloomy news in her letters with some good news. I can do that because, curiously enough, those years of unprecedented cuts were also years of unprecedented gifts. And that allows me to tell a couple of other stories, still about money, alas, but at least these are good stories.

Picture this: two intense, unsmiling men sitting on one side of a table. Easily mistaken for twins, their jackets, string ties, and general demeanour suggested recent participation in a poker game in the Far West. But this wasn't a gaming table. It was a long rectangle in a university office, and they were playing for higher stakes – looking to give, not to take away. Only to the right place, however, and they weren't showing their cards. Across from them sat a bevy of University officials, for the most part academics in disguise, all men except for the one in the middle directly opposite the two visitors. Brief introductions, no fanfare, the "twins" had no time to waste on pleasantries; a potential donor and his lawyer had business to conduct.

A nod from one and five words from the other: "What does the University want?"

Three words came straight back at him, the president's tone and expression matching his: "Scholarships for students."

Had it been a tennis match, the point would have been granted immediately to her, because the man opposite, poker-faced still, hesitated ever so slightly: "No other university has said that to me." (Aha! He gave away one of his cards: he had been shopping his donation around.)

"Well, that's what York wants."

With that, everyone went their separate ways, he to his gold-mining royalty company and my people to their offices. The next day – well, it might have been a week or so; it certainly wasn't long afterwards – I received the largest private donation ever to come the way of a Canadian university: $15 million from Seymour Schulich. It's been surpassed since then but at the time it was unheard of.[11] Less than twenty years later, the Schulich School of Business at York University is ranked by *The Economist* as among the best in the world. And many, many students have had the increasing financial burden of their studies eased by his philanthropy.

That Schulich and York made such a good match is not surprising. Given my history and culture of doing things differently and Seymour Schulich's unerring eye for a sound investment and a great adventure, we were bound to get along. But nor is it surprising that a few eyebrows were raised, both inside and outside the University, at the source and the magnitude of the donation. Leaving aside interuniversity rivalry (and there's a fair bit of that floating around), some academics actually find money and business ever so slightly distasteful. It's as if the old aristocratic cultural bias against money-making and business occupations had infected liberal, professorial minds. In its mildest form, the attitude colours the arts/professional school divide common to most universities and perhaps especially at York, where the Arts Faculty is huge compared to the professional schools. In its extreme form the attitude fosters the fear that the business world wishes to dictate what goes on in universities. I've seen the entire spectrum in my midst. Indeed, my governing structure lends some credence to such an attitude: a Board of Governors heavily weighted with businessmen oversees University finances while the Senate, heavily weighted with professors and students, determines academic programming and regulations. The two rarely meet; their only point of contact is the president, who is a member of both bodies but in charge of neither. Only she saw the intensity of commitment to York by both bodies. Only she saw the puzzlement of some Board members as to why a university did not in fact operate like a business, but she also registered the pride of all of them in being associated with York.

Very little of this came to the surface around the Schulich donation. The green glint in the eyes of other universities soon faded as they set about acquiring major benefactors of their own. Schulich was a pioneer in this regard, encouraging his peers to make similar donations and repeating his own generosity both at York and in different fields of study at other Canadian universities. What's in it for him? There is of course the tax deduction associated with a gift to a charitable institution. But there is also something only a university has to offer, something the nay-sayers within won't acknowledge: the prestige and longevity of a university connection. A big donation to a university, involving a named building or School or research centre or professorship, is about as close to immortality as one can get. Hence perhaps the high and rising price! Bigger gifts have gone to other universities since Schulich and I set the precedent back in the mid-1990s. And York has had increasing donations, too. Shortly after this presidency I acquired an Engineering School, now known as the Lassonde School of Engineering, thanks to a gift of $25 million from Pierre Lassonde. "Renaissance engineers" are to be trained there, drawing imaginatively on my interdisciplinary academic culture. And who is Pierre Lassonde? A long-time business partner of Seymour Schulich.

Needless to say, a president's three words to a potential donor are not a magic wand that produces instant largesse. My then-called Faculty of Administrative Studies and its ebullient dean (still there twenty years later!), along with the University's fundraising staff, had been carefully "cultivating" Mr Schulich for some time. It's a long process involving much planning and attention and care. Potential donors are not lined up at the entrance to universities, and even the sympathy occasioned by a president with her ankle in a cast at one point could not always loosen purse strings. But now and again a presidential word can do the trick. And that leads me to the second good story related to money.

Plans for a fundraising campaign had been slowly taking shape at the time. I now think the pace was in part determined by the unseemly nature of asking University folk themselves to contribute when all they saw around them were cuts, including their own frozen salaries. The goal, nonetheless, had been set: a modest $60 million, befitting my youth, perhaps – I was after all barely thirty years old then – and the fact that this would be my first major campaign. "Why not $100 million?" the president asked, knowing she had Board support for such a figure. Was there an audible gulp from at least one member of the University executive that morning? Perhaps, but that was the figure announced publicly and that was the figure (and then some) achieved. What the successful campaign permitted was an instant and huge increase (400 per cent!) in my very modest endowment of the time. It has gone on growing since then, and in 2014 my endowment sat most comfortably indeed at over $400 million,[12] and I can no longer complain, as I did a lot in those days, that other Canadian universities are better endowed (well, the older, wealthy ones are still ahead). The success back then was especially gratifying because one-quarter of the campaign goal was destined, at my president's insistence, for student scholarships. And just at that point, the provincial government announced a temporary program to match any funds the universities raised for student aid. The same hand that was taking away, decided to give, but no one looked for logic from government circles in those days.

So there we had the curious situation that miserliness and largesse went hand-in-hand during those years. In fact, if one does the math, it is clear in hindsight that the gifts actually amounted to more than the loss: $115 million given and $50 million taken away.[13] Maybe the gifts say something about my stature as a university in those days that I had not then recognized. But to make that math sound like a net gain would be to engage in "creative accounting," something university finances with their strict division of operating, capital, ancillary, and endowment funds do not allow.

Well, my activities during those years were pretty much determined by this peculiar context of miserliness and largesse. How to cope with the cuts and how to find some good through the coping – that was the agenda for the time. How to translate government-imposed reductions into specific cuts in every corner of the university. How to avoid student unrest over inevitable fee increases. How to maintain focus on research and teaching. How to keep alive the president's ambition to have my academic stature match my size and physical presence and to have everyone know it and believe it. How to maintain some kind of morale through all that. Change, especially when imposed from the outside, is not nearly as charming as that generated internally. And I had been used to fairly steady growth since the 1960s. Oh, there had been ups and downs, but the innovation for which I was known was usually of an expansive nature and based on ideas. That was much more invigorating and more fun than what was being asked of me now. My reputation for change and innovation was on the line.

I can't say that I took "the thunder and the sunshine" with quite the "frolic welcome" that Tennyson attributed to Ulysses' sailors, but I did keep my eye on the possibility that "some work of noble note, may yet be done."[14]

In fact my coping mechanisms were solidly in place. My tripartite system of governance – Board, Senate, administration – requiring politically astute intermediaries and numerous committees with frequently overlapping membership meant that everyone eventually talked to everyone: knowledge and ideas were widely shared. To a newcomer from outside, these structures and practices often appeared excessive, cumbersome, and time-consuming, but they clearly served to guide discussion and reach agreement. In addition, many planning exercises by the previous president had accustomed people to sorting through priorities and making choices. The existence of an academic plan for the University and the process of establishing and updating it made it much easier to determine, for example, that my academic endeavours remain paramount, through thick or thin. Indeed, the president would not have had it any other way. So the brunt of the cuts in the 1990s was to be borne by the administrative side of the University. I have to admit, of course, that it's always been easier to impose certain things on an administration than on the teaching staff, given the collegial system of academic governance. But in fact what the financial woes imposed on everyone was a greater appreciation of the interdependence of academic and administrative/financial matters. Gradually my Faculties began to reflect that awareness in their academic plans. In our favour, too, at the time was the fact that the Keele campus looked good (the Glendon one always did) thanks to the architectural and land planning of Harry Arthurs; the new and pleasing coherence of the campus may have helped to ease the general atmosphere, at least for awhile.

What certainly helped was that York had a mathematical genius among the vice-presidents. Sheldon Levy liked nothing better than a monster problem involving finances. He developed the idea of a three-year "rolling" budget, and he elaborated on the government's "social contract" hint that pension surpluses might be used to attenuate the impact of the cuts. In York's case, the surplus was sufficient for the administration to take a "pension holiday" for three years, suspending its annual contribution to the pension fund. These two measures, once approved by the Board, gave me the leeway to "roll" with the punches of annual cuts.

On my administrative side, that flexibility resulted in major adjustments to registrarial and housing services. Parts of each had been scattered, physically and structurally, across the campus, some parts in central student services, some in each of the ten Faculties, and still others in the seven colleges. In the hopes of cutting costs, inventing new ways of doing things, and easing the bureaucracy for students, both services were centralized. This removed a layer of admissions, record-keeping, and clerical functions from the Faculties and colleges, so they could concentrate respectively on academic, residential, and co-curricular programming. All this "restructuring" – the buzzword of the day – was accompanied by redesigned computer systems with their promise of more efficient handling of data. Among the results was my newly designed Student Information System, so promising that it evoked the dream of being offered to other universities – for a price, of course.[15] And such was the enthusiasm for computer-assisted reorganization that some people even foresaw harmonization of the myriad different regulations affecting students in my various Faculties. Now there was a task.

Besides nimble minds in administration, I had another ace in hand that might be played even in difficult times. The vast tract of land provided for me in the 1960s was both a place to construct the new Keele campus and a territorial bank account on which I could draw for further development. My land was, in effect, a modern version of a university endowment. Previous campus planning had divided that endowment into two sectors: an interior core reserved for future University buildings and large enough for the wildest expansionist dreams, and a peripheral sector that might conceivably have commercial development possibilities and thus bring in money to the University. During those bleak days of the 1990s, some additions actually were made to the interior core: a student field house, a "stadium" (a grand name for some bleachers at a playing field), and a new Chemistry and Computer Science building. Designs for another Science building (I'll spare you the inter-Faculty rivalry on that one) awaited only new capital funding. When that became available a few years later, the building won prizes for its "green" design that included a "natural" roof.[16] And in the interim, Fine Arts made its claim loud and clear to be the first in line for subsequent construction, a plea heard and supported by my next president. The Accolade buildings are the result.

Two quite different construction projects of that time – still within the interior core – involved unusual external cooperation. I doubt that joint undertakings, one with a private company and the other with a community college, would have happened without the financial noose around my neck. But they did, and they proved beneficial to my students. The first and more quickly realized project matched my interest in augmenting sports facilities with Lauridon Sports Management's interest in commercial skating and hockey arenas. The key to the cooperation was land, and I had it. So the agreement entailed a long-term lease of land by the company, which then arranged the financing and building of the sequentially named Sportsplex, Ice Gardens, and (in 2014), Canlan Ice Sports York. Together we would share both use and profits from the six rinks, fitness and training centre, and sports clinic. At the end of the lease, the entire complex would revert to me. An additional bonus during the final construction phase in the summer of 1996 involved the hiring of Fine Arts students to create artwork for the hallways of the new building.

The cooperation with Seneca College was more protracted because of the academic and financial complexities. It began in 1993, when Seneca sought new land for expansion and consolidation in the northwestern part of the Greater Toronto Area. Since approval and funding would necessarily come from the Ontario government (colleges being less autonomous than universities), a three-way mutual interest began to develop: the government was increasingly interested in practical education and training; Seneca wanted to be rid of many of its leased buildings; and I had all this land. But I wasn't about to give it away; there had to be some tangible benefit. As in fact there turned out to be. Capital funding for the project was initially allocated by the same NDP government that was "social contracting" us all (including the colleges) into severe restraint. Seneca and York were to have an agreed-upon share of that funding. Before any of it was in hand, however, let alone in the form of a Seneca shovel into leased ground at York, the subsequent Conservative government, cutting taxes in the name of "common sense," reduced the funding by a third. Would we proceed? Could we proceed?

In fact it was evident by then that collaboration with Seneca could entail more than monetary benefit. As the talks progressed – president to president, vice-presidents to vice-presidents, deans to deans, and physical plant directors to their college counterparts – it became clear that we had more in common than an interest in land. The academic possibilities of physical proximity began to take everyone's fancy. If Seneca brought to its new campus technical and applied programs that complemented University offerings in the Sciences, Communications, Fine Arts, and Liberal Studies, there might be all sorts of possibilities for cooperation and joint endeavours for both students and faculty. It was particularly the student interest that caught my attention. I wanted more students in the Sciences, and Seneca, with its larger network of incoming students, including international ones, might well encourage some of them to come on to York. And some of my own graduates could proceed to Seneca for more job-related training, a topic that was much in the public domain in those days. Once issues such as advanced standing for courses completed in either institution were resolved, well, it was a short step to actual joint programs in which students from either institution could acquire a college diploma and a BA or BSc in less time than it took to do each separately. At the time only the diploma/BA was defined and put through the approval processes of both institutions, but given the program offerings the college intended for Seneca@York, wider collaboration was definitely in the offing. And on my side, as originally planned, I would use my share of the capital funding to enhance laboratories and equipment for applied sciences. That too could lead to further collaboration with Seneca and even, just maybe, to the foundation for Engineering at York, something that the dean of pure and applied science in fact realized just a few years later.

Needless to say there was a bit of grumbling about the whole project. Both in my midst and at Seneca too, questions were raised about the appropriateness of trying to bridge the theoretical-practical division that supposedly characterized the difference between universities and colleges. Was there some sense that the two might contaminate each other if placed in close physical proximity? In fact, like all simplistic labeling, this one peeled away as the Seneca@York project proceeded through the multiple levels of approval. Indeed, the entire project – including its process – began to look like a model for post-secondary cooperation; there had never been anything like it in Ontario. York was maintaining its reputation for innovation. My own Glendon College began wondering about closer ties with the new (but short-lived) francophone community college, *Le collège des grands lacs,* and Durham College in Oshawa developed closer links with York, too. In the wake of the Seneca experiment, some preliminary plans were sketched for a possible presence of the Canadian Memorial Chiropractic College on my campus. Well, that never happened, but given that part of the rationale had been my numerous health-related programs, the proposal did set some people thinking about expanded health sciences at York. Years later and for different reasons, a new Faculty of Health was created. Long before then, however, construction for Seneca@York began in 1997. The splendid Moriyama-designed building opened for students in 1999.[17]

As these projects continued the slow filling-in of the interior core of the campus, the peripheral sector of my lands lay largely idle. They were under the purview of York University Development Corporation, a wholly owned subsidiary of which I was the sole shareholder. YUDC was created in 1985 to watch for and promote development possibilities on the outer reaches of the campus – those parts not intended for academic use. The new president reduced the size of YUDC both to fit the economic realities of the time and to assuage some academic uneasiness: should a university really be in the development business? In fact everyone at York had one thing very much in common with YUDC: the desire to see the Toronto subway extended northwest to York. That had been on my agenda since the Keele lands first came my way and long before YUDC existed. The purpose was not just to facilitate transportation to and from the campus or even to eliminate some of the horrid parking lots that scarred my landscape. Subway stations anywhere near me would increase the development potential of the peripheral sector of my land. Every one of my presidents inched the subway along; this one was led to believe by provincial and municipal politicians alike that it would be completed and running by 2002. Some of my people gleefully foresaw riding on it. Well, despite everyone at York exercising all sorts of pressure, the municipal politicians turned away and the subway didn't happen. At least not then. My subsequent president had one of her close colleagues attend to the file assiduously for nine years before the line to York was assured. Subway stations are actually being built on the campus right now, and "they" say a train might appear in 2017. I'm still not holding my breath, but the five presidents writing this book intend to be on that first train whenever it arrives.

Perhaps because tied to an eventual subway, other development projects of the time proceeded almost as slowly. Since the late 1980s, YUDC had been contemplating residential construction on the southern part of my lands. If the land were sold to an ambitious builder, perhaps an entire community, complete with housing, parks, roads, schools, and shops could fill in the blank space, embellish the area, and produce funds for me. Snags along the way meant that the project did not in fact get under way until well into the term of the next president. But there it is now, designed, built, landscaped, and inhabited within a stone's throw of the campus. Other YUDC musings, this time about my Glendon property, fortunately came to naught. Besides the fact that YUDC had no say, much less control, over those lands, Glendon was not in fact available for sale. The terms of the property's being given to me as my first home prohibited its being used for anything other than educational purposes.[18] But wouldn't the fancy condo developers have loved to get their hands on that glorious piece of land! Indeed, other Faculties on the Keele campus occasionally salivated at the possibility of displacing Glendon and moving in. Well, that didn't happen either.

The other far-fetched notion that came to naught was the president's own. She suggested spelling my name out in huge white letters on the roof of what was then the tallest building on campus. The Ross building was right on the flight path of all the incoming trans-Atlantic flights headed for Toronto's Pearson Airport just to the west. Millions of people would see the York name and remember it. Oh, the occasional snowstorm might obliterate the letters temporarily, but it would also halt the flights, so that was not a serious objection. It certainly would have been cheap advertising. But my facilities folk just grinned at the suggestion. Perhaps they had enough worries on their hands with the peregrine falcons nesting on that same roof and Canada geese leaving their mark(s) around the reflecting pool in front of the lovely new Vari Hall, designed to camouflage the starkness of the Ross building. It seems that York was on more than an airplane flight path.

The flight path that this president wanted for me was the ascendant one of academic achievement. Of course all presidents want that. The trick this time was to see if it could be done in a time of severe financial restraint. All that "restructuring" of services and structuring of space that I've just described was intended to spare the academic side of the University some of the severity inflicted upon us. But not all of it. The Faculties made the same percentage cuts to their own administrative services as occurred elsewhere on campus, and at the same time they tackled the only slightly smaller cuts to their academic functions. That meant scrutinizing everything from course offerings to class sizes and numbers of professors. It meant the likelihood of doing more with fewer resources, and that, in fact, is how most people remember those years: fewer courses, larger classes, overcrowded and understaffed libraries, fewer part-time instructors. But once the initial "social contract" cuts had been absorbed and the even larger "common sense" ones hit us, we had to imagine "doing less better," as an ambiguously titled Senate planning committee report put it in 1995.[19] It wasn't a matter of doing badly, much less worse; it was a matter of doing fewer things better. Nudged along by the vice-president (academic), Michael

Stevenson, the Faculties were encouraged to identify what they did really well and to look campus-wide, beyond their own units, to maintain and enhance those things. Only that way, it was thought, could I avoid what was happening elsewhere: the actual closing of programs and the reduction of professorial positions. And just maybe, some new things could be done if we did them in a different way. That was the fun part of those years.

One of the different ways was to conceive of the possible connection between academic change and monetary gain. Once that imaginative leap was made – and it was hard for many a professor – then programs conceivably could be altered or designed with the express purpose of saving or bringing in money. And that, in fact, is what was done. In Arts, for example, first-year courses were reorganized to consolidate the compulsory interdisciplinary Humanities and Social Science courses and add to them small-group tutorial supervision in critical skills for all incoming students. Monetary savings (and they were large) and academic benefit went hand-in-hand. The savings, in turn, permitted, among other things, the creation of new programs in Business and Society and in Criminology. In Fine Arts, rearranging of existing courses led to the creation of a hugely popular new program in Interdisciplinary Cultural Studies. This brought in so many students that the attendant revenue (a combination of student fees and government "formula funding" as fed through university operating funds) allowed for the maintenance of the more expensive studio components of programs in Art, Music, Dance, Theatre, and Film. The Music Department had a great idea for acquiring new pianos for its students by selling its old ones in an annual used piano sale that still attracts music lovers and piano seekers from all over the region.

Across the campus, the Faculty of Pure and Applied Science attracted a number of new students from the Toronto area, who, but for the economic recession of the time, might have gone elsewhere. Science also began a summer term of teaching. The increased revenue from both sources allowed the creation of more entrance scholarships, and that, in turn, enabled the Faculty to raise its entrance standards. The Faculty of Environmental Studies also attracted more students by adding an undergraduate program to its existing master's. Two other professional Faculties envisaged a different kind of new student and even a different location. Osgoode Hall Law School and the Faculty of Administrative Studies, soon to be renamed the Schulich School of Business, each began to offer part-time studies (the LLM and the MBA, respectively) in Toronto's downtown core to numerous adult students already in the workforce. Advertisements in the subway for the new location turned many a head: "This subway stops at York University" – effective if somewhat bittersweet publicity given the ongoing battle at the time for a major extension to the subway line. In all these cases of academic change for monetary gain, necessity was clearly the mother of invention, as "they" say.

Necessity gave a corresponding boost to inter-Faculty cooperation. After all, if I was able to do business with a private company and with a community college to create academic benefit, my Faculties ought to be able to do something similar internally. Science, in fact, led the way with overtures to Arts and Fine Arts, so that students in Science could pursue, as part of their undergraduate studies, their personal and increasingly professional interest in the Liberal and Performing Arts. Physics and Music, Physics and Philosophy, for example, have more in common than the academic structures of the time would allow one to think. And the new technologies being explored all over the campus were bound to encourage connections between Computer Science and Film, between Dance and Kinesiology. Not that making the actual connections was easy. All sorts of barriers stood in the way – from faculty regulations to timetabling to resource allocation and even geography – on a campus as big as mine, to say nothing of the protracted academic debates over core requirements in each discipline. And there was no money in any of it. But there might be eventually for the graduates of such cross-Faculty programs. An example from that time was the combining of artistic and business studies into a new program in Fine Arts Administration. Indeed, the whole point of exploring these interdisciplinary, cross-Faculty possibilities was precisely to keep my spirit of innovation alive, to keep the academic flame a-glow in those dark days.

And all that was merely at the undergraduate level. The Faculty of Graduate Studies was just as determined to ensure scholarly expansion, in terms of student numbers (from Canada and abroad), scholarship recipients, and new programs. Indeed, those three components went together as part of York's planning for growth. If I was to be a great university, I had to expand research and scholarship and broaden what I could offer to students. So I had to be sure – and this was one of the battles of the time – that my wings were not clipped in the name of "rationalization" and "differentiation." Curiously enough, one federal government cut actually facilitated things, although it did not seem so at first. "Fee waivers" for international students reduced the higher fees those students paid, but they also limited their number pretty much to the "fee waived." When the fee waivers were abolished in the mid-1990s, the artificial cap on foreign student enrolment was removed. I was free to attract more foreign students, and to use some of their higher fees for financial assistance for students in the form of scholarships, teaching, and research assistantships.

Of course, I wanted more Canadian graduate students, too. So, despite the times, my graduate Faculty went ahead with planning and implementing new graduate programs: the PhD in Women's Studies (the first in Canada to offer graduate work in this new interdisciplinary field), in Music, in Computer Science, in Education in the area of language, culture, and teaching, and the MA in Études françaises, housed at Glendon but drawing professorial resources from across the University. My PhD students in existing and new programs were mostly training for academic careers; for them, the Faculty of Graduate Studies designed another Canadian first: a teaching practicum, to add teacher training to the honing of research skills that are the essence of doctoral studies.[20]

Another way of expanding research was through externally funded research centres and chairs. I actually added a few even in those lean times. With the biggest individual donation ever to come to my law school, Osgoode created a Centre for the Study of Organized Crime and Corruption, still going strong today under a slightly different name and a wider mandate. Private money also came to Arts for a chair in Hellenic Studies and one in Jewish Studies. A new Centre for Applied Sustainability in the Faculty of Environmental Studies proposed to sustain itself on external grants; in 2004 it became the University-wide Institute for Research and Innovation in Sustainability. The already existing Centre for Health Studies acquired $2 million in federal funding in 1996 to become one of five Canadian Centres of Excellence in Women's Health. And when the Canada Research Chairs began in 2000, also with federal money, I scooped up a fair number of them on the basis of existing Faculty strengths, new research areas, and splendid young faculty members hired despite those dark days. Indeed, the policy was deliberate: York was not going to diminish the number of full-time faculty positions and, unlike most other universities, new young professors would go on being hired – I was in fact one of the few universities to do the latter.[21]

Along with this building and consolidating and safe-guarding within my boundaries, I was also looking abroad for possibilities. Many of my professors already had individual research links with their counterparts in other countries, and, of course, published their research findings in international journals. But what I was after was more institutional connections with universities overseas, more exchange possibilities for students, more potential for new programming. I had an existing structure for such activities in York International that looked after incoming foreign students, encouraged my students to go abroad, and established links with foreign countries. To build on that foundation, I stole away a new director from a rival university. And I shipped my president off to Israel for a study tour sponsored by the Canadian Jewish Congress; to Hong Kong to meet with York's many alumni, to attempt some fundraising and to solidify existing links with the Chinese University of Hong Kong; and to South Korea to establish university links – the one with Sookmyung Women's University led to its sending some thirty students to York for English-language study in the summer of 1996. Late in 1994, at the invitation of the German Academic Exchange Service (DAAD),[22] the York International director accompanied the president to Germany. Together they visited a number of universities and had talks with government and DAAD officials. The purpose was to promote a joint interdisciplinary and interuniversity program in German and European Studies between York and the Université de Montréal that the DAAD would sponsor financially. The surprising thing was how well known I was in European circles (and they were not confusing me with the University of York in England). And then we received the DAAD support, and the program was off and running! Once again, my penchant for, and practice of, doing things a little differently paid off – literally in this specific case, but also more generally in terms of continuing to build academically when the context could easily have dictated just hunkering down.

It's possible that the German connection was in my president's mind when she inaugurated an endowed scholarship for York students to study abroad.[23] People think it is named for her, but in fact it is in honour of her parents, both of whom died while she was in office. On two occasions they had facilitated her studying abroad as a young girl, and their home was always open to foreign travellers and newcomers to Canada. They even became the Canadian "parents" to a young couple emigrating from Germany in the 1960s. Years later, the woman of that pair provided the initial major donation for the scholarship.

But let me get back to the academic accomplishments of those years. They were many.

Far away from a president's office, the real work of a university takes place. In classrooms, in laboratories, and in the library, lively minds play with ideas. If the infrastructure for that play is crucial – space, facilities, equipment, books, journals, technology (the library, for example, went through the huge transition to electronic cataloguing and information retrieval in those years) – it's the result of the play that really counts. I use that word "counts" advisedly since it was the nub of one of the other catchphrases of the time: "performance indicators."[24] Here are some indicators – at least, ones that universities themselves recognize and value and that I deliberately set about to achieve: the number of doctoral fellowships from the Social Sciences and Humanities Research Council (SSHRC) doubled in those years, placing York among the top four universities in Canada for such awards; my incoming graduate students also acquired more Ontario Graduate Scholarships; the Science students among them picked up more awards from the Natural Sciences and Engineering Research Council (NSERC); and even internally we managed to add more than one hundred teaching assistantships to the eight hundred already on offer for the increasing number of graduate students.

At the undergraduate level, entrance requirements were raised and met. By 1995, more than half of the students entering Arts were Ontario Scholars with incoming grades above 80 per cent from their grade 13 studies.[25] The number of scholarship-level students in Science doubled. And, as demand for the undergraduate program in the Schulich School of Business rose by some 40 per cent, the entrance requirements for that Faculty rose to become the highest in Canada. York students won major external scholarships on graduation: Fulbright, Commonwealth, Queen Elizabeth II, and a Rhodes.

And they were being taught by professors who themselves were winning major awards and acknowledgments for their research and their teaching. Killam Awards, membership in the Royal Society of Canada, medals, awards, and prestigious prizes for books, for articles, for teaching – so many and in such profusion that *Maclean's* could say in 1994: "York full-time faculty have won more scholarly awards than those at any other university in Canada."[26] Needless to say, I was delighted to accept that assessment even though I remained sceptical about the magazine's self-imposed role of ranking universities. So many of the criteria used were in fact measures of age and wealth, of which I had little. To encourage new young professors to emulate their seniors, the president created an internal prize, the President's Prize for Promising Scholars, first awarded in 1994, the two recipients chosen annually from among the outstanding files coming through my hefty tenure and promotions process.

Actually, listed like that, it all looks quite daring for the time – almost as if the cuts spurred me to an "I'll show you" attitude. But don't get any false ideas: I don't want to go through that again just to prove I can.

In fact the whole question of how a university proves its worth was a vexing one at the time. All the language of business came at the universities in a torrent, from "value-for-money" to "accountability," "restructuring," "rationalization," "performance indicators," "globalization," and "competitiveness." Presidents and other university officials began to use the vocabulary themselves within and among our institutions. Few of them fought back to argue that these "measures" might not be appropriate for universities, that universities were not businesses, and did the business world really have the monopoly on best practices, much less behaviour? Universities had traditions much longer than those of business for "quality control": external peer review of scholarly worth; program reviews done by external assessors at the graduate and undergraduate levels; student and colleague evaluation of teaching. Oh, all that continued, and I prided myself on the frequently flattering results, such as the international assessors' comment in 1995 that my Centre for Atmospheric Chemistry was one of the best in the world.[27] But, long after the fact, I have the uneasy feeling that during those years I and all other universities began to lose our perception of ourselves as communities of scholars and to become instead a collection of competitive entities. Did I hear the word "student" replaced by the word "client"? Surely not. For it is those very students who ultimately show the value of a university by the way they lead their lives, professionally and personally, and the values they pass on to the next generation. None of that can be foretold, much less measured. My graduates from those years can be found in the media, in politics, in law, business, and teaching, in health services, academia, and the arts. Those are our real "performance indicators."

Well, I put on quite a performance myself at the very end of those years. And it was probably the worst indicator I could have chosen. In the spring of 1997, in the longest faculty strike ever in Canada (since then, there have been longer ones elsewhere), I let out a collective and very public howl of protest. It began in the wake of post–"social contract" negotiations with the eleven unionized employee groups on campus. Ten were concluded successfully; the one with the faculty union was not. The points in dispute were salaries (some of my faculty even thought they might "catch up" what they had lost) and a pre-existing early and post-retirement benefit, the costs of which had been underestimated and were now spiralling out of control. Well, that was where University finances and union horror of benefit "rollback" clashed, to the detriment of everyone. But what really fuelled the strike and kept it going so long was the perception of my faculty members that their status was declining and their working conditions were worsening. They had had enough of frozen salaries, crowded classrooms, new technologies, doing more with less, and even "doing less better." The bargaining table, designed solely for the two points in dispute, simply couldn't accommodate such unhappiness, and so the standoff lasted seven weeks, jeopardizing end-of-term classes and examinations and the recruitment of new students. Had there been an avenue for public protest during those years against niggardly governments, against "revolutions" that did not make "sense," against the new technologies and their implications for the classroom, against public questioning of the role of universities and the value of a liberal arts education, against loss of professorial prestige, against neoliberal economic ideas and conservative social ones, my faculty would have taken that route. Instead the strike had to bear the weight of all that malaise. Hardly surprising, then, that the eventual settlement – a slight salary increase and a big benefit rollback – satisfied so few. And so the strike wiped out, in the public eye and perhaps in my own spirit, all the accomplishments of those years. Needless to say, it added to my continuing reputation as a rowdy place.

That certainly cast a pall over things. It was almost as if, having coped with the financial cuts and all the subsequent changes to administrative and academic structures and programs, we decided to give ourselves a kick in the pants. The pall almost succeeded in blocking out the sky that filled so much of my Keele campus and served as a metaphor for the academic endeavour: "The sky's the limit," as the president used to say. Now that we seemed to have relinquished – temporarily, of course – reaching for the sky, she spread me out horizontally in her last presentation to the Board of Governors. "York on the Map," she called it, and pointed out my greater and growing academic, physical, financial, political, national, and international presence.

Then off she went to renew her love of research and writing. To her successor she left the task of expanding my presence on that map and, Penelope-like, of picking out some stitches, unravelling some knots, and adding new designs and colours to the fabric/work of art that is York University. As for me, I'm still here, and plan to be so for a very long time. I even got a chuckle recently to see my art gallery appropriating the name-calling I had endured for so long: the "Art Gallery of York University Is So Out There." Now that's the spirit.

* * * *

Oh, by the way, if you are up in space one day, out beyond a fringe of the Milky Way, you might come across galaxies MB1 and MB3, some eleven million light years away. That M is for McCall, an astronomer at York who discovered them in the mid-1990s. The sky really *is* the limit at York.

NOTES

This account is dedicated to the memory of Nancy Accinelli, Executive Assistant, Office of the President, 1993–98 and personification of the York spirit.

1 Alfred Lord Tennyson, "Ulysses" (32), in *An Anthology of Verse*, ed. Roberta A. Charlesworth and Dennis Lee (Toronto: Oxford University Press, 1964), 143–5. The reference to Tennyson's "Ulysses" by both Ian Macdonald in 2014 at the end of Chapter 2 of this book and by Susan Mann in 1992 at the beginning of this chapter speaks more to the similarity of the educational backgrounds of the two presidents than to any mutual influence. Once upon a time, students in Ontario secondary schools actually memorized poetry.

2 Installation address of President Susan Mann, York University, 12 November 1992, manuscript notes in personal papers. See also "Universities are places to wonder: Mann," *York Gazette*, 20 November 1992, 1–2.

3 York University, University Secretariat, President Susan Mann, "York on the Map," May 1997. This document combined the text of a presentation to a retreat of the Board of Governors in February 1997 with the various "maps" shown during

that presentation as well as the comments and suggestions of Board members in response to questions put by the president.

4 For example, ibid., 14.

5 York University Library, Clara Thomas Archives and Special Collections, Office of the President fonds, F0073, 2001-042/029(5), "Letters to the York Community (General)," 1994–1995; 2001-042/038(1), "Greetings to York Community," 1996; 2001-042/038(2), "Letters to York Community," 1996. The University collection of these letters is not complete; others are among Mann's personal papers and will be added to the York set.

6 Tennyson, "Ulysses" (55–6).

7 Ontario Council on University Affairs, "Sustaining Quality in Changing Times: Funding Ontario Universities: A Discussion Paper" (Toronto: OCUA, 1994).

8 See the opening sentence of Harry Arthurs, Chapter 3 in this volume.

9 Calculated from various communications to the York community, 1992–97. See, for example, "Provincial Budget Cuts, the Social Contract, and the Implications for York," letter of Susan Mann, 29 April 1993; letter of Susan Mann, 8 January 1996.

10 The provincial election in Ontario in June 1995 produced a Progressive Conservative majority under the leadership of Mike Harris. The campaign slogan of the PCs, "a common sense revolution," offered the electorate tax cuts and reduced public expenditure.

11 Thanks to Seymour Schulich for permission to quote his words from that meeting (e-mail communication to Susan Mann, 12 March 2015). If one dug into the nineteenth century and translated into current dollars some of the bequests to found or sustain the few universities of the time, one might find something equivalent to the Schulich gift. But in sheer numbers, there was nothing like it.

12 $414.9 million. See York University, Financial Statements, 30 April 2014, 7, 9; available online at http://www.yorku.ca/finance/documents/Financial_Statements_April_30_2014.pdf. Thanks to Vice-president Gary Brewer for providing this information.

13 Campaign results are recorded sometimes at $110 million and sometimes at $116 million. For the ease of readers who will have in mind the campaign goal of $100 million and the Schulich donation of $15 million, the text here rounds the figure by combining the two.

14 Tennyson, "Ulysses" (48, 47, 52).

15 Development of the Student Information System was part of the beginning of the evolution from mainframe to what is now Web-based computing. York needed to replace its mainframe computer and, after a vain effort to obtain interuniversity cooperation for a province-wide system, decided to leap on its own into what was then referred to as a "bleeding-edge client server system." That sounds somewhat dangerous, and perhaps foretold the real pain of the initial startup, but once the new system was fully functional, it permitted easier staff access, via Windows on

personal computers, to all student records: admission, enrolment, program of study, grades, completion, and graduation. The brainchild of Professor Alan Cobb and under the direction of Registrar Gene Denzel, the system was inaugurated in the summer of 1996 and is still going strong, although integrating the normal evolution of computing since then. Thanks to former registrar Gene Denzel for these precisions; e-mail communication from Gene Denzel, 11 June 2014.

16 Now (2016) known simply as the Chemistry building, the new space was initially shared with Computer Science until the construction of the "green" building into which the Department of Computer Science and Engineering moved. That building, now called Lassonde for the engineering benefactor, did not quite live up in practical terms to its environmental celebrity. Bugs from the "natural" aspects of the building got into the scientists' experiments! (e-mail communication from Lorna Marsden, 1 June 2014).

17 Material related to the agreement with Seneca can be found in the files of almost all administrative offices at York. See, for example, York University Library, Clara Thomas Archives and Special Collections, Office of the President fonds, F0073, 2001-042 (67), File 4450-50: "Institutions of Higher Education, Partnerships/ Affiliations, Seneca – January 1996."

18 York's founding in 1959 is intimately connected with the University of Toronto, which housed the new university initially on the downtown campus and then, in 1961, on its Glendon property, acquired in 1951 as a bequest on the death of Agnes Euphemia Wood. The land became a financial burden to the University of Toronto and so was transferred officially to York for $1.00, with the proviso that it be used for educational purposes only or returned to Toronto. See Horn, *York University*, 12, 21–2, 67; Edward Spence and Robert Everett, *Glendon College and Academic Planning: The Context for Consideration of Options* (Toronto: York University, November 1999), 2.

19 York University, University Secretariat, "Doing Less Better: The Context of 1995 Academic Planning," Report to the Community from the Academic Policy and Planning Committee (North York, ON, 20 July, 1995); received by the Senate, 28 September 1995.

20 Thanks to former deans Dyane Adam, George Fallis, Seth Feldman, David Leyton-Brown, Robert Prince, and Stan Shapson, and former University librarian Ellen Hoffmann for sharing their recollections of the good and the bad of those years. Errors of omission and commission are those of the author.

21 We managed the second, but not the first. Overall faculty numbers declined somewhat during those years. See York University, *Fact Book*, 2012–13 (Toronto: York University, 2013), 181; available online at http://www.yorku.ca/factbook/ factbook/2012%20-%202013/Section_08_Employees/A%29_Full_Time_Faculty/ 01_Full_Time_Academic_Staff_1976-77_Through_2012-2013.pdf. See also Mann, "York on the Map," 13.

22 Deutscher Akademischer Austauschdienst, known as the DAAD, is the German national body that promotes and coordinates international academic collaboration.

23 The Mann Award of Excellence for Study Abroad. Since its inception, the award has helped more than twenty students to study for a term or two in the United Kingdom, Europe, Australia, and Asia.

24 Performance indicators, an import from the business world of production and sales, caught the fancy of the UK government in the late 1980s, as it attempted to contain expenditures and exercise more control over the universities. The institutions in turn thought they could control the process by designing their own indicators. The UK drama was watched closely and emulated by government and universities in Ontario through the 1990s. Although the phrase is still used and its attendant mountains of data still produced in such circles, the business world has moved on to the somewhat more precise "management statistics." See Martin Cave, Stephen Hanney, and Maurice Kogan, *The Use of Performance Indicators in Higher Education: The Challenge of the Quality Movement* (London: Jessica Kingsley, 1988, 1991, 1997).

25 Mann, "York on the Map," 12.

26 Since 1991 *Maclean's*, the weekly news magazine published in Toronto, has been ranking Canadian universities in a special November issue. Always controversial within the university community for its methodology, criteria, weightings, and rankings, the institutions nonetheless pick out what makes them look good – as is done here, from the November 1994 issue.

27 York University, Centre for Atmospheric Chemistry, *Summary Report of the External Review Committee, Centre for Atmospheric Chemistry York University*, Memorandum to Dean K.A. Innanen from United States Department of Commerce, National Oceanic and Atmospheric Administration, 4 March 1994, 2. Thanks to department chair, Professor Robert McLaren, for digging out this document.

Figure 5.1. Lorna Marsden, 1997

5 Years of Transition, 1997–2007

LORNA R. MARSDEN

"It's Wonderful" – "It's Impossible"

On being asked to consider the presidency of York University, I sought advice among my friends and colleagues. Their responses ranged from "It's wonderful" to "It's impossible" and sometimes both from the same person. Clearly this was a challenging organization.

At the heart of the position of university president is the nurturing of the academy: the faculty members, students, Faculties, and programs, and how these are understood in the wider community. This nurturing takes good governance and significant resources. The academic strengths of this University were clear. They included leading academic programs in many traditional fields and professions as well as highly innovative programs, a student body reflecting Toronto's cultural and economic diversity, interdisciplinary achievements, and ambitious plans. Among the faculty members were many distinguished scholars and scientists, writers, artists, and professionals.[1] Renowned in their specialized fields, their dedication to York and their students was unquestionable. Many faculty members and staff had served the University for most of their careers and shared its larger academic ambitions expressed in strategic and academic plans. All had ambitions for the University and, like all well-trained minds, thoughtful critiques. The governance of the University appeared to be straightforward, and certainly the chair of the Board who invited me to accept the presidency led a well-organized committee. The problem of resources was serious, although, in the context of the late 1990s all universities were stretched, as I knew from my position as president of Wilfrid Laurier University. The full state of the challenges York faced, however, became clear to me only after I was in the job. Furthermore, between the time I accepted the appointment in January and the time I took office in the summer of 1997, there had been a protracted and bitter strike of the faculty members. Although it had been settled, emotions were still running high.

By the time I arrived at York University, I had accumulated a lot of experience in organizations large and small. York, however, is an organization that requires much more than experience. It has a powerful culture of its own and a fiercely independent and committed faculty and staff. At the same time, York's recovery from the faculty strike involved a legacy of mistrust, especially between the union leadership and the administration, faculty, and students.[2] There was much misunderstanding of the issues that had been involved in that dispute. The University's reputation had once again been battered in the Toronto media. To reach York's strategic objectives, we had to secure and direct the resources that would allow the academy to get on with its work of teaching and research and to protect it from outside interference.[3] Nonetheless, all I spoke to had confidence in the academic plans.

I was an outsider, like nearly all York's presidents, and needed help to understand the culture and organization. Every president wants very talented advisors, and for me that person was Professor Edward (Ted) Spence. He was highly analytic, numerate, and loyal to York. Having been at York for many years as professor, associate dean of arts, dean of environmental studies, and member of the Senate and countless other committees, he was invaluable not only in providing background information but also in setting me straight on many issues. Happily, he joined my office. Since we both believed in evidence-based decisions, he eventually became the head of the Office of Institutional Research and Analysis and continued to do superb work.

Other top talents were the chiefs of staff in my office, first the late Nancy Accinelli and then Sylvia Zingrone, both of whom were first rate. They helped me to get thoroughly briefed by all the right people,[4] who provided excellent advice and information about the ambitions and strengths of the Faculties. Some of the immediate requirements not mentioned in the recruitment interviews were laid bare. These included tackling the funding issues,[5] inadequate classrooms and other academic space, student accommodation on and around campus, the need for more tenure-stream faculty members, problems in more than one of the Faculties, and union-administration relationships on this almost totally unionized campus. York suffers from the classic problem of being a new university in a city with a powerful, well-established university.[6] Above all we were still a very young institution, with decades to go before realizing all our ambitions. We had to build self-confidence, identity, community, and respect.

The sheer complexity of York's organization was a challenge. Some Faculties were small, but the Faculty of Arts was enormous. On campus there were tensions arising from the recent strike, the change of presidents, and the loyalties still bruised by these events. Our relationship with the community college, Seneca College, which was building a subcampus on our Keele campus, had complicated issues. My predecessor had left some great opportunities, such as initial plans and funding for a new science building[7] and a fundraising campaign that was well under way.

By November I had a list of internal projects of considerable length: one Faculty was approaching bankruptcy; the leader of the fundraising organization had recently left; construction projects needed attention; the graduate student union, CUPE 3903, included teaching and graduate assistants along with part-time faculty, and was being led by a group with some aggressive tactics.[8] For the first six months I was obsessed with all the work to be done. But the powerful programs and strong Faculties, the ambitious plans, the student energy and involvement, the loyalty of faculty and staff to York, the sheer excitement of a young university, more than balanced the challenges.

A Mandate

As I had requested, the Board of Governors prepared a Presidential Mandate for my first five-year term. At my previous presidency, a written mandate had proved to be a useful document. We publicized it widely to the community so that everyone would know what the governors expected and what my priorities would be. It set out the goals for my annual performance review by the Board. It is reproduced here to illustrate the priorities as seen by the Board. Much of my work and this chapter reflect these initial requirements.

Presidential Mandate for 1997–2002

The President is responsible to the Board of Governors for the leadership and all aspects of the management of the University. The President and her administration shall be characterized by a willingness to be open, receptive and responsible to the views and concerns of individuals and groups in the University community while striving to achieve the agreed vision and goals of the University.

1 The President shall lead the University in the development and enunciation of its vision and goals and the establishment and implementation of comprehensive strategies to achieve these goals.

2 The President will work closely with the Senate and Academic Officers of the University to establish the academic mission and focus of the University.

She will encourage an international standard of academic excellence in all Faculties, Colleges and Centres of the University in undergraduate, graduate, professional and non-credit programs and courses. The President must ensure that academic standards are maintained and improved. She should be responsive to rigorous evaluations of all programs on a regular basis in both academic and non-academic departments.

3 The President shall foster positive relations and communication within all parts of the University community and, where necessary, restore civil relations among colleagues. She must ensure the development of mutual respect and a common sense of purpose among constituent groups. Students, staff, alumni and faculty shall all receive attention.

4 The President shall spend up to fifty per cent of her time raising the external profile and understanding of the University (locally, nationally and internationally) and increasing its influence in its relations with municipal, provincial and federal governments and agencies

5 The President must ensure that the University maintains balanced budgets and prudent management of the University's assets. She shall enhance the University's financial self-sufficiency through ongoing solicitation of private funding, both endowed and operating, cooperative ventures and the maximization of benefits which can be realized from the University assets.

6 The President shall seek creative ways for the University to become more accountable while protecting academic freedom and the necessary elements of institutional autonomy.

7 The President should look for co-operative ventures with other universities, institutions and corporations to enhance its academic mission while reducing the University's costs and spreading its risks.

8 The President shall establish annual goals with respect to this mandate and shall report to the Board of Governors at the end of each year on progress achieved and plans for the next year. The President will assist the Chair of the Board in Board development and together they will work to improve the effectiveness of the Board in governance of the University, and representation of the University externally.

The Organization

The mandate was very helpful for organizing our work, but it left out issues that remained to be solved, such as the long-standing underfunding issue, the reputational challenges, and faculty morale. After the tensions of the previous year, how could we work together on these priorities?

My preference is always to work with a team. We had a good team of vice-presidents, deans, and advisors who knew more than I did about the history and issues at York. At our weekly Wednesday morning meetings of the executive core, we looked at the priorities and developed solutions. Some presidents prefer a smaller group of direct reports, but I preferred to see the debate and planning go forward with all the key voices represented. In effect, the entire leadership team has to know in some detail what the others are doing in order to avoid chaos and overlap, and so each part of the University can help accomplish the common goals. Although some of the people changed over the decade, the positions were always represented at the weekly meetings and are diagrammed in Figure 5.2.

Readers might note that at one point from mid-2000 to mid-2002 five of the eight most senior positions were held by women, what one wit described as the "ovary tower."

The Academy

The only reason for a university to exist is to teach students and carry out research that rests on the body of accumulated knowledge and documentation kept in libraries, archives, and in the minds of scholars and scientists who advance and perpetuate that knowledge. From the start, York University created a contemporary approach: performance and professional programs were not peripheral to the academy but fully integrated. The walls between the disciplines were scarcely visible, and students knew many professors outside their own degree studies. It was only at the doctoral level that deep specialization became visible. The atmosphere of learning was wonderful. I envied the faculty members teaching in this atmosphere. It is on their work that the reputation of the University is built. Attracting and retaining excellent faculty members is accomplished by the deans and their search committees, and in this the administrators provided all resources they could muster. Between 1997 and 2007 our deans were dedicated to this task despite serious resource challenges.

Without students a university becomes solely a research institute. Spread over ten faculties and two campuses, in 1997 York had nearly 40,000 graduate and post-graduate students,[9] full-time and part-time undergraduates, and mature students in bridging programs. Enrolment plans were built carefully each year, and recruitment of students to fulfil those plans was one of the major annual exercises in the institution. The student numbers were formed in part by the desires of the Faculties, but driven greatly by changes in government policy

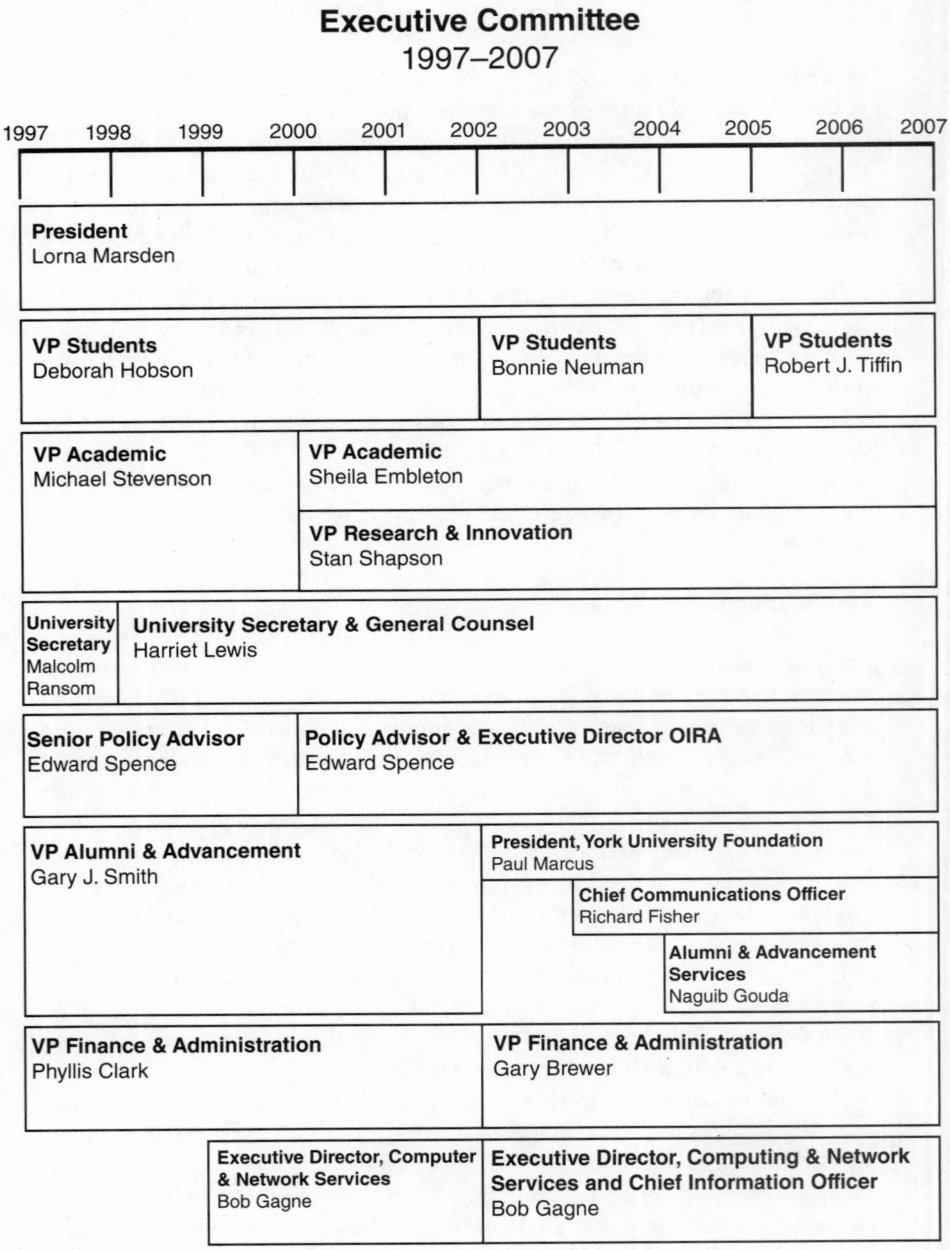

Executive Committee
1997–2007

1997	1998	1999	2000	2001	2002	2003	2004	2005	2006	2007

President
Lorna Marsden

VP Students Deborah Hobson	**VP Students** Bonnie Neuman	**VP Students** Robert J. Tiffin

VP Academic Michael Stevenson	**VP Academic** Sheila Embleton
	VP Research & Innovation Stan Shapson

University Secretary Malcolm Ransom	**University Secretary & General Counsel** Harriet Lewis

Senior Policy Advisor Edward Spence	**Policy Advisor & Executive Director OIRA** Edward Spence

VP Alumni & Advancement Gary J. Smith	**President, York University Foundation** Paul Marcus
	Chief Communications Officer Richard Fisher
	Alumni & Advancement Services Naguib Gouda

VP Finance & Administration Phyllis Clark	**VP Finance & Administration** Gary Brewer

Executive Director, Computer & Network Services Bob Gagne	**Executive Director, Computing & Network Services and Chief Information Officer** Bob Gagne

Figure 5.2. York University's executive committee, 1997–2007

and the ability of our resources to accommodate more students. We wanted to enrich the lives of students on campus. This, too, was a challenge.

The leader of the life of undergraduates[10] is the vice-president students, and at the start of my first term we were able to attract back Professor Deborah Hobson, who had been on the faculty at York and knew the landscape well.[11] In addition to the usual work, her job was made more complex because of the structure laid down in the early years of the University, with residential colleges (with dining rooms, masters, and staff), and special activities of all kinds, including academic advising, pubs, art galleries, and sports teams. It was observed earlier that the college model created by the founding president for a much smaller institution was a poor fit with a very large commuter university. Only about 5 per cent of our students lived in campus residences, although they were a vibrant part of campus life.[12]

The competition for the best students is an ongoing and vital part of the annual university cycle. Having attractive programs of study and advertising them is only part of the process. Offering good scholarships and bursaries, housing, sports, and extramural programs are also important. We wanted to be the first choice of more students in all our programs and to provide good financial support, an attractive social environment, and strong academic advising for them. This required a well-focused team of staff in student recruitment, finance, sports, and health, academic and career advising, discipline, housing, and food services.

Graduate students are a precious commodity for faculty members and departments. Each student must have an adviser and then a thesis supervisor, a package of financial support, and a good fit with the academic program. The deans of graduate studies during my years, David Leyton-Brown, John Lennox, and Ron Pearlman, worked endlessly to ensure that standards were kept high and students were able to complete their degrees in a timely way.

Students were engaged in all levels of governance, including student governments for the University and each college, but the vast majority of students came to campus for a few hours for classes before they commuted out to jobs and their homes. Many of them joined no clubs or sports teams, attended none of the other campus events, and were disengaged. Students who are the first in their families to be at a university seldom have knowledge of the "varsity" traditions to guide their behaviour. Particularly in my first term, a small number of disruptive activists and college pub nights[13] were troublesome issues. The eight college masters[14] focused on their own members, so our vice-president students coped with the overall nonacademic territory. There were significant frustrations for the masters, academic deans, and all three who served as vice-president students during my ten years.[15] Together, however, they kept me briefed, made reforms, and built greater social density among students through athletics and campus spirit groups: the YorkisU program for those who were York boosters, York's "birthday" celebrations, and the most successful of all, multicultural week.[16] With a great deal of dedicated work by the staff, the atmosphere improved, but commuter student connections remain a challenge for York as it does for most commuter universities.[17]

In 2005, much later in my years, Vice-President Students Rob Tiffin led a process of consultation on the colleges that resulted in a report called "Strengthening York's Neighbourhoods."[18] Its recommendations emphasized the student experience and reflected the changed nature of the student body – in particular, part-time students. It was an excellent response to changing times, and has added to the evolution of the colleges from their first inception in the days of our founding president to the large commuter university we have become.[19]

Throughout this decade, we raised student admission standards, coped with the double cohort of students, helped graduate students complete their degrees more quickly, improved our sport and exercise facilities, and kept all our Faculties filled with very good students. By 2004, York was second only to the University of Toronto in Ontario in the number of high school graduates who made York their first choice on the application form to Ontario universities. We also increased the amount spent on student scholarships and bursaries from about $7.6 million to about $52.5 million, and always had the best contract conditions we could negotiate for graduate students who worked as teaching assistants.[20]

Academic Plans, Processes, and Problems

By 1997 York had established strong academic plans and planning processes that we could modify and adapt as circumstances changed. In 1988 the first University Academic Plan (UAP) was approved by the Senate. Almost each year after, revisions and additions were made to that plan, but I saw no reason to embark on a major strategic review.[21] Between 1997 and 2007, however, circumstances changed quite dramatically. In 1998, our vice-president academic, Michael Stevenson, drew on the previous academic planning documents in a report entitled "Strategic Planning for the New Millennium 1999–2010." Then, in 1999, we reported to the governors with a document entitled "A Strategic Plan for York University Towards 2009," which incorporated revised enrolment plans as well as information technology and research proposals. The landscape was changing so rapidly that we were constantly revising our plans. Finally, in 2004, as events led to the need for a new coherent academic statement, the Senate Academic Policy, Planning and Research Committee made a major effort to present an updated UAP that could be used to guide not only Faculty work and budget planning, but also our new capital campaign, *York to the Power of Fifty* (June 2005). In addition, that plan gave priority to research and health education, paving the way for the next steps in the reorganization of some of the disciplines and Faculties.

Evolution of Programs and Faculties

Many of the Faculties went through changes in their programs, recruitment, and research priorities between 1997 and 2007. External reviews of existing programs by peers were helpful exercises, and all new programs were to be reviewed to be eligible for funding. With Senate colleagues, we rethought how our Faculties were responding to student interests and social demand.[22] One of the more dramatic changes included an engineering program established in the Faculty of Pure and Applied Science, preparing the way for an engineering school.[23] Expertly led by Dean Bob Prince, the name of the Faculty was changed to Science and Engineering. Schools of Nursing and Social Work had been housed in the Atkinson Faculty of Liberal and Professional Studies. Eventually the plan for a new Faculty of Health developed, drawing from other Faculties' departments such as Psychology and Kinesiology. In a consultative process led by Vice-President Academic Sheila Embleton, most of those departments chose to join the new Faculty of Health and, in 2006, we recruited a dynamic first dean, Harvey Skinner, to provide leadership.

Atkinson College (later Faculty) for part-time studies had been built in the 1960s with its own faculty members, programs, buildings, fee structures, and policies.[24] Because this Faculty taught in the evenings and on weekends, York now had three departments of English, History, Sociology, Mathematics, Computer Science, and virtually all other programs in the Arts. Atkinson, Glendon, and the Faculty of Arts had separate hiring and promotion practices and separate courses and cultures. Many applicants and students were confused by these issues. They were not the only ones.

The student world had changed. By the late 1990s nearly all students at a university such as York were holding down part-time jobs, studying part time, and very often managing complex family relationships as well. Fewer took a full course load. More took longer to complete their degrees. Finally we realized that all undergraduate Faculties needed to enrol part-time students, and it was impossible to sustain Atkinson College as the only locus of part-time studies. Bringing the Faculty of Arts and the Atkinson departments together was a monumental task undertaken by VP Sheila Embleton and the team she developed. The dean of Atkinson, Rhonda Lenton, ensured that the special aspects of her Faculty were retained. They spent endless hours in hearings, debates, negotiations, and planning before a final proposal went through the Senate to create a gigantic Faculty of Liberal Arts and Professional Studies. This became a reality in 2009 under Dean Martin Singer. We had hoped this would be an interim step to a division of this large and unwieldy Faculty into further Faculties, but as I write, this has not yet happened.

Although most of our Faculties were very successful, a few went through bad times. In 1997 our bilingual Glendon Faculty was in trouble with dropping student enrolment, low retention, weak recruitment, and poor morale. The Board of Governors instructed me to find a solution or close the campus. After thorough review, we built a plan to save the Faculty, but a great deal had to change: student recruitment had to improve in quality and numbers; faculty complement needed boosting; and we had to find an effective leader to restore the Faculty to good health in all its dimensions. This was accomplished. Under Principal Kenneth McRoberts, this Faculty has succeeded in attracting top national and international students as well as improving its campus facilities, student relations, and program offerings. In my second term, the Faculty of Environmental Studies was in deficit and floundering. Again, with the vice-president academic, we carried out a vigorous review and analysis. Programs had to be changed, student complaints had to be resolved, but in the end the Faculty recovered and has gone on to be as successful as it had been earlier. In both these cases, persuading faculty members, students, and alumni of the facts and their consequences was the most difficult part of the exercise. Faculty had important goals, but they were not always aligned with changing student interests or available resources. But evidence-based planning does work, and more than enough of the people involved in each case saw the need for change, were imaginative in finding solutions, and committed themselves to work in new ways to make a success of these near-failures.

Research: Responding to New Challenges

The research enterprise in Canadian universities is massive. Although the provinces have always supported their universities, after World War II the federal government began to be the major supporter of research through granting councils that provide competitive grants programs for researchers. York's specialized research in many areas, from Canadian literature to space science and beyond, had long been overseen by an associate vice-president reporting to the vice-president academic. Although York had many distinguished researchers and specialized research centres making contributions to basic knowledge and to applied problems, we did not encourage research-only faculty positions as some universities did. We wanted students to be taught by researchers.

By the mid-1990s Ontario universities had begun to divide between those that self-described as "research intensive" and everyone else. The "intensity" was measured by the number and amounts of external research grants received. This measure ensured that universities with medical and engineering schools were always in the research-intensive group, and it was difficult for those without such faculties to meet that criterion. It became impossible not to move in the direction of "research intensity" because the federal government, among others, appeared to accept this situation uncritically. No doubt in an effort to focus diminishing resources, it began to discuss giving most grants and research chairs to these "research-intensive" institutions.

This differentiation was the first step in demolishing the merit-based funding system in which individual researchers or groups of researchers, not institutions, were seen as the points of funding. The system based on individual proposals had allowed first-rate researchers at any university to compete for funds. This meant that many small or new universities could attract and retain top-rank researchers in some fields. Gradually the institutions, rather than the researchers, began to predominate. There were some good reasons for this as the research infrastructure became more and more expensive in a few fields, but it had some bad effects in the sense that universities not in the "research-intensive club" began to be seen as inferior places to study and to work despite having excellent researchers among their faculty members. They became poorer in academic reputation as well as in funding as the ranking of institutions, rather than researchers, slowly predominated.

In 2000 we created a new separate portfolio of vice-president research and innovation. Professor Stan Shapson moved from AVP research to this new position. He devoted many years to tasks already in train, such as assisting faculty members in their search for funding as well as ramping up our knowledge about York's researchers, increasing our relations with the many granting agencies, and raising the profile of our research. The results have been salutary for our faculty, graduate students, and the country. We also advanced a long-standing proposal for a medical school at York. In this process, a good friend at another university who was deeply knowledgeable explained to me in detail how extraordinarily difficult – nearly impossible – that quest would be. Indeed, he proved to be correct at least at that time. The Faculty of Health we created has entirely different objectives from a Faculty of Medicine, and has proved to be a major attraction to students, research funds, and new fields of graduate employment. If York is ever successful in establishing a Faculty of Medicine – and I hope it will be – research grants will immediately increase.

Advancing Identity and Reputation

Earlier chapters described the difficult relations with the media that had long been a problem for York's reputation. There is a paragraph in founding president Murray Ross's memoirs that I wish I had studied in 1997.[25] He describes how Claude Bissell handled public relations when he became president of the University of Toronto by hiring a senior journalist. "Toronto was a good university when Bissell came but no one in Toronto seemed to recognize it. He and (the journalist) convinced both faculty members and people in the community that it was so. Confidence in the institution grew." Bissell's precedent is one I should have followed. We had a small communications department at York working with the media, internal communications, and each of the Faculties. They all worked very hard, but we needed a strategic media leader and many more experienced communications staff than our budget resources would allow to turn around York's long-standing problems. We had to try to reach our goal by another route.

Through a survey research firm,[26] we found that York had no positive identity in the public mind or among the media. We consistently reported on the accomplishments of the faculty and students and placed some success stories, but all too often it was the unflattering incidents that attracted media attention. Why did this happen? Part, at least, stemmed from the crises of the early 1970s and our reputation for nonconformity and politics, aspects of campus life that were present but much exaggerated.

York has a lively campus and outside speakers on many controversial topics. Our established internal policies provide access for a multiplicity of views. The invitations to speakers come from departments and individuals and from student clubs and other groups on campus. To ensure that there were fair opportunities for all speakers, we negotiated use of space rules that applied to student clubs and other associations on campus. There were more than a few incidents of outside agitators trying to enlist our students to their causes, of maverick students or faculty who simply took up positions in high-traffic areas with amplified sound to expound their beliefs, sometimes disrupting classes, intimidating students and faculty, and abusing all the negotiated protocols.[27] This was tiresome for those who had to divert their work from more crucial projects to deal with these situations. Those most hurt by these disruptions, however, were the time- and cash-strapped students who, focused on completing their courses, resented such interruptions.[28]

At one point, a highly controversial speaker on the politics of the Middle East, Daniel Pipes, was invited to speak by a university group. Some controversy erupted, as it did on many campuses, over the Israel-Palestine issue on which this speaker had well-known views, and the group cancelled the invitation shortly before the event. At this point the controversy grew fiercer, and my executive committee decided that, in the interests of free speech, the invitation must stand. York University has a clear rule that all speakers will be heard so long as they are not preaching hatred, breaking the law, or contradicting university policies. We took no position at all on the views expressed, but only on York's value of freedom of speech. In this instance, we brought in security at considerable expense, moved the venue to allow a larger crowd to attend, and secured the speaker's safety as well as crowd control. The event went ahead without problems. The principle was protected. For years after, however, we had to deal with the fallout from the faculty association and from many individuals worried about fairness or procedures.[29]

These events attracted a lot of media, but did not advance our academic reputation. To deal with these problems, we developed with what we came to call "the four pillars" of university advancement: (1) fundraising; (2) marketing/communications/media; (3) alumni relations and advancement services; and (4) special events (including convocations, ceremonial occasions, conferences, and care of visitors). Creating these pillars involved a struggle with what had become a highly decentralized workplace, with Faculties, colleges, campuses, and some programs duplicating efforts and working without reference to rules and practices required in such a complex organization. The budget duplication, the complaints about their events, the colours of other universities used to advertise York events instead of our own red and white, and some students and faculty members speaking directly to the media as if they were speaking for the entire University upset not only the senior administrators but particularly the University governors and all too often parents, politicians, and neighbours of the University. We aimed to reduce this chaos and build York's positive identity.

Over the years we found experts to lead in each of the four areas.[30] In 2001 we created a separately incorporated foundation (pillar 1), and by 2002 had found an experienced senior fundraiser, Paul Marcus, and a dedicated Board of Directors, chaired by Governor Tim Price, to oversee and work exclusively on fundraising. In 2003 we hired Richard Fisher, a branding/marketing/communications expert (pillar 2) from a private firm who reorganized communications at York, created a York University brand and presence in the city, and for all external and internal communications. In 2004 we brought on board a head of alumni relations (pillar 3), Naguib Gouda, who tackled the problems of inspiring our alumni association and developing accurate record-keeping of alumni and donors. Finally in 2004 we established an office called special events and community relations (pillar 4) to run our eighteen annual convocations, ceremonial events, care for university visitors, and manage conventions held on our campuses.[31] This office was led by Sylvia Zingrone, who also served as my chief of staff. This "four pillars" project was a major undertaking, but had many benefits, including the enhancement of York's overall reputation.

Cooperative Ventures

"The President should look for co-operative ventures with other universities, institutions and corporations to enhance its academic mission while reducing the University's costs and spreading its risks," declared clause 7 of the presidential mandate. Many cooperative relations, both academic and otherwise, were already in place, including those with other universities, governments, and community groups.

Like previous presidential teams, we maintained a vigorous calendar of meetings with governments at all levels. For this, we needed timely and factual information. The Office of Institutional Research and Analysis was brought into my office and produced data of all sorts, statistical tables, maps, and reports. There were wins and losses in our government campaigns, but it helped a great deal when government officials and our team understood each other's challenges.

We worked closely with the municipalities surrounding the Keele campus, with excellent support from our federal MP, Judy Sgro, our provincial MPP, Mario Sergio, and several municipal politicians. Over the years these relationships involved the subway extension, research, cooperative work between specific Faculties and the municipalities, and the expansion of our special relationships in the Jane-Finch communities. York Region was our home for relationships of all kinds. After all, we were separated from York Region only by a few yards across Steeles Avenue. The vice-president research and innovation, Stan Shapson, worked indefatigably on this with the school boards and hospitals, with the cities of Markham and Vaughan and the Town of Richmond Hill, as well as the surrounding areas. Those city governments, especially the successive mayors of Markham, proved to be excellent partners. Building on work that the Faculty of Education had pioneered many years before, this resulted in a great cooperative spirit among neighbouring institutions. So strong was the reputation of the Humanities and Social Sciences at York and of the Business and Law schools that some of the not-for-profit and business organizations near the campus had not realized the depth and extent of research in science and medicine carried out at York.

That research had spawned a series of businesses created by faculty members and alumni, but unlike most universities, York did not own the intellectual property of faculty members' research.[32] So, as faculty members went on to commercialize their work in the private sector, it was not clear that it was at York University that the innovations had developed. Early on, with the cooperation of the City of Markham and IBM, the Innovation Synergy Center in Markham was created that has helped many researchers to make this research visible and take their inventions and innovations into development.[33]

The public schools around the Keele campus all have long-standing relationships with faculty members and staff. With an increasing number of projects undertaken in the neighbouring Jane-Finch area, a first-settlement community for many new immigrants and refugees, it became clear that we needed to coordinate our work. In 2006, with a major, ten-year gift of support from TD Bank, we secured space in the neighbourhood for a Community Engagement Centre.[34] Our staff work with the residents on skills training and services has helped to build our relationships with this vibrant community and bring many superb students to York.

In the late 1990s the government of Ontario wanted to ease the flow of students between the community college and university programs. President Mann had agreed to York's becoming the first university in the province to include a community college (Seneca College) facility on our campus, building on some existing joint academic programs. Seneca College and York were able to expand our joint programs. We also developed a strong joint program with Sheridan College, among other college relationships.

As in other universities, York's faculty members work with colleagues in their fields of specialization wherever in the world is appropriate. Some of these are with other academic institutions and some with municipal, commercial, and other not-for-profit organizations. From the start, York had cooperative exchanges with other universities and research organizations around the world. Notable among them was the University of York in England, which opened in 1963 shortly after our York.[35]

During my presidency, "internationalization" was an important concept in Ontario, and at York[36] international exchange programs were already extensive for students and for faculty on research leave. Both academic VPs Michael Stevenson and his successor Sheila Embleton were tireless travellers who trimmed or expanded these links regularly with the help of their AVPs international. In 1997 York won the competition to establish a Centre for German and European Studies in conjunction with the Université de Montréal, as President Mann describes in her chapter. In the early 1990s the government of Premier David Peterson had built cooperation between Ontario and Baden-Württemberg in southwest Germany as part of the Four Motors project.[37] The mix of industries and agricultural economies in the two jurisdictions was remarkably similar, and educational exchanges were arranged. When the provincial government changed in the mid-1990s, these links were neglected. So the competition sponsored by the German federal government through its academic exchange programs (DAAD) promised to revive those relationships. Our Centre started with an official opening in November 1997 at the Université de Montréal. Our University had several faculty members dedicated to its success, and the project strengthened relationships between Germany and Canada.

Many other student and academic exchanges were built, especially with universities in Asia and the Americas, based on common scholarly or scientific projects and the exchange of students. York's well-established York University English Language Institute (YUELI) served students arriving without the needed language skills.[38] On more than one occasion we invited all the consuls general in the Greater Toronto Area to a day on campus, which proved successful. In September 2005 we hosted twelve university rectors from Japan on our campus. This was a return visit after twelve Canadian university presidents, of which I was one, went to Japan in 2001. With co-host Wade MacLauchlan, then-president of the University of Prince Edward Island, and the support of the Department of Foreign Affairs, the Association of Universities and Colleges of Canada, and the ambassadors of both countries, this visit built closer understanding.

Several of the Faculties at York built their own international joint degrees. For example, the Schulich School of Business has a joint Executive MBA program, begun in 2001, with the Kellogg School at Northwestern University in Chicago; since 2005 the Osgoode Hall Law School has had programs with the Stern Law School at New York University. These two high-profile relationships were by no means the only ones in our Faculties serving research faculty and students. Cooperation, moreover, extends well beyond academic programs. For decades, Tennis Canada had held the Canadian Open Tennis Championships in facilities it built and managed on the Keele campus. In the late 1990s, Tennis Canada approached us to expand its facilities in the northeast quadrant. After many months of discussions, we agreed on a piece of land beside Black Creek where Tennis Canada built a beautiful new centre court, winter facilities, and the grounds for the annual Open Championships, which opened to great acclaim in 2004. We own the land, and Tennis Canada owns and manages the facilities. We hold our convocation ceremonies in its winter facilities, and Tennis Canada uses our parking facilities during the championships. Like so many other cooperative ventures, this all became possible because of the personalities involved and the willingness to make a deal.

Despite the constraints of resources and government policies, the academy at York grew increasingly focused and absorbed in building a strong and distinctive reputation. Some of this was because the governance institutions were so strong.

Governance

From my first meeting with the York Senate, it became clear to me that this was a powerful governing body.[39] It was highly effective and a place where well-considered planning discussion occurred both in its committees and in monthly Senate meetings. Senior scholars, researchers, and former deans were elected as representatives to the Senate along with many others. Everyone was held to account. It was chaired by an elected faculty member, and that post was always contested.

Although governance in a university is similar to that of a government or a business only at the most general level – in the sense of having regulations, policies and financial requirements, executive bodies, and legal provisions – the assessment of academic quality and institutional history are more important considerations in a university. Assessing academic quality can be done only by scholars and scientists, whom John Lombardi calls the "quality engines" of a university.[40] York's senators keep a close eye on everything associated with the academic standards and plans.

In the context of this culture, the massive challenges of the "business" of the University, which must work to a brisk timetable – attracting and retaining good students; funding salaries, benefits, and research; complying with federal, provincial, and municipal laws and regulations; providing heated, cooled, and cleaned buildings; and ensuring campus security – is often seen as a secondary consideration. The negotiations to achieve budget reductions and organizational changes in such a culture often take far longer than in other types of organizations. Unlike a business corporation, where employees are "let go" with severance, faculty members once tenured can be asked to leave only for the most dire behaviour.[41] Considering that academic administrators return to faculty ranks after their term in office, it is hard for department chairs, deans, and even vice-presidents to hold firm on painful decisions. The brilliance of many academic administrators at York was their ability to deal with many personalities and constrained budgets while keeping the majority of their colleagues well informed and forward-looking.

This is why it was so worthwhile to ensure that the governance bodies remained strong. York's bicameral system of governance – a Board of Governors and an academic Senate – is laid out in the York University Act of 1965. By 1997 there was a need for some changes. The Board had asked me to revisit the mission statement, achieve more transparency and accountability in the University documents, and clearly state goals and timetables. The system has two important cultural divides that the president must tend: one with lay governors for whom the academic world is mysterious, and another between administrators and the academy of faculty and students.

During my terms, among many changes to governance to move the processes of decision-making forward and bridge the divides, five stand out: revision of the mission statement, realigning the senior administration and the Board of Governors, improving the rules of the Senate, decreasing the size of the Senate, and improving the transparency of information and accountability.

In 1997 the University's mission statement ran to two pages, and contained the desires of all parts of the University. How could we shorten it, make it crisper, and less declarative? In April 1998, in a memo to the Joint Executive Committees of the Board and the Senate,[42] I outlined all the past documents dealing with York's mission – from the 1957 project of the North Toronto YMCA to establish a new university to the *2020 Vision* exercise of 1992 – and asked for a consultative body to carry out the task. By July 1998 a draft mission statement for comments had been circulated by the chairs of the Board and Senate to the entire York community. The short draft statement received many responses, including requests to put favourite phrases back in the statement.[43] After considerably more work, a 108-word statement in English and a 139-word counterpart in French were approved; they can still be found on the University's website, only slightly revised in 2003. To achieve more transparency, we created a new annual document called *Planning, Budgeting and Accountability*, described in detail below.

The York Board of Governors is autonomous and has no members appointed by governments or church bodies, as at some other Ontario universities. There are several committees of the Board, dealing with matters such as audit, finance, and pensions. As part of our effort to respond to the mandated goal of positive relations in the University and to increase the trust and confidence between governors and faculty members, we reformed the committee structure to ensure that each vice-president was attached to a Board committee. Their assignment was to help in the preparation of agendas and to bring the appropriate materials to the committee. Some of these reforms, in areas such as finance and land use, were very successful; others were less so.

Since all major academic decisions are the province of the Senate, we established a Board academic resources committee. We prepared for this carefully: a memo to the Board in 2006 said "your largest investment as a Board is in tenure stream faculty and permanent staff ... Yet apart from the listing of new hires and promotions with some sketchy career information you receive almost no information about the faculty members, our most precious resource."[44] The goal was to help Board members from quite different walks of life understand how academics carry on their work, while the vice-presidents got a much clearer idea of governance concerns. It allowed the vice-president academic and vice-president research to bring forward issues relating to faculty complement and retention, the link between finances and issues such as research grants, libraries, computing, and major academic plans as they advanced. Committees staffed with vice-presidents allowed a great many issues to be aired and some of the "we-they" sentiments to be resolved. The composition of the Executive Committee of the Board was changed to consist of all the chairs of the committees. Information then flowed well, and was a great source of guidance to our team. I served with three chairs of the Board, each quite different, but all deeply interested in supporting the university: William Dimma, who was finishing his term as I came into office; Charles Hantho, who served for three years; and Marshall Cohen, with whom I worked for the subsequent seven years. The University owes all of them a debt of gratitude.

Until 1972 the chair of the Senate at York was the University president, as in many other universities. Thereafter the chair was elected from among the faculty members on the Senate for a one-year term; this was changed in 2003 to an eighteen-month term,[45] when we elected at the same time a vice-chair to provide for succession. As each new chair learned the rules, processes, and powers of the Senate, this was much helped both by the *Senate Handbook*[46] and by the Secretary of the University, Harriet Lewis,[47] and her staff. Over my ten years, we had some excellent chairs and committee chairs. The *Senate Handbook* is extremely detailed, and is amended from time to time, indicating the evolution of procedures. But the issues each chair faced and that person's style in office greatly affected what could be accomplished. So we turned our attention to how we could adjust Senate procedures to help the chairs.

The York Senate is the academic governing body, and although the committees of the Senate got their reports and recommendations through efficiently,[48] quite often the monthly Senate meetings were long and frustrating, partly because of the rules governing their conduct. Senate rules set two-hour meetings that could be extended by a vote, which often happened when a contentious issue was on the floor. Since meetings began at 3 p.m., an extension meant that parents with children and senators with other duties had to leave before issues were resolved. At that time, the Senate operated largely under Bourinot's Rules of Order, the same as used in the Parliament of Canada.[49] For example, York's Senate rules required three readings for statutory matters such as the creation or dissolution of Faculties and the creation of new degrees. To work, Bourinot's Rules require a government to propose legislation and an organized opposition to dissent and recommend amendments. There is a great deal of necessary tension between the parties in such a governing structure. The Senate of York, however, was a group of individuals – more like a town hall meeting at which individual voices dominate, rather than parties. A town hall discussion would be guided by Robert's Rules of Order. Furthermore, policy proposals brought to the Senate had already been through a Senate committee, as had all proposals for new programs, new Faculties, timetables, and virtually all the statutory business of the Senate. It was quite unlike the Parliament of Canada.

I found the process laborious and confusing. It seemed to me that the use of Bourinot's Rules had the effect of turning the administration into the government and everyone else into a rather chaotic opposition – not helpful to coming to decisions. After many revisions, and with the help of the chair of the Senate and secretary of the University, the rules were modified. When I left the presidency, they had evolved into a more effective mixture of Robert's, Bourinot's, and York's homegrown rules. They continue to improve as experience changes.

We also undertook a Senate reform to reduce its size and rationalize its committee structure. By 1998 the Senate had ballooned to 226 members under a formula derived from the York University Act. Attendance was poor. Few could speak. Following the conclusions of a Senate sub-committee, a new formula was recommended in 2004 to take effect in 2005 with a goal of about 157 senators. The debate in 2004 became strident as the then Faculty of Arts was to lose a great many of its senators. The proposed changes were saved by a brave speech by Dean of Arts Robert Drummond, a professor of political science, on the many forms of democratic representation.[50] The change improved participation and focused the work on academic governance issues without sacrificing the representation of the many constituencies with a stake in academic governance.

These changes to the mission statement, Board organization, and Senate procedures and size were intended to improve governance and participation in the affairs of the University, and I believe they did so.

Accountability

Item six of the presidential mandate called on the president to make the University "more accountable while protecting academic freedom and the necessary elements of institutional autonomy." In short, we were to report in a way that would satisfy the governments at various levels, while not giving in to the intrusive desires of some parts of government. The provincial auditor, for example, had a long-standing ambition to audit universities' books using a value-for-money audit. This type of audit would give an auditor a great deal of power to impose his values on those of the University, in addition to absorbing vast amounts of staff and administrative time.[51] We managed to escape that proposal. The province did force the universities to come under the Freedom of Information and Protection of Privacy Act, which added considerable costs and workload to the institutions without a corresponding increase in transparency, since so much in universities was already done collegially or publicly.

To focus attention on accountability to the community, I followed the lead of David Strangway, who, as president of the University of British Columbia, had produced a very detailed annual report describing to the stakeholders all the activity of that university.[52] At York we modified his document and, starting with fiscal year 1998/99, produced *Planning, Budgeting and Accountability* (PBA), an annual report that detailed plans, revenues, expenditures, and explanations for each unit, academic and nonacademic. The first PBA describes it this way: "The PBA Report will replace a number of publications that are now presented at various times throughout the year. It will appear each year in the beginning of the Fall term and is both retrospective and prospective in nature. Essentially the PBA Report answers the following questions for each major unit in the University: What were the plans for the year just past? How did the budget link to those plans? How did the actual results vary from those plans and why? What are the major plans for the coming year?"

With input from each of the vice-presidents and deans, we produced the PBA every year until the end of my second term, and it stands as a record of what was accomplished by each Faculty, the major nonacademic departments, and the Office of the President. The PBA reported on York's initial work on environmental accountability measures – we signed the Talloires Declaration in 2002[53] – linked to a range of issues, including waste management, power and water usage, and fertilizer and pesticide use.[54] The PBA was made available to each governor, the provincial government, and anyone else who wanted a copy.

Did this satisfy everyone? Certainly no one expected it would, but many deans, vice-presidents, and governors could refer questioners to this document with the assurance that we stood behind the numbers. Many faculty members, senators, and students used it regularly.

My personal accountability was laid out in the presidential mandate in the form of an annual review with the Executive Committee of the Board. It was invariably helpful in improving and focusing our goals. The Board held my feet to the fire on many issues, but constructively. One difficult period for everyone was during "my strike."

It seems to be a ritual at York that a strike occurs in each presidential regime. In my case, it was the union that represented graduate students (who worked as teaching or graduate assistants) and the part-time faculty members. They struck after we were unable to conclude a contract agreement in the fall of 2000. Although many issues arose and were settled through negotiations, money remained the contested issue in the form of automatic increases pegged to graduate student fees. The strike strongly affected the undergraduates, and involved many sympathetic faculty members who withdrew their services. There was a great deal of emotion and outraged drama at picket lines, in the offices of some of the University governors, and outside my house in downtown Toronto. The Senate met constantly as classes, examinations, and other matters had to be changed. The chair and leaders of the Senate were very professional in all their dealings with both sides and had the trust of us all. Some students dropped out of York. Other students, however, came forward to see how they could help. At the fall convocation ceremony, many students crossing the platform urged us to "hold firm." One particular group of undergraduates supported the vice-president students and me, and continued to do so for several years afterwards, a most remarkable act of friendship and generosity. They remain active alumni at York and in the wider community.

It was a painful period finally settled in early January 2001. Afterwards, we reorganized our employee relations staff and operations and brought in outside negotiators to avoid some of the emotion raised by conflict among people who work together every day. There were no more strikes in my presidential terms, but there was almost continuous contract negotiation with the many unions, and always grievances to be settled. I strongly support collective bargaining, but the industrial model seemed quite inappropriate and ineffective for most people working in the university setting.[55] However, no alternative model was found during these years.

For my second mandate (2002–07), the Board accepted a new set of objectives.[56] These included reorganizing to create a Faculty of Health,[57] building the independently incorporated Foundation to develop first-rate fundraising staff, preparing for a capital campaign for the fiftieth anniversary of York's founding, and building a sustainable plan for alumni relations.

Two years before I intended to leave the presidency, I urged the Board chair to reform the search process to make it possible for the widest possible set of presidential candidates to come forward. The chair of the Board, Marshall Cohen, wisely enlisted the help of Peter Hogg, Dean Emeritus of Osgoode Hall Law School and constitutional expert. The goal was to modify the search for my successor from the "beauty contest" approach in use when I was selected to a "consult and decide process." Due no doubt to the earlier problems of presidential selection described in the Introduction to this book, the process when I was recruited in 1996 was to create a search committee that would recommend a few names to the Board and the Senate. Each candidate then had to speak to and be questioned by the Senate, after which the senators would vote in a secret ballot. The governors voted later.

There were three main difficulties in this process. First, it was a public process, with lobbying and pressures on voters. Second, under this public system, many desirable candidates would not allow their names to stand for fear of losing the position they already held should they fail to be selected for York.

This was most stressful for candidates inside the University, who were put in an awkward situation if they then had to remain as unsuccessful aspirants. Third, if the Senate or Board rejected the name put forward at the end of the process, the committee had to start all over again with a new set of viable candidates.

In 2006 we modified the process. Now, after wide consultation with all the University's constituencies, the skills and characteristics of the next president are determined and agreed to by the community in a written document; a selection committee of governors, senators, staff, and students is established and, with the help of a search firm, candidates are assessed, interviewed only by the committee, and recommended to the Board of Governors. There is no public process in the Senate before the selection is made. This new process made it much easier to select my successor and, I hope, will aid the search for all future presidents.

Together these governance, accountability, and procedural changes, although not highly visible, contributed to a more resilient institution and, by reducing those gaps between the academy, administrators, and governors, were among my greatest satisfactions while in office.

Bringing in Resources: Money Matters

All studies of the work of contemporary university presidencies emphasize the importance of increasing and managing resources. Between 1997 and 2007 at York we faced all these challenges. Here we look at the impact of the cuts and a few of the ways we increased operating, capital, and endowments in order to achieve our goals.

Big cuts

As President Mann describes in Chapter 4, in 1996, the Harris government of Ontario announced massively reduced university budgets that, added to the budget cuts of previous years, created a shock wave through all institutions. As a result, all sorts of efficiencies were put into effect with an impact on staff, students, and campus development. Most significant for academic operations, the cuts led to a reduction in the full-time faculty tenure-stream appointments. From 1993 to 1998 the decline in faculty complement in the Ontario university system was an average of 11.7 per cent. At York this decline was "only" 2.7 per cent.[58] The reduction had the effect of increasing the faculty/student ratio and weakening graduate enrolments. Even as these cuts were under way, my team was determined to ensure that the faculty complement would be brought up to or beyond previous standards. We knew that the proportion of tenure-stream faculty members raised the reputation of the University. The access of students to faculty members improved the quality of their education and satisfaction with their University experience. But the Ontario government demanded that additional funding be accompanied by higher enrolments, resulting in further dilution of the faculty/student ratio.

The problem of increasing enrolments because of government requirements was not a new one at York. That policy had changed York from its original small student size back in the 1960s (see Chapter 1, in this volume). All universities struggled with these demands, especially since the government also implemented what it described as "quality" measures.[59] The older universities were somewhat buffered by very large endowments and well-embedded fundraising systems. York University was too young to have achieved either, so getting to that strength became a priority for the governors and for me.

From 1997 to 2007, among the myriad changes in government funding policies, two stand out. The first was the shift away from per capita grants towards tuition increases. In December 1997 the government announced the deregulation of graduate and professional program tuition fees. Fees and, therefore, university incomes rose, but then in 1998 grants to universities were not increased. We were all losers. University budgets had to be adjusted once again.[60] Significant tuition and ancillary fee increases continued for the life of the Harris government, along with incentives to increase student financial aid through charitable donations. To address the problem of grants, we tackled the long-standing issue of the funding formula.

Fair funding: The formula revisited

The system by which the province of Ontario funded universities – under a formula and funding corridor described in Chapters 1 and 3 in this volume – had unfortunate impacts on new universities, and certainly on York University. For example, we received fewer dollars per student in standard courses such as English, in which the content and the costs were nearly identical at all universities. The unfairness of the system was manifest. The results of this system were highly detrimental to our budget and ability to hire faculty and improve student services.

In 1996 President Mann had captured a talented finance and administrative leader, Phyllis Clark, from the Ontario government. In 1997, as our vice-president finance and administration, she picked up the campaign developed by her predecessor[61] to try for funding at levels comparable to those at other universities for students "outside the corridor." She followed the earlier campaign by neatly promoting this complex issue as the "94 cent dollar." It indicated that York got only 94 cents for each dollar provided to some of the other universities with comparable programs. Together we persuaded the government that we could not take more students without full funding. Dave Johnson, MPP, was minister of education and training from October 1997 to June 1999. He both understood the issue and acted on it. In 1998 we were able to report an additional $12.5 million was being added to our base funding in increments over a three-year period.[62]

Capitalizing on directed funding: The Access to Opportunities Program

Governments generally prefer to direct the expenditures of universities in conformity with their view of the needs of the economy. In the late 1990s the Harris government, through the Access to Opportunities Program (ATOP), focused on skills to prepare students for an era of computer-based work. Its program was designed to support computer engineering and computer science programs. It also required universities to find private sector sponsors to match the government contributions. This was of immediate benefit to those few universities with engineering and especially computer engineering programs and loyal and generous donors. But all universities tried to benefit from the program by examining their offerings to see what would fit in its confines.

Although York's Department of Computer Science was strong, we decided to develop a program for Arts and Science undergraduates in Information Technology (ITEC), a "multi-disciplinary programme, providing a solid ground in computer science, enriched by an understanding of computer applications and the social, policy and ethical implications relating to computing."[63] Eventually, jointly with Seneca College and inspired by the insights of the new vice-president research and innovation, we built the Technology Enhanced Learning (TEL) building, which houses programs from both institutions.

Over the period of the ATOP program, York was able to benefit substantially both in academic programs and financial support. ATOP and Fair Funding allowed us to improve the tenure-stream complement by hiring more faculty members in the Faculty of Pure and Applied Science and in the ITEC programs in other Faculties. In addition, many more scholarships were funded with a matching program from the provincial government, creating more opportunities for our students.

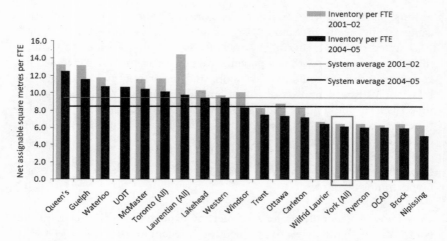

Figure 5.3. Total space per student, Ontario universities, 2001–02 and 2004–05

FTE = full-time equivalent student
Source: Council of Ontario Universities, "Space Inventory," various issues.

Capital funding: Creating space for the double cohort

The second dramatic policy change came in 1998. Ontario had long required a fifth year of high school, known as grade 13, for students entering university. The Harris government announced this fifth year would be eliminated in 2003, creating a "double cohort" of graduates. Accommodating such numbers was an immediate challenge to all universities, but it was a particular problem for universities in Toronto, where the surge of high school graduates was dramatic. In response the government announced a competition for capital funds named "Superbuild." The government's approach was to call for bids under a set of criteria that included partial government financing. The rest of the funding the university would have to raise itself.

At York, because of our rapid growth, the need for more and improved space was very great. In fact, as Figure 5.3 shows, our amount of built space, such as classrooms and other academic space, was one of the worst in the province. We desperately needed to build.

Every York president has had to deal with the problem of capital resources. We were struggling with parking requirements, stormwater drainage problems, and the rising costs of heating, cooling, and powering our many buildings. Deferred maintenance costs were a preoccupation for all universities. Now we faced two major tasks: to accumulate enough capital for these Superbuild competitions, and then to win the government part of the funding. In facing these tasks, some real innovation occurred.

At York we needed more physical space to accommodate the double cohort as well as our normal rising enrolment. We already had a list of space priorities. All our buildings and classrooms were used to capacity during the week and for some weekend classes. The estimate of the growth at York before, during, and after the double cohort was daunting. So when the call came out to apply for capital under Superbuild, we were more than ready.[64] Our vice-president administration, with years of government experience, had come up with a proposal of how to tackle the issue. We prepared our arguments carefully, and submitted our list of priority building projects to the ministry.

First on that list was the need for additional Fine Arts space. Due to high enrolments, this Faculty was stuffed into buildings across the campus, with Music students practising in rooms the size of telephone boxes in basements, the dancers competing for turns on the single sprung floor, and Theatre and Visual Arts students struggling with old existing facilities. The Faculty had very high admission standards, and attracted stellar students. They needed to be together and in better space. Many other Faculties – Science, Business, Education, Arts, and Environmental Studies – also needed better space, and the libraries had to be updated.

In February 2002 the government announced the first round of capital grants. York University received the largest grant to a single campus: $77.5 million for two projects, of which $54 million would come to York and the balance to Seneca at York. The ministry, consistent with its priorities, had selected the business school, which had been sixth on our list, for capital funding.[65] The very capable dean, Dezsö Horváth, with the vice-president advancement, set to work to raise the additional funds required from private sources, and our campus development group held a competition for the architect.[66] Fortunately our great benefactor Seymour Schulich was extraordinary in his interest in and support of the new building for the business school on the east side of the Keele campus, which is named in his honour. Also in this round of Superbuild, we responded to the government's request that we join with the Ontario Colleges of Applied Arts and Technology to share space. So the second project funded in this round was jointly with Seneca College at York for the TEL building, a large, airy, well-lit structure that is a favourite of students. Both buildings were ready for occupancy by 2004.

In the second call for capital grants proposals a few years later, our vice-president suggested we ask for a "general academic building" to meet our priority for more space for Fine Arts, with lecture halls and classrooms physically joined to existing Theatre and Film buildings. So the west-side building would consist largely of classrooms and academic space, the focus of the Superbuild program, while on the east side we would have a performing arts building with full facilities for all programs, including a theatre and concert hall. Given our successes in round one, we knew we were low on the government's list for more capital funding. Using all the new financing knowledge and skills of our team, York submitted a bid that cost only $7,500 per student space, while our nearest competitors came in at $10,000 per student space. It was a very happy day when our success was announced.

Dean of Fine Arts Phillip Silver had a clear vision of the standards and requirements for his Faculty.[67] He worked tirelessly with our finance, facilities, and fundraising teams, as well as with the construction leaders on acoustics, space needs, and standards. Again our volunteers sprang into action to secure private funding, and by the end of the Superbuild initiative, York had a handsome new business school building, a new, technology-rich building with Seneca, and a complex of Fine Arts buildings, freeing space elsewhere on campus. We converted the former administrative studies building into space for the Faculty of Environmental Studies and the newly created School of Nursing. In addition, we built a new residence,[68] with accommodation for students with disabilities and an innovative heat-saving system. We changed some of the little-used two-storey high college dining rooms into two rooms used for lectures and other events. Since parking was always a major issue, we developed a program of parking garages wrapped with administration offices in front. In these front buildings, we put a variety of student and other services, which made them convenient walk-in locations.

The impact of the Superbuild program on York University was very positive in many ways. Added to other funding from generous benefactors and borrowing, it allowed us to create a number of new buildings to accommodate the sharp intake of students, to convert other buildings extensively to serve new academic needs, and to build out much of the campus plan developed earlier by President Arthurs. For example, we were able to complete the buildings envisioned around the central Harry Arthurs Common on campus, including eventually the colonnade that protects pedestrians from the weather as they move among buildings.

It was a race against time to have all the space ready and certified for occupancy before the double cohort arrived. Since some students came early (before 2003) and some remained in high school for an additional year and came in 2004, the actual enrolment increases attributable to the double cohort were spread over three years. York's all-in enrolment numbers skyrocketed from about thirty-eight thousand full-time equivalent students in 1997 to nearly fifty-two thousand students when I left in 2007.[69]

Innovation and necessity: New and improved capital funding

Prior to the Harris government, raising funds from generous donors had been incremental to capital grants from government. The changes requiring universities to find donors for competitive funding brought further innovations to York's financial armoury. We had to step up our long-standing fundraising operation and raise capital by other means than borrowing from the banks.

FUNDRAISING: CREATING A NEW FOUNDATION

I arrived at York in 1997 while President Mann's National Campaign was still under way. We continued it with enthusiasm, ending in 1998–99 with over $108 million.[70] The success of this campaign for York, under the leadership of our Board volunteers and, after 1998 our vice-president advancement, Gary Smith,[71] resulted in the addition of twenty endowed chairs and professorships – hugely helpful in building the faculty membership. This inspired us in our next major fundraising campaign under a reorganized fundraising foundation. In 1997, due to staff changes, the records relating to fundraising were incomplete, making proper stewardship difficult. At York, as elsewhere, fundraising staff turned over quite quickly, and the ideas and practices of professional fundraising were not yet embedded in the policies or culture of the University. This had to change.

In 2002 the York Foundation was separately incorporated, and installed its own Board of Directors. We found an experienced president, Paul Marcus, who had a history of successful leadership of philanthropic projects. He assembled a good team, and we set to work to raise funds in a systematic way. The president of the Foundation and Governor Tim Price, who became chair of this Board, created a powerful group of governors who implemented best fundraising and stewardship practices in time for our campaign.[72]

The campaign was a major challenge for the entire University. All the deans had to be convinced to identify and clear prospective donors with the central campaign office. The Faculties that were successful on their own were reluctant to join in, and had to be told firmly that there was only one way to give charitable receipts: through the Foundation.[73] Cooperation was mandatory. Gifts made prior to the creation of the Foundation had to be respected. The database of alumni and donors had to serve the alumni department, general University uses, and fundraising. This was not easy.

After formidable amounts of work, it all came together. The alumni sprang to life, staff and volunteers worked hard. The campaign ended on our fiftieth anniversary in 2009 with $207 million for academic needs, buildings, and endowments for scholarships and other programs. The success of the campaign – concluded by my successor – was only part of the value.[74] Embedding the best ways of record-keeping, stewardship, alumni recruitment, and research has remained valuable. Alumni, corporations, and friends of the University were extraordinarily generous, and their names are to be found in the naming of rooms and buildings and in scholarships, professorships, and many other ways. I was deeply grateful for this generosity, which helped so many students and the institution to move forward.

DEBENTURES

How could we pay for all the capital costs of the buildings that were needed? The universities of Ontario were challenged by the Ontario government to behave in a more market-driven, competitive fashion. Two of the older and well-established universities – the University of Toronto and the University of British Columbia – had issued bonds; we had to show government that we had a competitive approach to funding our projects. Virtually all York's endowments were tied to academic purposes such as student scholarships and faculty positions. Our vice-president finance and administration had attracted a superb financial officer, Gary Brewer, who is both an engineer and an accountant and who, in turn, brought on Trudy Pound-Curtis as chief financial officer. Now there were three senior officers with a strong grasp of financing, as well as of construction and maintenance, and they led a major funding project of issuing debentures. In order to do this, the University had to be assessed by credit agencies Standard & Poor's and Dominion Bond Rating Service, which gave us an AA (low) rating in 2002. Preparation for this project was a very major task taken on principally by our three senior financial officers with the support of the Board[75] and staff. In 2002 we issued a very successful first tranche of debentures for $200 million, and went on to issue a second tranche of $100 million in May 2004. This was not the end of the innovation and competitiveness we introduced in funding capital.

A NEW APPROACH TO CAMPUS CONSTRUCTION: P3 FUNDING

Having moved both phases of the Superbuild program forward, our VP finance and administration – now Gary Brewer, as Phyllis Clark had moved to Alberta in 2002 – had accumulated great knowledge, experience, and contacts in the construction area, and York needed still more space. In the newspaper, we read a call for proposals from the government of Ontario for the building of a new Ontario Public Archives. This was a competition open to commercial and other bidders. With the president of the York University Development Corporation (YUDC), Bud Purves, our vice-president set about planning a bid that could accomplish both the objective of new archives and more space for York. Their goal was to mobilize all the available resources on all sides to win the competition: the archives needed a highly specialized building, but had no land; we had the land and academic needs, but could not stretch our financial resources. Furthermore, we were in the throes of making our case for a subway link, and access to the archives would be an important reason for better public transit. The University set out to attract all the necessary business partners to create an archives building that would be designed and built on our campus and operated by us for thirty years. In addition, we proposed to add six additional floors of space to the project for use by the University. It was a very complex deal with many challenges, but it was successful. The University and partners competed against the commercial sector and won. We now have an academic partner in the archives, new space housing research centres and institutions, as well as the senior administration, and subway trains eventually will stop at the door of this building in the core of the campus. The space freed elsewhere on campus has allowed the rational relocation of academic programs that had been at the periphery.

Communications and the New Electronic Era: A Key Resource

Between 1997 and 2007 there was a transformation in communications as personal computers, access to the Web, and cell phones began to take over from computer commons and printed communications. These technological improvements had a major impact at York. Previously, contacting faculty, staff, alumni, and students quickly involved printing on paper and delivering to mailboxes. More important, in a commuter university spread across dozens of buildings on two widely separated campuses, there was no way to contact people in case of weather or other emergencies. Now everyone began – slowly – to be online.

The arrival of the new technology required a more extensive staff to service the software and telephone systems, as well as to deal with hardware, storage of digital information, and, as the millennium approached, to ensure that the anticipated Y2K disaster was averted. In 1999 we attracted a senior leader, Robert Gagne, who was both an expert in information technology and computer network systems and a loyal alumnus of York.

It is difficult now to recall the panic that surrounded the Y2K problem: the changeover of internal clocks in computers to the new century.[76] Expert opinions differed on the threat, and corporations invested millions in new equipment and software just in case. Like everyone else, we spent an inordinate amount of staff time and resources in the run-up to 31 December 1999, when disaster was predicted to strike around the world. I spent a very tense New Year's Eve on campus with Vice-President Phyllis Clark, who was responsible for all aspects of the preparation. At 11:55 we were in the nerve centre trying to be calm. But midnight passed and absolutely nothing at all happened, except that we overheard miserable staff phoning home to their partners to wish them happy New Year and ask how the parties were going. The campus was quiet. Of course this was good news, but it was a letdown after all we had been through to prepare during the previous years. Then a partying student pulled a fire alarm in one of the residences and the fire trucks – all sirens blaring – roared through campus. It was the biggest excitement of that Y2K New Year's Eve.

The eventual arrival of personal computers, personal devices, and electronic news changed everything.[77] Internally, since 1970 a weekly hard-copy newspaper, the *York Gazette*, had been the vehicle for keeping the York community apprised of issues and events. The *Gazette* was the journal of record on decisions of the Board of Governors and the Senate, but it was hard to produce in a timely fashion. Soon budget cuts reduced it to a twice-monthly publication. It ceased publishing in 2002. On 9 September 2002 we launched a daily e-news bulletin called *YFile*, which appears in all electronic mailboxes early every morning. It keeps the campus informed about developments in many parts of University life, and alerts the University community to emergencies. The media/communications group also produced the alumni magazine, *YorkU*, annual reports, and a range of other important publications, highlighting in all of them the York "brand." In 2001 we began live-streaming the convocation ceremonies, allowing families all over the world to see their graduate crossing the platform.

Much else changed as we adapted to a more aggressive communications style in recruitment. In 2004 the media group bought advertisements for York called "subway domination," plastering the downtown St George subway station stairs and walls with York logos and messages at a crucial decision-making time for entering students. We were the first university in Toronto to take this aggressive step. It was a very successful move and a credit to the imagination of our staff.

In addition to our comprehensive logo and the consistent use of the York colours and tag line on all our communications, we worked on updating our identity in the city and among universities. A major multiyear project was the introduction of new, consistent signage and way-finding across our campuses. In another example, people were unhappy with the names of our sports teams: the Yeomen and Yeowomen. I could see why, and strongly supported and engaged with an alumni and student consultative process to change them. In 2003 we held a referendum and built a new brand campaign to announce our new name, the York Lions. It has been a great success.

By 2007 every aspect of University life had been altered by the new technologies, including registration, fee payments, lecture materials, the libraries, payroll, planning, and virtually all our activities. The innovation continues.

Two Other Successes

All the time that our team was focused on academic issues, enrolment, and construction, we were also working on other challenges. One was the long-standing campaign to bring the subway to the campus, made more urgent by the endless pressure for parking spaces. Another was the use of the lands south of Pond Road, the partial sale of which had already been attempted, as President Arthurs describes in his chapter.

Getting on and off campus

I was not the only University president to say that parking was a top issue on campus. With nearly seventy thousand people moving onto and off campus during terms, parking lots occupied too much land. In the summer of 1997, we opened the first parking garage on the Keele campus, to accommodate 325 cars at rates that eventually would pay for the building. Two other larger parking buildings were provided on my watch. But our main goal was to persuade commuters to use public transportation. We kept the parking rates sufficiently high to make it worthwhile to use the city buses, GO trains, and other services. We operated a shuttle bus between the Glendon and Keele campuses, supported car-pooling, and provided bicyclists safe indoor racks and showers. All this was good, but we needed the heft of the Toronto Transit Commission (TTC) and governments at all levels to achieve our major goal of a connection to the city subway system and to the regional transportation systems.

For well over thirty years, York administrators had been lobbying for a subway extension to our campus. Many plans were made, and the Spadina subway line was extended to Wilson Avenue in 1978 and to Downsview in 1996, but our campus was still out of reach.[78] In 1998 the Board and I agreed this was a priority, and from then until the $2 billion in funding was completed by all three levels of government, the environmental assessments finished, and the project assured in early 2007, we never rested. All our campus and construction planning was done with a subway extension in mind. Many senior administrators, the York University Development Corporation, the chancellor, alumni – notably our alumnus Greg Sorbara[79] – and many others, including everyone on campus, worked nonstop to make this happen.

In the meantime, regional transportation systems began bus services to the heart of the campus from across the top of the city. With GO Transit's 407 bus service from Hamilton to Oshawa, and YRT and VIVA buses from York Region, nearly 2,000 buses a day were arriving on campus. As well, a new York University station opened on the Bradford/Barrie GO Train line. In 2003, after a TTC

Figure 5.4.   Aerial view, looking west of York University station, under construction, 2015. Source: Copyright Toronto Transit Commission 2015. Reproduced with permission of the Toronto Transit Commission

ridership growth report, the City of Toronto decided on a rapid transit bus route between the Downsview subway station and the centre of campus. This multimillion-dollar project took until 2009 to complete, and shaved only seven minutes off the regular bus ride, but certainly helped with congestion. But nothing could compare with an underground subway. Heroic efforts were made between 1998 and 2006, described by Edward Spence in his article, "The Spadina Subway Extension through York University – Reflections on the Struggle for Approvals."[80] The subway extension with two stops on campus opens in 2017.

The south lands sale

Very early in the 1970s, under the presidency of Murray Ross, the University Board had expanded the lands granted for the Keele campus by buying over 200 acres south of the campus for future expansion. In the 1980s, under President

Arthurs, the campus master plan had been revised and the lands required for future University uses had been identified. As President Arthurs describes in Chapter 4, the University then sought to develop some of the surplus lands on the southern edge of the campus, and sold a portion to developer Bramalea Limited for high-rise buildings. But the lands were not developed, and the University was able to repurchase them later for a very favourable price. In 2000, when Marshall Cohen became chair of the Board, we took another hard look at the development possibilities of those south lands.[81]

Many points of view were expressed on this in the various consultative committees established on campus and through the YUDC. Eventually the decision was made to monetize a portion of the lands for housing. The conditions for their sale included low-rise buildings that would not cast shadows on the campus, the creation of a community, a sufficient financial return to the University to make it worthwhile, and a reputable and dependable developer.

We also had to settle other matters, such as stormwater drainage, which required building a large pond, obtaining permissions from the municipality (which demanded land for a park), and getting agreement from the York community. I was keen to see this development because of student safety issues. Developed lands would have roads open to policing by the city police, with lit sidewalks, and be a safer area. The sale of lands would also produce funds for academic purposes. Fortunately we had knowledge and expertise on our Board of Governors and on the Board of the YUDC with its new president, Bud Purves. Working together they eventually found two major companies qualified to bid, but at a late date one withdrew. We agonized over moving ahead with the remaining developer, but in the end did so, and under favourable terms for that era. The deal was signed in 2002. The land was to be sold in two tranches and the preparation for development of the first phase begun.

In early 2005 we learned that some faculty members unhappy with the sale had been talking to a *Toronto Star* investigative reporter. When he got in touch, we supplied him with the key documents and urged him to talk with the YUDC president, who had the best grasp of all the issues, dates, and outcomes. In February 2005 we picked up the *Star* to see a front-page article, "Did York bungle university land deal?" The article made a series of accusations, among them that we had sold the land at less than the maximum price because we were "favouring" the developer, who was a friend of the chair of the YUDC. The facts were twisted to put them in the worst possible light. While we were confident we had done nothing wrong, the issue was a public relations problem. The Board of Governors was unhappy, the faculty and staff were confused, our donors were shocked, and we had to deal with the fallout.[82] We visited the editorial board of the *Star* to no avail. On helpful advice from our chancellor, Peter Cory, we asked retired judge Edward Saunders to investigate. After interviewing nearly everyone involved, he prepared a detailed report concluding that, although some things might have been done better, no illegal or even wrong actions had been taken. On 4 June 2005, the *Star*'s public editor published a rather sulky column, "Did story treat York fairly?" basically defending its reporter, but on 21 June it published a complete retraction.[83]

By the time I left the presidency, we had the beginning of a village. Returns from the first tranche of that sale, in addition to paying the University's costs of the project, provided a million dollars to each of our Faculties as matching funds for their fundraising efforts for faculty chairs. The second tranche of returns was to be disbursed by my successor.

In effect, over these ten years the leadership team of York, with its capital fund creations and some exceptionally generous volunteers, alumni, and donors, raised many millions of dollars to create both a better physical plant and much better funding for students and faculty, laying the groundwork of York University's second fifty years.

Conclusion

In a large and complex organization such as York University, almost every project a president undertakes is a continuation of a previous decision or another attempt to solve a long-standing problem. Most of what I contributed was some sort of continuity with the past, although the problems presented themselves in new ways. For example, the "double cohort" looked like a new problem, but in the 1960s Murray Ross had been told by the government of Ontario that his plan for a university growing slowly to about twelve thousand students was dead, and he would have to take many more. The strike of the graduate student and part-time faculty union (CUPE 3903) between 26 October 2000 and 10 January 2001 seemed unique during its many weeks of turmoil, but it happened all over again to my successor.

The happy occasions such as convocations arrive in the spring and the fall each year, and each one feels unlike any other for the president as well as the graduates. There are very distinguished individuals to be presented with honorary degrees, and dinners to mark the occasion. There are the many celebrations of faculty research grants and other accomplishments. Faculty who are appointed to eminent societies such as the Royal Society of Canada and who receive medals and other honours are celebrated, as are long-serving faculty and staff. There is the annual "Hail and Farewell" dinner celebrating governors and administrators. With the head of the University Events & Community Relations group, we developed several celebratory occasions, such as a special annual dinner for the many staff awards that have been created over the years, giving us a chance to thank and recognize all those who make the University work on a daily basis.

Dedications of new buildings and installations of chancellors and deans are great gatherings, with many friends of the University and officials in attendance. The celebration of major anniversaries – such as the fortieth anniversary of the founding of York in 1999 that we so much enjoyed – only intensified for the fiftieth anniversary in 2009, soon after I left the presidency.

The complex cultural mix of students changed during my decade as president as the population of the Greater Toronto Area changed, but we remained committed to attracting students from the most recent immigrant families as well as from all Toronto's diverse communities. In the late summer we held special sessions for entering students and their parents on campus to welcome and advise new students. Homecoming in the fall involves the famous Red/Blue football game with our University of Toronto rivals, and I was happy to see that, during my decade, we won that game every year. The annual sports banquets, college celebrations, awards, and performances by students draw parents to campus.

There were some real and substantial accomplishments between 1997 and 2007. These were due to a dedicated and creative team of individuals with whom it was a joy to work. New faculty appointments enriched the academy. The creation of the position of vice-president research, and of the new Faculty of Health, the continued internationalization of the University, and the funded promise of the subway extension to and through the campus at Keele were significant accomplishments. The great leap forward in fundraising and in building alumni relationships, the many new buildings to better house the Sciences under the first "green roof" in Ontario, the splendid Fine Arts faculty, the famous Schulich School of Business, the staff offices in the new buildings for student recruitment, and services such as security improved working conditions. Proper donor recognition in a pavilion at the formal entrance to the Keele campus allowed us to acknowledge so much generosity.[84] Funding for a new building and other improvements at the Glendon campus were put into action. Important new relationships in both the Jane-Finch community and the York Region communities became institutionalized to our mutual benefit. Equally satisfying was to have rescued the failing Faculties in their bad moments and left them thriving, and to have created dozens of new sources of financial support for students, faculty, and a competitive environment for their research and scholarship.

In particular I was pleased to have left major improvements on both the academic and the business sides of the University. An improved governance system, including the search process for presidents, the operation of the Senate and the

Board of Governors, and all the preparations for the fiftieth anniversary were in place, including an "official" history of the University authored by Michiel Horn.[85]

The University gave me a great sendoff in the late spring of 2007 with a gala dinner at the Toronto Botanical Gardens, a party on campus, and many other celebrations, all of which I enjoyed and appreciated. Inevitably many threads were left unfinished, and projects we had begun, such as the fiftieth anniversary celebrations, the completion of the research tower and Ontario Public Archives building, and several academic projects, were passed on to my successor's capable hands.

Perhaps universities are doomed to experience over and over the essential problems born of their founding cultures as well as the joys of their special occasions. If that is the case, it is good thing that presidents are changed every five or ten years so that the issues and occasions feel fresh and inspiring.

My successor has taken up the big challenges, changed much, and built the School of Engineering and many other aspects of the University. He has faced struggles, as have we all, but, like me, has been captivated and enlivened by the spirit of York.

NOTES

1 For examples, see the York University publication for the fiftieth anniversary, *Faculty Honours 1959–2009*, an updated version of Professor Robert Haynes's project, *Forty Years of Faculty Honours, 1999*.

2 Canadian universities are highly unionized compared with their US counterparts. York University in the 1990s and early 2000s was among many that endured strikes. See Christine W. Wickens, "The Organizational Impact of University Labor Unions," *Higher Education* 56, no. 5 (2008): 545–64; and Deborah Zinni, Parbudyal Singh, and Anne F. MacLennan, "An Exploratory Study of Graduate Student Unions in Canada," *Industrial Relations* 60, no. 1 (2005): 145–74.

3 This is not an original view and is shown in much of the literature on universities I had read in graduate school, but it has been recently best summarized in Lombardi, *How Universities Work*. Nor is the view that a university presidency is an "impossible" job. "Personally, I wouldn't touch it with a barge pole," says David Kirby, director of the University of Manitoba's Centre for Higher Education Research and development, referring to the top job. "The Challenges are so enormous today." See Tamburri, "Evolving Role of President Takes Its Toll."

4 The importance of interpersonal relations in the work of the university president is studied in D.W. Sloper, "The Work Patterns of Australian Vice-Chancellors," *Higher Education* 31, no. 2 (1996): 205–31.

5 Vice-President Phyllis Clark, memo to the Board of Governors, 26 February 1998, "The Planning Context: Future Resource Needs – a Background Paper," York University Libraries, Clara Thomas Archives and Special Collections, 2008-003/009 (09).

6 See also Horn, *York University*, 255–7.

7 This became the first cold-weather "green" academic building in eastern Canada. Designed by Van Nostrand di Castro & Peter Busby of Vancouver, it won a Governor General's Medal in Architecture in 2002.

8 At an early Board of Governors meeting at Glendon Senate Chamber, these students prevented the meeting from continuing, blockaded the chamber, and damaged the cars of governors, preventing some of us from leaving. This particular small group was rehearsing for a larger demonstration in the city.

9 The York University *Fact Book* shows about forty-seven thousand "basic income units" (BIUs) and just over thirty-one thousand full-time equivalents, which worked out to about fifty thousand students on campus at one time or another. This grew to over sixty-eight thousand BIUs by 2007. For details of York's enrolment numbers from 1960 forward, see *Fact Book*, available at the website of the Office of Institutional Planning and Analysis, http://www.yorku.ca/factbook/.

10 Graduate students are selected by the graduate departments through the Faculty of Graduate Studies.

11 Professor of Classics at York, Deborah Hobson served as vice-president students from 1997 to 2002, when she retired from the University.

12 For married students, in addition to housing, there were childcare centres and health services, all of which were available to all students, staff, and faculty.

13 During my ten years the majority of student pubs on campus closed. When the double cohort arrived in 2003, they were usually under the legal age for drinking. This was the perfect opportunity to reduce the licensed outlets on campus, and the York Federation of Students was a good partner in this decision.

14 In my ten years there were eight colleges; a ninth was added in 2009.

15 Deborah Hobson was succeeded by Bonnie Neuman (2002–05) and then by Robert J. Tiffin (2005–12).

16 These events, led by the vice-president students, were intended to build York's sense of community, and are described online at http://alumniandfriends.yorku.ca/, accessed 18 June 2014. Multicultural week attracted a massive array of ethnic and national groups of student to display their traditions in food, artefacts, dancing, flags, and other manifestations of cultural identity in a mall on campus. It was wildly successful in building attachment to the University. However, we resisted the proposals of some of Toronto's major ethnic organizations to build their own halls on our campus. Our goal was to bring students together across all cultural, religious, and political divides, not to segregate them.

17 For several years I attended the Coalition of Urban and Metropolitan Universities, whose members are largely US commuter institutions, which was helpful in working on our own challenges. See www.cumuonline.org.

18 York University, Task Force on the Colleges, "Strengthening York's Neighbourhoods" (Toronto, November 2006), available online at http://www.yorku.ca/vpstdnts/pdfs/TFOC_execsummary.pdf, accessed 18 June 2014.

19 Memo to Robert Tiffin, VP Students, "Executive response to the Report: Strengthening York's Neighbourhoods," 28 November 2006, author's papers.

20 The graduate students might not agree that they were well off, but as we prepared for negotiations with CUPE 3903, we always compared our pay, benefits, job security, and working conditions with the other major universities in Ontario. Other universities conceded that York was the leader in this area.

21 It should be noted that Vice-President Academic Michael Stevenson set to work almost immediately on revisions to the academic plan, drawing on *2020 Vision*. Approved by the Senate in 1999, this sharpened up our thinking and remained the plan for my first term.

22 For details, see the chapter in each *Planning, Budgeting and Accountability* (PBA) document by the VP academic, who details program changes, faculty member awards and recognition, Canada Research Chair appointments and renewals, and other details. All issues of the PBA are available in the Clara Thomas Archives at York University.

23 In 2014, President Shoukri established a Faculty of Engineering, with its own new building, and strengthened the Faculty of Science.

24 There had been a most generous gift for its creation from the Atkinson Foundation and constant student support from the Honderich family.

25 Ross, *Way Must Be Tried*, 65.

26 Martin Goldfarb's firm provided a survey and analysis pro bono, one of the many generous gifts to York University by Joan and Martin Goldfarb and their family. The Goldfarbs' best-known gift is a spectacular collection of twentieth-century paintings and the funds (amounting in total to nearly $4 million) to create a centre in the Faculty of Fine Arts for the study and storage of these works of art.

27 See for example, L. Anders Sandberg, "Vari Hall: A Public or Private Space?" *Alternative Campus Tour*; available online at http://alternativecampustour.info.yorku.ca/sites/vari-hall, accessed 18 June 2014.

28 See Lorna Marsden, "Recent Disruptions on Campus in Vari Hall," recording my comments to the Senate, 27 January 2005, author's papers.

29 See, for example, Clive Seligman, President of the Society for Academic Freedom and Scholarship, to Marsden, 19 March 2003; available online at http://www.safs.ca/issuescases/marsden.html, accessed May 2014. See also David Frum, "Something's seriously wrong at York University," *National Post*, 20 February 2014.

30 The "President's Message" in the 2001–02 PBA deals almost exclusively with this issue.

31 The number of social events presidents attend is extraordinary. For example, the 2000–01 PBA reports: "During 2000–2001 the president hosted more than 100 receptions, lunches and dinners with guests including members of the faculty, staff, students, governors, donors, international visitors and government officials. She also attended a large number of events at the invitation of others" (15).

32 Since 1976 the collective agreement with the Faculty Association has contained the agreement about the ownership of intellectual property. For details, consult Article 23.

33 See the website of the VP research and innovation at http://www.yorku.ca/~research/partnering/.

34 See the Centre's website at cec.info.yorku.ca/.

35 Among the University's documents are watercolour sketches of a campus plan. The plan is almost precisely the plan for the University of York in England as it now exists. This is said to have resulted from the friendship between the first vice-chancellor of the University of York, Lord James of Rusholme, and the chair of the Board of York University in Toronto. But see also Horn, *York University*, 31.

36 See the PBA 1999–2000, 46, concerning this, including a special task force carried forward by the vice-president academic.

37 The Four Motors are industrial areas of Germany and France with economies not unlike that of Ontario. Premier Peterson's including academic relations in the mix of links was a most welcome development both at Wilfrid Laurier University and at York University, where German Studies were a strong part of the Faculty of Arts. For the basic documents, see *Declaration of Partnership and Memorandum of Understanding on Cooperation*, 25 June 1990, Archives of Ontario, RG 3–83.

38 YUELI and York International are departments of the University that serve international students and international linkages.

39 The unicameral system adopted at the University of Toronto, which merged the Senate and the Board, led to a great deal of backroom planning and negotiation in my limited experience of it; at Wilfrid Laurier University, the Senate was important, especially in its debates on the annual budget, but since as president I chaired the Senate, it was impossible to truly participate and hard to observe.

40 See Lombardi, *How Universities Work*, chap. 1.

41 It is important to note that, during my years as president, about 5 per cent of tenure-stream faculty members left or failed to acquire tenure, roughly the same proportion as leave business organizations. Post-tenure, however, it is most likely that faculty will leave only for a more congenial position, rather than from pressure from their colleagues or university.

42 Lorna Marsden, memo to Joint Executive Committees of the Board and Senate, "Project to Refocus the University's Mission," 6 April 1998, Clara Thomas Archives, York University, 2008-003/009(05).

43 Many faculty members simply ignored the entire exercise. As Lombardi points out, "criteria for distributing money create much stronger incentives for guild behavior than do strategic plans and mission statements articulated by institutional leaders for inspirational purposes" (*How Universities Work*, 8).

44 Lorna Marsden, "Board of Governors Committees: A View from the Administration," 7 September 2006. In June 2006 my executive team had a session with governance expert Carol Hansell to help us line up our strategic priorities, risks, budgets, and reputation/marketing issues. See Marsden to Marshall Cohen, "Administrative Reporting to the Board," 22 September 2006, author's papers.

45 These reforms to the Senate were the product of a March 2000 report of the Senate Sub-Committee on Aspects of Senate Reform, which commented on attendance (only 40–50 per cent for over a decade) and made several other recommendations; Robert Everett, Notes from Associate Secretary to Marsden, 24 June 2014, author's papers.

46 The *Senate Handbook* can be found online at http://secretariat.info.yorku.ca/files/ SenateRulesAndProceduresSeptember2012RevJuly2013RevJan2014RevMar2015.pdf.

47 Harriet Lewis was originally hired by President Arthurs to serve as legal counsel to York. In 1998 I determined to add University secretary to her position to streamline governance. She served those two functions brilliantly, and has been a model for other universities in Canada.

48 One example of the work of Senate sub-committees is the Honorary Degrees and Ceremonials Committee, which carefully reviews candidates for honorary degrees. We changed some procedures to create a five-year limited pool of approved candidates, so that when a president was inviting honorary graduands to a particular convocation, they could be selected for their relationship to the graduate students, as well as for a balance of men and women, Canadian and international, and so on. At one point, I asked the chair of this Committee, Professor Bernie Wolff, to come up with guidelines for honorary degrees in absentia (York had previously given them to Nelson Mandela and Anatoly Sharansky) and post-mortem degrees.

49 The rules for Parliament were written in 1884 by John Bourinot, drawn from Westminster and adapted to our federal Constitution. In Parliament, each Bill has three readings: first, for a vote in principle as to whether the legislation should proceed to the next stage; second, to send it to the appropriate committee, which may hear witnesses and propose amendments and clarifications before the legislation is returned to the House for third reading debate and a final vote.

50 I am grateful to Professor Marty Lockshin for reminding me of this particular Senate meeting.

51 For a splendid account of such issues in the United States, see Lombardi, *How Universities Work*, chap. 14.

52 David Strangway, with whom I worked when he was provost and then president of the University of Toronto, was a believer in open budget documents. On becoming president of the University of British Columbia, he had published a very detailed annual report on the planning, budgets, and accountability of that university, first in *UBC Reports* and then in fiscal years 1995/96 and 1996/97 as separate documents. It was on those latter two reports that we modelled our own PBA. David Strangway, personal e-mail correspondence to Marsden, 15 July 2014.

53 See Association of University Leaders for a Sustainable Future, "Talloires Declaration" [2001], available online at http://www.ulsf.org/programs_talloires.html.

54 In 1999 I had asked leading environmental economist Professor Peter Victor to chair a committee on environmental activities at York. The report was made in June 2001 and is described in PBA 2002–03 (13–16). As a personal initiative, I involved students and staff in my Pink Lung Project, an attempt to reduce smoking on campus. We offered smoking cessation programs, moved smokers 9 metres away from buildings, and tried to improve health on the campus.

55 For a description of events, see Wickens, "Organizational Impact"; Zinni, Singh, and Maclennan, "Exploratory Study"; and the 2002 Senate Sub-Committee Report on the State of the University.

56 Lorna Marsden, Confidential memo to the Board on these objectives, 25 May, 2004, author's papers.

57 On 24 November, 2004 VP Embleton took a proposal to create a new Faculty of Health Sciences to the Academic Priorities and Planning Committee of the Senate. We foresaw an eighteen-month process before such a Faculty would be operational. Lorna Marsden, Memo to the Board of Governors, 22 November 2004, author's papers.

58 See PBA 1998–99, 29. Of course, percentages are not entirely satisfactory as a way of measuring impact.

59 For a compelling US view on these, see Lombardi, *How Universities Work*, chap. 14.

60 To see the impact of these measures on the York budget, see Phyllis Clark to the Board, "The Planning Context: Future Resource Needs, a Background Paper," February 1998, York University Libraries, Clara Thomas Archives and Special Collections 2008-003/009(09).

61 Sheldon Levy had left York in 1997 to become president of Sheridan College and eventually the dynamic president of Ryerson University.

62 See PBA 1998–99, 88.

63 Ibid., 35.

64 See "York University: Superbuild Proposal," February 2003 a deck of materials presented to the Board of Governors and others in preparation for our specific requests for the second round of the Superbuild program.

65 See PBA 1999–2000, 111–12.

66 This building has two parts: the Seymour Schulich Building (2003) and the Executive Learning Centre (2004), which has a hotel and restaurants and space for executive groups in residence. Architect Siamak Hariri won a Governor General's Medal in Architecture for this building in 2006. The same architecture firms (Hariri Pontarini and Robbie/Young + Wright) designed the Bennett Student Centre. Dean Dezsö Horváth and Seymour Schulich were deeply involved, and Professor James McKellar, also an architect, oversaw the project with the University's committee.

67 The Accolade East (2006) and West (2005) buildings were designed by Zeidler Partnership and Bregman & Hamman. Tarek El-Khatib was the lead architect, and Dean Phil Silver worked with him, acoustics engineers, and other designers, as well as budget officers, throughout.

68 Designed by Architects 'Alliance; completed 2004.

69 See enrolment numbers in issues of *Fact Book*, at http://www.yorku.ca/factbook/.

70 See "Thank you, The National Campaign for York University," York University, November 1999.

71 Gary Smith, a distinguished former Canadian ambassador and York alumnus, was our vice-president advancement until 2002.

72 Timothy Price, long-serving York governor, is a man of infinite patience and great generosity. His business offices were invaded by student strikers, but nevertheless he has led financial planning, investing, and fundraising. We owe him a large debt.

73 The situation was somewhat more complex. Every university – by provincial fiat – already had a foundation, but its restrictions made it not very useful for a major campaign. In addition, York had been receiving philanthropy since its inception for scholarships, buildings, and many other purposes, and they remained in the University. So it was new gifts that were receipted only by the new Foundation.

74 As the appendix table in Chapter 7 shows, there was a drop in endowments in 2009–10 as the campaign ended, but this was a result of the sharp financial crisis of those years; when the markets returned, the endowment was restored.

75 Once again Tim Price gave his time and influence to help on this project.

76 York put aside $1 million in its budget for adjustment to the Y2K challenge.

77 In addition, such aspects of personal computing as direct deposit payrolls and similar services changed the work of human resources, e-books changed the library collections, and numerous other parts of the University were transformed.

78 For a detailed description of the subway plans and decisions, see Spence, "Spadina Subway Extension."

79 The Honourable Greg Sorbara, a double graduate of York, represented a riding in York Region near the campus. He had been minister of finance, among other ministries, in the Ontario Liberal government, but when he became involved with the subway project, he had stepped away from cabinet while a potential conflict

with his family's firm was settled. The timing was extraordinarily lucky from our point of view. He remains a favourite son of the University.

80 Spence, "Spadina Subway Extension."

81 This had been anticipated in my original mandate.

82 See Memo to Members of the Board of Governors, 27 February 2005, "Toronto Star Campaign re: York," author's papers.

83 See Sharon Burnside, "Did story treat York fairly?" *Toronto Star*, 4 June 2005; Kevin Donovan, "Report clears York U in housing deal," *Toronto Star*, 21 June 2005; along with a sulky commentary justifying the *Star's* attack.

84 This building, designed by Stephen Teeple, with its courtyard of stones naming our major donors, its welcome centre staffed by the transportation group, and its washroom and location near the main entrance to the Keele campus, won an architecture award in 2002. The building was made possible by a generous donation from Seymour Schulich. When I retired in 2007, it was named the Lorna R. Marsden Honour Court & Welcome Centre. I am very honoured.

85 See Horn, *York University*. Augmenting this history have been autobiographies by administrators such as deans John Saywell and James Gillies and publications by former dean and my senior policy adviser Edward Spence on the years of struggle to build a subway extension to York; some of these publications are listed in the bibliography.

Figure 6.1. Mamdouh Shoukri, 2007

6 This Is Our Time: Into a New Era at York University, 2007–14

MAMDOUH SHOUKRI

Introduction

When I was invited to participate in the writing of this book, I initially hesitated. Unlike other contributors I would be writing in real time, while my tenure as York University's current president is still under way. Ultimately, I agreed to participate as I believe that my contribution, although incomplete, would represent both a sense of continuity and a look to York's future. I was able to review other contributions before I began writing my chapter, and read with great interest the accounts of my predecessors, which reflect their individual visions as well as York's history as they saw and helped to create it. In some sense their accounts are also influenced by the unravelled consequences of decisions made and events that took place during their presidencies. My account, on the other hand, is largely a day-by-day one as I still live the experience of leading one of Canada's largest and most promising institutions.

I believe that York University today is on the verge of great change, and has all the ingredients necessary to assume a more significant leadership role among Canadian universities. Above and beyond the persuasive power of Marshall Cohen, who served as chair of York's Board of Governors from 2000 to 2009, the opportunities I saw for York were the reason I applied for and later accepted the job as the seventh president and vice-chancellor of York University. As I considered letting my name stand for the position, it was clear to me that York was indeed one of Canada's leading educational and research institutions in Humanities, Social Sciences, Fine Arts, Business, and Law. It had pioneered many interdisciplinary programs, such as Environmental Studies. Although it was relatively small, York's strong Faculty of Science hosted "boutique" engineering programs. Just prior to my arrival, the Faculty of Health had been established, bringing under one roof a number of excellent programs, including the largest Department of Psychology in Canada, Kinesiology, Nursing, and Health Policy, thus creating a more focused effort in health research and education.

Since I believe the stature of a university is directly related to the quality of its academic programs, I saw York as having significant ingredients to build on; and perhaps more important, I could see clearly what was missing to achieve York's greatest potential. For me, the strategic direction was clear: we needed to protect the University's existing strengths, expand Science and Health, and build a significant presence in Engineering, together with a renewed focus on research intensification. I was encouraged to find frequent references to what I saw as the proper strategic direction in earlier planning documents, which assured me that I would find the necessary support for my vision. The clarity of the strategic direction needed for York, at least in my mind, and the opportunities associated with the future of the region surrounding the University, were the primary incentives for my interest in the job.

There is no question that I was also drawn by the University's long-standing commitment to social justice, equity, and accessibility – values that are totally aligned with my personal beliefs. Another draw was York's remarkable diversity. As one of the most ethnically diverse universities in the world, York in my mind reflected the future of Canada.

Thus, in retrospect, it is now clear to me that my interest in York was driven primarily by academic considerations – namely, the opportunity to build a more comprehensive and research-intensive university that already enjoys the credibility of academic strength and size as well as York's location in the centre of a growing urban area and its well-known commitment to social values. I felt I had the experience to lead this effort, having enjoyed a career that nearly covered the spectrum of activities in the academy as a professor with significant research accomplishments, graduate program director, department chair, Faculty dean, and vice-president. I had been successful in promoting research and innovation, both in academia and industry. Nevertheless, as I learned during my first few months in office, I may have underestimated, despite some gentle warnings by colleagues, other issues related to the evolution of York University. My predecessors' accounts have covered some of these concerns, so I will not reiterate them, but I will offer below some of my own experiences thus far. While my predecessors have spoken of York's first fifty years, and of its founding principles and values, I would like to describe the York of today as well as a vision for the University in the next fifty years.

My Time in Office

The beginning

Although my appointment began on 1 July 2007, I was a frequent visitor to campus starting in April 2007, when I met with senior members of the administration and a number of faculty and staff. During this period, President Marsden was particularly generous with her support and advice, and I received excellent briefing files and had access to as much information as I needed. In terms of preparing for the job, I should mention the incredible generosity of the chair of the Board, Marshall Cohen, and his wife Judi. Recognizing my need to engage the Toronto community, they organized four dinner parties at their home over the spring and summer of 2007 to introduce my wife Susan and me to York's friends and donors as well as to other influential people in the city. Not surprisingly, the Cohens continue to be among our dearest friends.

While my appointment was welcomed by the media and the academic community, an unexpected amount of media attention initially focused on my ethnic background. "York's new president to make history," trumpeted the headlines. "Engineer is first Muslim to be named permanent head of Canadian university"; "Shoukri is first Canadian Muslim to hold [job of university president]"; and "York's new president vows to be inclusive." Obviously for me, this came as a surprise. As I indicated in media interviews at the time, I saw my appointment as nothing exceptional in a society as diverse as Canada's. Faith is a very personal thing, and I define my ethnic background in many ways, as an Egyptian as well as a Muslim. I knew that my decisions would be made with one thing in mind – the interests of York University and our student body as a whole. As I said then, "I intend to be the president of the entire, diverse university, and I will be a person who will value every member of the York community – which group they come from is, with respect, truly irrelevant."[1]

I certainly expected to face some headwinds in this role, and for the University to face headwinds as other universities advanced their designs on expansion and with a provincial government dealing with multiple demands on public money. Indeed, if the media headlines came as a surprise, so too did an early occurrence on campus that opened my eyes to some of the realities of my appointment. In my first few months, I became accustomed to being stopped on campus by colleagues and students greeting me and wishing me well; these were gestures that I enjoyed a great deal, and continue to enjoy today in my travels across campus. One early evening while walking on campus accompanied by the communications manager in my office, Ken Fasciano, I met an elderly man walking a dog. He introduced himself and welcomed me to York. He turned out to be a professor teaching an evening class. As we exchanged pleasantries, I could not resist playing with his very friendly dog. He told me that he takes the dog to class, where it sits quietly, and that students typically play with the dog after class. Then he added, "Even Muslim students play with him." As it seemed clear he did not intend to offend me, I maintained my friendly demeanor and asked what he meant. He said, "I understand that Muslims do not like dogs," to which I replied, "But clearly your dog likes one." We maintained a friendly conversation, but the incident reinforced the realization that I would be seen by some through a very specific lens.

This was a valuable lesson, particularly as it sensitized me to some of the dynamics on campus – dynamics certainly not unique to York. Indeed, York is an institution that justifiably prides itself on its commitment to progressive social values. Since these early experiences, my background has been an issue on a very few occasions. While I am tremendously proud of my heritage, my faith, and where .I come from, I am even more proud of Canada and all that it stands for, not least of which is its incredible diversity. In fact, I have always thought that Bill Clinton got it exactly right when he said, "In a world darkened by ethnic conflicts that tear nations apart, Canada stands as a model of how people of different cultures can live and work together in peace, prosperity, and mutual respect."[2] The few occasions on which my heritage or faith has been an issue have served to remind me that, as a society, we need to continue our efforts to sustain and advance our achievements in this regard in order to create a world that truly reflects Clinton's words.

Academic planning at York

As Frank Rhodes, the former president of Cornell University, once said, "The first and greatest task for a president is to articulate the vision, champion the goals, and enunciate the objectives."[3] As I began my first term as president, I believed that over the next decade York's focus should be on transformation in the following areas:

- strengthening the University's academic capacity to become a truly comprehensive university, including the creation of a school for Engineering and a school of Medicine;
- expanding York's research capacity and innovation and becoming recognized as a research-intensive institution;
- transforming the administrative structure of the institution to make it function more effectively; and
- overseeing the urbanization of the Keele campus in conjunction with the arrival of the subway.

As I outlined in my inaugural remarks to the Senate in September 2007, I felt very optimistic about York's prospects and an eagerness to work closely with the academic community to realize the objectives of the University Academic Plan (2005), formed under President Marsden's leadership, while articulating York's ongoing commitment to building on our strengths of access, social responsibility, and interdisciplinary excellence.

In its early years, York University was described as a "quasi-federal institution." This allowed significant creativity in the development of innovative academic programs at the local level. With relocation to the larger Keele campus, however, enrolment increased at an unprecedented rate, reflecting the growing demand for post-secondary education, and consequently, the University was expected to become a comprehensive institution. Maintaining the "quasi-federated" model, while allowing academic innovation locally, did not support the development of a truly strong, integrated academic plan to facilitate and encourage the growth of the breadth of programs and activities typical of a large, comprehensive university.

Accordingly, the University's previous academic plans appeared to be largely a reflection of a federated institution, perhaps with the exception of *2020 Vision* (1992), which was, to my mind, the first attempt to create an integrated plan. This was exacerbated by the fact that York did not appoint a vice-president academic or a provost to lead the implementation of an integrated academic plan for close to a decade in its early years on the Keele campus, and when a VP academic was appointed, it was with a fairly limited mandate. An interesting example that captures this incongruity in academic planning is the absence of strong Engineering or large Life Sciences programs in the second-largest university in the province, despite the incredible demand for and frequent reference to these programs in academic plans. In my view, this was a continuation of the small university model applied to an institution that was growing to be among the largest universities in North America.

As a result, at the outset of my term, I acknowledged the need for a senior academic leader, and accordingly changed the position of VP academic to VP academic and provost. I developed a plan to broaden and strengthen the mandate of that portfolio to ensure effective academic leadership of the University to integrate both the Faculty plans and the institution's long-term aspirations in a single academic plan, one that would provide the strong input of academic perspectives into financial and budgetary planning. Patrick Monahan was appointed VP academic and provost with the new mandate in 2009. Together we set out to establish a clear strategic direction for the University, including advancing the strategic priorities of academic excellence, student success, and community engagement.

Prior to the development of the University's Academic Plan (2010–15), or UAP, Monahan, with the able help of his vice-provost, Rhonda Lenton, undertook a major consultative process involving the Faculties, faculty members, students, staff, and various external groups. Working closely with members of the Academic Policy, Planning and Research Committee (APPRC), he developed the Provostial White Paper (2010), which was subsequently used as the basis for the UAP. Unanimously endorsed by the Senate, the White Paper and the UAP were explicit in identifying initiatives under the general area of academic excellence.

Being a more comprehensive university included the explicit objectives of expanding Science, particularly Life Sciences; building a Faculty of Engineering; and expanding Health, including the aspiration to establish a Medical school. These initiatives were suggested while protecting York's traditional strengths in the Humanities, Social Sciences, and Fine Arts as well as its leadership in multidisciplinary education. The explicit objective of research intensification included the development a strategic research plan, reforming research policies, and reviewing the structure of graduate education at York. Accordingly, York's first comprehensive Strategic Research Plan was developed and approved by the Senate in 2013, outlining areas of research strength to build upon as well as areas of opportunities for strategic development. This plan informs new policies for facilitating research intensification.

My primary mandate from the Board of Governors was to lead, facilitate, and implement the UAP. In this, my key priorities were intensifying York's research culture, expanding the Sciences and Applied Sciences, and enhancing graduate student enrolment and the student experience. In the first years of my first term, York was at a critical point in its history. I truly felt that no other university in Ontario – perhaps in the country – had York's potential. But I knew that, before we could realize that potential, before we could build the York University of the future, we needed to address the shared challenges we faced, as well as the threats to the institution that were holding us back.

Supporting the demand for Life Sciences

The first opportunity to implement the plan came through the announcement of the Ontario government's Knowledge Infrastructure Program (KIP). This was timely for York. The demand for Life Sciences was growing significantly, and the University responded by increasing our enrolment significantly and hiring a number of talented new young faculty. However, it was clear that the instructional facilities were not adequate to meet the demand of these new faculty and students. In fact, one of the earliest letters I received as president was authored by a number of new Life Science faculty members, who complained of the lack of research laboratories they had been promised. The situation threatened our claim to academic excellence and commitment to our students, and represented a potential loss of future research talent.

It is not surprising, then, that the first of the two KIP proposals submitted was to support the construction of a large Life Sciences building. The KIP program was jointly funded by the federal and provincial governments. Having spent a considerable amount of time explaining our strategy to, and securing the support of, the province, it was no surprise that the provincial government would provide the strongest endorsement of the project to its federal partners. With $70 million in government funding, the new Life Sciences building was completed in 2012, and stands now as the home of students and researchers in high-demand disciplines such as Biology, Chemistry, Biochemistry, and Kinesiology. This state-of-the-art facility, in addition to helping us to recruit new talent from around the world, has allowed us to build the excellence of our Life Sciences programs – a key part of our vision to make York a more comprehensive university.[4]

Engineering

While York's original curriculum focused on general and liberal education in arts and science, by the late 1960s there was talk of adding three additional Faculties – Education, Engineering, and Medicine. Although Education was established as the focus, the aspiration to expand in professional fields – specifically in Engineering and Medicine – was reflected in the University's strategic plans.

Indeed, building engineering at York had been a long-standing aspiration since the University moved to the Keele campus. I keep in my office a campus map dated 1963 that projects two engineering buildings. Engineering was mentioned in numerous planning documents over the years, and was clearly identified in *2020 Vision*. I attribute the reasons for not moving forward with it earlier to the nature of academic planning described above as well as to a possible concern about the provincial government's willingness to invest in engineering.

During those years, however, a number of small "boutique" engineering programs were developed within departments in the Faculty of Science. One of the strides made during my predecessor's term was to secure the accreditation of three approved streams for York's engineering program. By 2007 York had programs in Computer Engineering, hosted by the Department of Computer Science, and Geomatics Engineering and Space Engineering, hosted by the

Department of Earth and Space Sciences. The total enrolment was 146 students. Due to the lack of mainstream engineering programs, small enrolment, and location within the Faculty of Science, it was impossible for these programs to gain credibility within the engineering profession or among potential students. In fact, I was frequently asked why York did not have engineering programs.

Coming to York, I was aware of the 8–9 per cent annual increase in applications to engineering schools in Ontario over the previous five years, a trend that continues today. As such, building a large engineering school at York was not only a simple approach to becoming a more comprehensive institution and fulfilling an old promise; it was also a necessary response to a societal need. The demographics of the York Region and the continuing growth of knowledge-based industries in the region provided another strong incentive.

As an engineer myself, I have always believed that engineering education should be complemented by broader elements of general education in the Humanities, Social Sciences, Arts, and Business to enable future engineers to play a more prominent and effective role in society. Engineers who appreciate the thought processes of humanists, social scientists, and artists will likely, in my opinion, be better able to fulfil their professional responsibilities. Given its strength in these areas and commitment to social justice, I felt that York University was uniquely able to prepare future generations of engineers for the twenty-first century.

In 2009 I appointed an expert committee of leading engineering academics to examine the need for, and the nature of, a future engineering school at York. The committee confirmed the need and advised on potential structure and costs. The appointment of Janusz Kozinski, former dean of engineering at the University of Saskatchewan, as York's dean of science and engineering in July 2010 marked the beginning of our pursuit of a separate Engineering Faculty.

The objective was to develop an engineering school for more than two thousand students, covering the breadth of engineering programs with substantial research activities and graduate enrolment. To fund the first phase, including the construction of a major new building, we were able to secure a $50-million grant from the province towards the cost of constructing the building and $25 million from Pierre Lassonde, the visionary engineer and entrepreneur. Recognizing that we needed it to build the new Faculty, Mr Lassonde agreed to make his donation totally expendable. In his honour, the Faculty has been named the Lassonde School of Engineering. Close to $20 million has been raised in support of the project, and a groundbreaking ceremony for the new building was held in June 2013. Opening its doors in September 2015, the innovative five-storey structure has been named the Bergeron Centre for Engineering Excellence, thanks to the generous support of York alumnus Doug Bergeron and his wife Sandra, whose record-breaking donation of $10 million in 2014 represented the largest amount ever given to the University by an alumnus.

The story of the Lassonde gift is worth mentioning here. During one of my frequent long walks with Seymour Schulich, I brought up the subject of Engineering at York. Schulich is indeed a unique person in his commitment to post-secondary education and his willingness to invest generously in preparing young Canadians for the future. He was very supportive of the idea of Engineering at York and introduced me to his business partner, Pierre Lassonde. I knew his late wife, Claudette MacKay-Lassonde, as a very gifted fellow engineer in the nuclear industry back in the seventies. Pierre was very excited about the vision of the school, particularly as it related to the breadth of education and the commitment to recruit more women to engineering. It was interesting that, following our meeting, he phoned me to say that he was "almost" in agreement but wanted to meet the dean before making his final decision. As he put it, "it is good to have the commitment of the president, but the dean is the one who can turn the vision into reality." Needless to say, following several more meetings, he agreed. As the Lassonde School of Engineering grows and I see the new building completed, I have a strong sense of gratitude that finally York has a new school that will prepare engineers for the twenty-first century.

Glendon College

York, through Glendon College, is the only university that offers bilingual post-secondary degrees in central southwestern Ontario. As such, Glendon College is an important distinguishing feature of the University. Located in a picturesque setting on Bayview at Lawrence, in the heart of Toronto, Glendon continues to be a jewel in York's crown. With growing interest in bilingual university education in Ontario, the case for growing the enrolment and broadening the program offerings at Glendon has been encouraged by both the provincial government and the local francophone community.

Just prior to my arrival, a proposal was submitted to the province to fund the construction of two buildings on the Glendon campus. One building was intended for expanding the program offerings of Glendon College, while the other was to accommodate the aspirations of Collège Boréal to offer college programs in Toronto. The idea was to transform the site into a Centre of Excellence for bilingual education, offering both university and college programs on the same site, and facilitating close collaboration and credit transfer between universities and colleges.

As I reviewed the proposals and had extensive discussion with all concerned, I realized that the plan for academic collaboration with Collège Boréal had not succeeded and was unlikely to develop in the foreseeable future. As such, I could not justify a proposal to use the limited land available at Glendon for a Collège Boréal building without a serious prospect of future collaboration. I was warned by senior York colleagues and government employees that abandoning the second building would be politically unwise and might result in government rejection of the entire project, including the proposed York building. However, I was not prepared to accept their argument, and felt strongly that the case for expanding our programs was strong enough on its own merits. I was delighted that the government, while encouraging us to work closely with the colleges, approved the new building. Today, the new Centre of Excellence stands at the entrance of Glendon campus, allowing us to provide learning facilities and an environment of the highest quality for bilingual education in Toronto.

York's commitment to bilingual education continues to grow, reflecting the academic excellence of the programs and the growing demand by young Ontarians as well as international students. We are currently working closely with the government of Ontario to further expand program offerings at Glendon and to establish it as the central hub of bilingual university education in central southwestern Ontario.

Internationalization

Having the most ethnically diverse student population and being located in the heart of the Greater Toronto Area (GTA) with its diverse population, York provides a model for university internationalization in every respect. This includes internationalization of the curricula, providing opportunities for students to study abroad, student and faculty-exchange agreements, and joint research and recruitment of international students. Internationalization was cited as a priority in both the White Paper and the UAP. With more focused recruitment plans, the number of international students has nearly doubled since I arrived at York, reaching close to 10 per cent in 2014 and with plans to reach 15 per cent by 2020. We were particularly successful in ensuring a more uniform distribution of international students among academic programs, with a significant portion of the growth directed to the Humanities and Social Sciences. The past few years have also seen a growth in the number and percentage of our students who are engaged in international student exchanges.

Perhaps one of the most exciting recent developments was the opening in September 2014 of the new campus of York's Schulich School of Business in India. Located near the Hyderabad airport, this campus promises to be a global hub for students from all over Asia who wish to attend our renowned MBA in India program.

University Organization: Continuity and Change

The fast pace of change and the continuing evolution of the University from a small liberal arts college also left its mark on York's organizational structure. Prior to my arrival, the number of offices reporting to the president at the senior level was larger than usual. This was necessary during a period of significant growth, but, as I arrived at York, enrolment growth was slowing down. I felt that the University had reached a level of maturity and stability requiring a more streamlined organizational structure that promoted efficiency and empowered other leaders on campus in effective decision-making. I made a number of changes during the first few years of my first term that significantly reduced the number of divisions reporting directly to the president from twelve to seven.[5] These changes included:

- creating the provost function to ensure that the academic vision for the University is reflected in institutional policies and day-to-day operations;
- changing the position of vice-president students to vice-provost students, reporting to the provost, which helped to consolidate student affairs with the academic enterprise;
- bringing University Information Technology, which reported to the vice-president finance and administration, under the chief information officer division to streamline IT functions in the University, with the consolidated office reporting to the VP finance and administration;
- combining the fundraising function and alumni affairs in a new Division of Advancement under a new vice-president advancement;
- consolidating the University's planning function by combining the Office of Institutional Research and Analysis and the planning functions of the offices of the vice-provost academic and VP finance and administration into a single office – the Office of Institutional Planning and Analysis (OIPA), reporting to the provost; and
- maintaining the Office of Communications and Public Affairs' direct reporting relationship to the Office of the President, to keep direct involvement in this critical area for the University.

Although most of these changes took place smoothly, some of the cultural behaviour continued to persist. The historic centrality of the Office of the President was difficult to change simply by modifying the organizational structure or individual mandates. It took time for many campus leaders to feel truly empowered and to act accordingly. Nonetheless, with fewer direct reports, the weekly meetings of the president and vice-presidents became an excellent forum for discussions, assessment, and, at times, vigorous debates. This suited me very well, as I try to hear as many opinions as possible and to seek convergence on important decisions.

Fundraising

The experience of moving the fundraising function from an external foundation into the newly created Division of Advancement was particularly interesting due to its complexity. Surprisingly, it went much more smoothly than I had expected.

To strengthen and enhance the fundraising function, the York University Foundation was created in 2002 as a separate entity with an external board comprised of University friends and donors, including some members of York's governors. As president, I was the only University employee serving on the Board. The Foundation was funded by an annual allocation from the University as well as an annual levy from individual Faculties. The sole function of the Foundation was to raise funds for the University. An experienced fundraiser, Paul Marcus, was appointed president and CEO of the Foundation.

Over the following five years, the Foundation was successful in building a strong support base for the University, developing a professional fundraising team, and enhancing the culture of philanthropy and fundraising in the York community. The Foundation also successfully completed a $207-million major campaign to mark the University's fiftieth anniversary, "York to the Power of 50," the largest fundraising campaign in York's history.

As we approached the end of the campaign, however, I felt the need to recalibrate the relevant activities. As York's alumni body grew both in number and stature, it became clear that York's alumni would be its major future donors. As such, it was essential that alumni relations, which was a separate division within the University reporting to the president, and the fundraising functions come under the same roof – particularly as I was worried about signs of unnecessary competition between the two groups. I also felt that bringing the two functions together and within the University structure proper would better align York's academic priorities and its fundraising activities, as well as allow better collaboration with the deans. I shared my views with Paul Cantor, chair of York's Board at the time, as well as with Marshall Cohen and Tim Price, chair of the Foundation Board, and we agreed to appoint Ketchum Canada Incorporated (KCI) to work with us on the development of a post-campaign structure. After extensive work, KCI recommended the creation of the Division of Advancement within the University to be responsible for fundraising as well as alumni and community relations.

The Foundation president was very cooperative, supported the review, and agreed with the conclusions. Members of the Foundation Board were equally supportive, as the success of the Foundation in achieving its original goals was acknowledged and it was time to move to the next level of developing advancement at York. Most of the Foundation employees were transferred to the new division and, as of May 2011, the York University Foundation became part of York's new Division of Advancement. The new model proved very successful. Having one Division of Advancement, as well as the alignment of and close collaboration with the deans, resulted in securing more significant gifts, in terms of both their amount and their impact on the University, as well as significant growth in the number of donors who are York's alumni. Moreover, the cost of fundraising has been drastically reduced over the past three years.

Community engagement

The concept of engagement has been gaining increasing prominence and acceptance in higher education across North America. In this context, "engagement" represents collaboration between higher education institutions and their broader communities (local, regional, national, and global) for the mutually beneficial exchange of knowledge and resources in a context of partnership and reciprocity.

An early initiative at York was to launch the President's Task Force on Community Engagement, led by Dr Rhonda Lenton, who subsequently became York's provost and VP academic, succeeding Patrick Monahan. The Task Force is credited with bringing to focus and advancing York's long-established commitment to community engagement. The Task Force's final report with recommendations, issued in February 2010,[6] identified over one hundred examples of current community-University partnerships, catalogued initiatives already under way across the University, and highlighted opportunities to build on those initiatives in relation to learning and the student experience, partnership and community collaboration, campus culture, and knowledge exchange.

The Task Force report was acknowledged in both the White Paper and the UAP, and community engagement, broadly defined, was identified as a major priority for the University. In the consultation process for the White Paper, however, York community members emphasized that engagement should not be limited to relationships between the University and the broader community, but that it should also be a vehicle to strengthen relationships and connections on campus, particularly as there is a clear and well-established link between engagement and student learning. Indeed, community engagement at York comes in a variety of forms, from community-based learning that takes our students outside of the classroom to comprehensive initiatives that foster post-secondary education among community groups facing barriers to accessing university education.

As a large university with a large student population, York faces a special challenge in engaging students and increasing their opportunities to engage faculty and their peers in learning and co-curriculum contexts. The widely used National Survey of Student Engagement (NSSE), conducted every three years by the Center for Postsecondary Research at Indiana University, is organized around the theme of engagement, recognizing that students learn best when they are actively engaged in the learning process. The NSSE offers an opportunity for universities to gauge the quality of their undergraduate education by providing evidence-based information telling us what our students feel we do well, what we need to do better, and where we should focus our efforts to improve. A higher response rate yields better data that allow universities to develop the right programs and enhance existing programs and services. In 2011, York's participation rate in the survey was much lower than the provincial average. Starting in 2011 we launched a campaign to raise the completion rates of our first- and fourth-year students. In 2014, thanks in large part to the support of University leaders and a coordinated campaign involving staff, faculty, and student groups across campus, our response rate significantly increased, reaching levels consistent with those of other universities in the province.

Facing Challenges

Labour relations

The labour relations environment on university campuses is an important and complex issue. Although it is not my intention to engage in a broad discussion of the subject, having faced very early in my presidency one of the longest strikes on a university campus, I feel compelled to reflect on this particular event.

I arrived at York knowing of its history of labour disputes, but also with a strong sense of appreciation for the critical role the labour movement plays in democratic societies. The optimist in me felt that my natural sympathy with the labour movement would be an asset in fostering better relations on campus.

The 2008 labour disruption at York was undertaken by the Canadian Union of Public Employees (CUPE Local 3903), which comprises three units repre-senting teaching assistants (graduate students), contract faculty, and gradu-ate assistants. As a discussion of university labour relations or even a detailed account of York's 2008 labour disruption is beyond the scope of this book, I will limit my comments to the central theme of the strike, some personal reflections, lessons learned, and the impact it had on subsequent decision-making.

The initial set of proposals from the union included a variety of compensation increases and job security provisions that amounted to a 196 per cent increase in costs to the University over the previous agreement. The proposals covered a wide variety of demands related to compensation and job security for members of the three units represented by the union. It became clear, however, that job security and career development for contract faculty was the central issue. The union's positions on job security for contract faculty (unit 2) were increasingly tied up in union communications with the issues of precarious employment and the casualization of labour – issues with which I sympathized. Central elements of the union's approach to job security included a guaranteed volume of work for longer-service contract faculty and a conversion program to tenure-track faculty positions. The union's initial proposal was to convert all contract faculty with certain levels of service and intensity of teaching automatically into tenure-stream positions. A major thrust of the union's approach to compensation parity with full-time faculty was an initial proposal to increase the course directorship rate by approximately 75 per cent.

I consider the growing dependence of universities on part-time and contract faculty to be a serious issue in need of long-term solutions, and one tied to the overall underfunding of universities. I also appreciate the legitimacy of the social and academic concerns associated with the evolution of a two-tier system of university teachers. Nevertheless, it is impossible for any university to accept a scenario for recruiting permanent tenure-track faculty that is not based on a completely open competition.

Negotiations began on 16 July 2008, a strike vote was held 14–17 October, and the strike commenced on 6 November. Although we were disappointed that a settlement could not be reached prior to the strike deadline, the University continued to negotiate with CUPE 3903 during the labour disruption in an effort to reach a fair and reasonable settlement. Consistent with the guiding principles of academic integrity and in fairness to students, the deans of all Faculties, together with the chair of the Senate, agreed that academic activities (with some exceptions) would be suspended for the duration of the strike. This was a difficult time for everyone, but particularly for our students.

Following a number of failed attempts to reach a settlement, the premier announced a recall of the provincial legislature on 24 January 2014 to introduce back-to-work legislation, which was passed on 29 January; classes resumed on 2 February. A tentative settlement was reached by the University and CUPE 3903 on the evening of 7 April with the assistance of a mediator appointed under the back-to-work legislation.

I cannot come close to describing my feelings during these eleven weeks, which I consider the worst period of my professional life. I had many sleepless nights thinking about the fifty-two thousand students who were unable to attend classes, and the impact of this situation on their lives. Moreover, being faced with this situation shortly after arriving at York, and with great aspirations after thirteen years of success in senior administration elsewhere, I found this a very challenging time personally as well.

Early on, I made a decision to keep a low profile and not to engage in the rhetorical arguments typical of a labour disruption. I felt that as president I would have the ultimate responsibility of being the healer following the strike, and should be able to reach out to all community members, including those on strike at that time. Although the passage of time has proved I made the right decision, I was criticized by many for not being more visible. My presence on campus every day during the strike did not prevent one of the major papers from describing me as "MIA" (missing in action) for my reluctance to speak to the media or to respond personally to statements made by representatives of the strikers. During that period, I participated in the Senate and Senate committee meetings, held daily meetings with the senior administrative team, and continued to seek advice on ways to deal with the situation.

Unfortunately this policy of keeping a low profile might have been carried further than I had intended. During this period I issued two messages to the community. Upon reflection, and after hearing from members of the community, I believe I should have done more to communicate with our students and to let them know that we were doing everything we could to resolve the dispute swiftly and fairly. Even though there was not always progress on which to report, in hindsight I do believe that more could – and should – have been done to stay in touch with and to reassure our students during the nearly three-month period they were unable to attend classes.

Despite the challenges of this period, there were a number of bright moments. Strolling through campus one cold day, I saw Professor Fran Wilkinson, a renowned expert in vision research, who, in an attempt to lift my spirits, invited me to visit her laboratory. There, I met a young faculty member, Dr Jennifer Steeves, and a number of graduate students, who had continued to carry out their research despite the strike. I continue to recall those encouraging moments every time I see Professor Wilkinson or Dr Steeves.

On a personal level, the strike affected me in a profound way. For a number of years, I had developed the habit of going to see my aging father in Egypt, and holding a birthday party for him during the holiday season. That year, my travel arrangements had been made prior to the strike. With the encouragement of the chair of the Board, I decided to maintain my travel plans, assuming that nothing important could happen in the last week of December. After a great deal of hesitation, however, I cancelled my travel plans on the day of the scheduled departure, as I did not feel comfortable being away from the University during a strike, even though it was the holiday season. Sadly, my father passed away the following March, so I missed the chance to celebrate his eighty-ninth and last birthday with him.

Every time I am reminded of this challenging time, I cannot help but think of the irony of a strike occurring on an issue about which I personally sympathize, yet whose resolution remains frustratingly elusive given that it is part of a broader systemic issue facing post-secondary education in Canada and beyond.

Post-strike initiatives

As the University went back to normal operations, I became engaged in internal and external discussions on lessons learned and, most important, on the way forward to enhance relationships on campus. I received a great deal of advice, much of which encouraged me to create highly publicized events to discuss labour relations as a general challenge facing post-secondary institutions. Although I agreed that the issues are system-wide in nature, I rejected these types of initiatives because I felt that I should focus our energies on healing the York community first.

After extensive consultations, we decided to develop a multiyear strategy for addressing employee relations at the University. I appointed Jim Thomas in July 2009 as a senior advisor to the president. A labour lawyer who served as Ontario's deputy minister of labour in Bob Rae's government, Thomas is known for his deep understanding of the labour movement and close relations with unions. Thomas's early role was, on my behalf, to engage in exploratory discussions with both unions and senior University management over ways to improve relations with York's employee groups and to avoid labour disruptions in the future. These exploratory discussions proved useful, and gave me a greater understanding of the issues and concerns from both sides.

It became clear that central to these relationships are issues of trust and mutual respect. In the later stage of these exploratory discussions, I became personally involved in meetings with leaders of all unions facilitated by Mr Thomas. These meetings were carried out throughout winter and spring 2010, and were extremely useful in building a higher level of trust and in informing me of issues and concerns that might not be part of labour negotiations, but most certainly affect them.

In 2010, I launched the Creating a Better Workplace initiative, which commenced with a listening phase involving community and union consultation.

Creating a Better Workplace was a multiyear, pan-University commitment to enhance the workplace culture, build more harmonious labour relations, improve employee satisfaction, and address challenging policy issues that could become obstacles at the bargaining table. Phase 2 of Creating a Better Workplace was launched in January 2011, and four working groups were established to address employee awards and recognition; leadership and management development; information sharing and communication; and change management and culture change. In late fall 2011, we appointed a project director for the initiative, and transitioned from a Better Workplace Management Committee to the appointment of a Better Workplace Advisory Committee for ongoing oversight and to support a fuller integration of the initiative into departments and divisions across the University.

York's first Employee Engagement Survey (for faculty and staff) was conducted in fall 2012. Our goal was to offer an environment for employees to speak up, be heard, and share with us what was and was not working on campus. We also decided to establish a baseline against which improvements could be benchmarked. The survey questions explored twenty-two different drivers of organizational and role/work engagement. Some of the institutional strengths identified by York's faculty and staff included support for diversity, role clarity, job control, and workplace safety. Institutional opportunities for improvement identified included opportunities for advancement, collaboration between departments, and workload. The findings of this first engagement survey provided a vital tool in helping us to realize our vision of a better workplace by clearly identifying where we were and what we needed to do to move forward.

In 2011–12, the University and CUPE 3903 had a constructive round of negotiations for new collective agreements that focused on finding solutions and reaching agreement, including on long-standing issues. More broadly, since the 2008–09 strike, the University and its other employee groups have successfully negotiated eleven renewed collective agreements and one first collective agreement. The University and its employee groups, which formed a York all-Union Pension Group (YUPG), also successfully negotiated changes to the University pension plan at a common negotiating table. Many of the changes were aimed at addressing the financial health or sustainability of the plan.

Despite these strides in enhancing institutional relations and communications, labour negotiations between teams for CUPE 3903 and the University, which began in September 2014, ultimately led to a strike mandate vote by the union in January 2015. The labour disruption that followed, which began on 3 March and was over by 31 March, was unfortunate. Although we believed we were working towards a tentative agreement as we entered the final scheduled days of negotiations, it appears that the situation at the University of Toronto, in which CUPE Local 3902, representing teaching assistants, went on strike at the same time, had a role in activating the strike at York. The strike initially suspended all classes at the University, but many classes were resumed after contract faculty (Unit 2) accepted a new deal on 9 March.

From the outset, we were committed to reaching fair and competitive settlements that reflect the valuable contributions of our graduate students and their important role in supporting our learning environment. York, like other institutions in the broader public and university sector, faces fiscal challenges. But even with these challenges, the compensation and other collective agreement improvements we offered were highly competitive with recent settlements elsewhere, with CUPE 3903 leading the post-secondary education sector in a variety of bargaining areas. On 31 March, union members in Unit 1 voted overwhelmingly (750 to 37) to accept a new contract and end the strike, while Unit 3 voted 175 to 6 in favour. Measures of the new three-year collective agreements included a tuition offset for international graduate students, reducing the potential out-of-pocket cost of tuition; an increase in the overall funding package for graduate assistants by $2,000; and a tuition freeze for the length of the collective agreement.

The 2015 labour disruption, though briefer and ultimately less detrimental than previous strikes, made it clear that our efforts with regard to faculty and staff relations must be ongoing. Labour relations and, relatedly, graduate funding continue to be serious matters in the province and across the country. As Meric Gertler noted at the end of the University of Toronto's strike on 27 March 2015 after union members voted to accept a university proposal to resolve the dispute through binding arbitration, a concerted effort among all institutions in the province to call for an increase in funding per student would be welcome.

I cannot mention our recent labour relations history – and the hard-won successes we have had – without acknowledging the cooperation and commitment of the leadership of various unions on campus, as well as the dedication of the senior management team, led by Gary Brewer, in helping to shape these initiatives and support them.

Student activism and engagement

One of the perceived challenges at York University has been associated with student activism. Since arriving at York, one of my primary objectives has been to encourage a culture of inclusivity. I believe in fairness and a commitment to giving people opportunities to show their excellence and to share their views openly and frankly. I imagine that there is not a political issue existing anywhere in the world that will not be debated on York's campuses, and I encourage that.

The role of the University is to make sure freedom of expression and academic freedom are exercised to the fullest extent within the law.

Given this, I always expected – and in many respects, celebrated – the existence of student activism and considered it a positive characteristic of a university and a force for positive change in society. Indeed, I witnessed, and to some extent participated in, such activities as a university student in the sixties. Nevertheless, as the following description of several incidents suggests, I learned again that it is my position as president, and not necessarily how I feel personally about an issue, that defines my level or type of engagement. These incidents are significant not only because they reflect the mood on campus in my first year in office, but also because they provide a contrast to the more positive environment that exists today.

In January 2008, only a few months after my arrival, the York community was shocked by racist graffiti found on the doors of the office space for the York University Black Students' Alliance (YUBSA), as well as the walls of an adjacent washroom. An anti-racism rally was called by YUBSA, in which many external organizations participated. An atmosphere of shock and anger prevailed on campus, and I issued a statement calling the acts "deplorable and unacceptable." Although I had not been invited, I decided it was important to attend the rally, against the advice of senior colleagues. At the rally the mood was volatile, and I stood in a corner listening to a series of angry speakers. When my presence was noted, I walked to the front of the crowd assuming that perhaps I was expected to address it. However, the organizers of the rally prevented me from speaking. Media reports described the incident as "a university president denied the freedom of speech on campus." Nevertheless, I stood there, intending my presence to indicate my support of the students, and when I was interviewed by the media I relayed my total sympathy with the protesters and acknowledged the legitimacy of their anger.

Less than two months later, we experienced another, very different, student rally. Members of the York Sustainable Purchasing Coalition called for a rally to take place on 6 March 2008 urging the University to implement a "no-sweat" policy guaranteeing that all clothing sold on campus would be produced using ethical standards. I was informed of the planned rally a day earlier by the then VP students, Rob Tiffin, as I was on my way to the airport for a two-day trip. I was very surprised that York, with its commitment to social justice, did not already have a relevant policy on this issue. I was also aware that, contrary to some views, implementing such a policy does not impede the purchasing power of the institution. I asked Rob Tiffin to inform the students of my total support, with a commitment that by the end of April we would have a clear policy on this matter even if we had to use an existing, acceptable policy from another institution.

As it turned out, the students held their rally and listened to Vice-President Tiffin's assurances of my commitment, yet decided to hold a sit-in in my office until I returned so that they might "hear it from me directly." York's security officials accommodated the dozen or so students participating in the sit-in and even provided them with food. Returning home on Friday night, I was assured that the sit-in was very peaceful and the students were likely to go home later that evening for the weekend. I called Security early on Saturday morning to learn that most of the students were still there, so I drove to the office around 8 a.m. I found the students camped out in front of my office, which was in the Ross Building at the time, with sleeping bags and surrounded by empty pizza boxes. They were very polite, and accepted my invitation for morning coffee in the Student Centre, though one of the students declined the offer of coffee as I could not assure her it had been traded fairly. The students and I had an extensive conversation in which I was able to assure them of my commitment. The sit-in ended very peacefully, the students felt they had won, and York's policy was developed and implemented. York subsequently became a member of the Fair Labor Association (FLA) and the Worker Rights Consortium (WRC), ensuring that all vendors selling our licensed products follow the codes set out by the FLA and WRC.

With several more incidents of varying degrees of seriousness, it became clear to me that, although student activism is central to campus life, it does not necessarily have to be associated with bitter confrontation with the administration. In general I felt that a number of key issues needed to be addressed, including better communication, the building of trust, and the removal of ambiguities in University policies. As a result, I established a number of presidential task forces to develop recommendations on a variety of topics related to enhancing the overall environment on campus.

I asked Patrick Monahan, who was dean of Osgoode Hall Law School at the time, to lead a task force on Student Life, Learning and Community. The committee, which was comprised of faculty and students, undertook extensive consultation and held town hall meetings with various groups on campus. The task force report made wide-ranging recommendations, including creating a standing committee on campus dialogue, changes in the student code of conduct and in security procedures, and enhancing student space. Today, with the ongoing implementation of these recommendations, the student environment on campus has been markedly improved.

I have also made a special effort to reach out personally to student groups, both graduate and undergraduate, and to participate in student activities on campus, including attending varsity games, hosting the annual President for a Day contest (where I trade places with a York undergraduate student), and speaking at our biannual campus-wide Red & White spirit days. Participation in these kinds of events and initiatives, as well as the regular meetings I hold with the leadership of the various groups on campus, has helped me to understand and appreciate the legitimate concerns and aspirations of these groups. Reciprocally, I believe they appreciate that I share many of these aspirations.

The President's Sustainability Council is another initiative that continues to serve the community well. The Council has provided an excellent forum in which the administration joins with representatives of the community to discuss a wide variety of sustainability issues and to undertake new initiatives. This has led to widespread recognition of York University as a leader in sustainability among Canadian universities, which is discussed in further detail below.

Building on Strength: Defining York's Future

What has made the past seven years such an exciting time is the sense that York really has come of age. We can now look towards the future with clearly defined aspirations, having developed a reputation for excellence in teaching, learning, and community-engaged research.

In addition to being a Canadian leader in the delivery of bilingual education through our distinctive Glendon College campus, over the past decade York has expanded and strengthened its business and professional education. The Schulich School of Business has established a reputation as one of the world's leading business schools, and significant business and professional programs have been developed in the Faculty of Liberal Arts and Professional Studies. Our Osgoode Hall Law School has also been consistently ranked as one of the top Canadian law schools, recognized for its outstanding faculty, commitment to achieving justice through law, and innovative approaches to legal education that combine theoretical and practical perspectives. We are world renowned in the Humanities, Social Sciences, Fine Arts, and Basic Sciences. We also are making significant progress in building additional strengths and gaining growing recognition in Life Sciences, Engineering, and Health.

In October 2015 we were delighted to announce that York alumnus Victor Phillip Dahdaleh, a Canadian business leader based in the United Kingdom, had made a transformational donation of $20 million in support of our global health initiatives. This historic gift, the largest by an alumnus in the University's fifty-six-year history, will enable us to expand our global health teaching and research activities, in keeping with our academic priorities, to better prepare the next generation of global health leaders and advance our commitment to building stronger, healthier communities. In 2014 our Faculty of Health launched the first Global Health Bachelor of Arts and Bachelor of Science programs in

Canada, to produce graduates who will work with health practitioners, educators, non-governmental organizations, governments, and businesses around the world. This donation will have a major impact at the University and the world beyond through the expansion of this innovative Global Health program and related research initiatives.

The first goal of any university is to advance knowledge at the highest level. At York we believe that means pursuing a broad education. It is clear that now, more than ever, universities are global institutions, and, as such, we have a role to play in addressing the challenges facing the world today – pandemics, climate change, poverty, racism, bullying, and extremism, to name a few. It is exciting to see York's faculty, researchers, staff, and students playing an increasingly active role in addressing these problems.

A leader in sustainability

Founded in 1968, the Faculty of Environmental Studies at York was the first of its kind in North America, and today remains the largest environmental studies program on the continent, with nearly thirteen hundred graduate and undergraduate students. Thanks in large part to this pioneering program, and to concerted efforts over the past decade to foster a culture of sustainability on our two campuses, today sustainability is a core value at York.

In addition to pursuing innovative research and teaching in this area, we continue to expand our on-campus efforts to make York a healthier, more efficient, and more sustainable place to work, learn, and live. We have conserved resources, improved our building operations and waste diversion, enhanced public transit, and reduced our greenhouse gas emissions. The Computer Science Building (renamed the Lassonde Building) was one of the first "green" buildings constructed in Ontario, and York now has ten buildings that meet green building standards, including the Kaneff Tower, which is a LEED Silver certified building. These accomplishments support our research and teaching mission by lowering operational costs and increasing efficiency, efforts that we must continue to support and strengthen in the months and years to come.

Our efforts are being recognized. In 2012 York received the SmartCommute Regional Employer of the Year award for our commitment to improving alternative transportation solutions for members of the York community. We were named one of Canada's Greenest Employers for three consecutive years – in 2013, 2014, and 2015 – and we consistently rank in the top 10 per cent of schools in the UI Green Metric ranking of World Universities on sustainability. In July 2013 the University received an Award for Environmental Excellence from Ontario's minister of the environment for being a provincial leader in sustainability and environmental protection initiatives. In terms of academic programming, the MBA program at Schulich School of Business continues to be the world's top-ranked MBA program integrating sustainability into the curriculum. Moreover, in keeping with our commitment to be a leader in sustainability strategies and to work as a community to reduce our environmental footprint, in April 2012 the then president of the York Federation of Students and I publicly committed to phase out the sale of bottled water at the University by 2015. This was achieved in September 2015, and reflects the University's shared commitment to being a leading socially responsible and progressive post-secondary institution for sustainability and environmental conscientiousness. Finally, in 2013, we issued our first University-wide Annual Sustainability Report, which illustrates the progress we have made towards becoming one of the greenest universities in Canada and, indeed, the world.

We are fortunate to have so many committed environmental ambassadors and innovators here at York, including colleagues serving on the President's Sustainability Council as well as the many student, staff, faculty, and alumni leaders who drive our greening efforts and are helping to make York a leader in safeguarding the well-being of the planet today and for future generations.

An evolving mandate: Knowledge transfer

With the current emphasis on the need to maintain the world's prosperity through the effective transformation of knowledge into social and economic activities, universities worldwide are seized with knowledge transfer and innovation as an evolving mandate. In 1960 York's founding president, Murray Ross, said, "To have specialization but nothing else is to possess but half an education … we shall try to break down the barriers of specialization." Ross's words are even truer today. York's reputation for interdisciplinary education is already well-established. Since most real social, economic, and health issues facing society today are multifaceted and multidisciplinary in nature, a university with such a tradition is well-suited to offer its research results and prepare its graduates to deal with these issues. Increasingly, York researchers in the Humanities, Social Sciences, Law, Business, Sciences, Health, and Environmental Studies are addressing through their research and education real-world issues and providing relevant solutions.

To become a leader in innovation and knowledge transfer, York's challenge is to become both more comprehensive – that is, by expanding Engineering, Science, and Health-related studies – as well as more research intensive. Combined with a continuing commitment to interdisciplinarity, York would then be in position to be a true leader in innovation. This will also require the development of policies and incentives to encourage a spirit of innovation and entrepreneurship among students and faculty.

Intensifying research and increasing the commitment to innovation at York does not mean a diminished emphasis on teaching. On the contrary, it means that our students are taught by individuals who are world leaders in their fields and exposed to leading-edge knowledge. It also means that our students are more aware of the potential for using what they learn or create to address real-world problems. I believe that research and teaching are inseparable; they form a continuum. But pursuing knowledge at the highest level is not enough. The greatest responsibility of the University is to disseminate that knowledge, to ensure that it is applied rapidly and does not sit on a shelf, and that it is shared with every part of society. This is York's mission today.

How do we ensure the timely dissemination of knowledge? In a time of growing global competitiveness, universities need to develop effective mechanisms for the deployment of new knowledge to ensure society is able to rapidly adapt that knowledge. That said, the best mechanism for the effective dissemination of knowledge remains our students. Knowledge transfer happens through our graduates as they enter the workforce, through our faculty and researchers, and through scholarly publications. Experiential learning is another form of knowledge transfer, and over the past few years we have placed special emphasis on making sure that our research results are readily available for the purposes of social and economic development. We now need to invest in new vehicles to make our knowledge available to a world in which knowledge is a primary driver of social and economic development.

Building on our traditional strengths in the Humanities and Social Sciences, York today is taking a leadership position in conducting socially engaged research and helping to define social innovation. Our researchers are conducting work on timely and socially relevant issues such as bullying, the health care experience, civil justice, corporate social responsibility, and income inequality, and this research is being used by policy-makers, not-for-profit organizations, and in the private sector.

We have also developed Innovation York, an office that supports the entrepreneurial activities of our students and faculty by providing the necessary services and space to facilitate start-ups. Moreover, York was a founding member of VentureLab, a provincially funded organization supporting university-industry collaborations and the commercialization of research results. As our engagement in knowledge transfer continues to grow, I believe it will have a major impact on the economic development in the region. This is becoming evident with the growing engagement of our researchers in Health, Sciences, and Engineering with local industries, particularly small and medium-sized knowledge-based companies. I was delighted to visit Innovation York recently and meet young innovators who are starting new companies fueled by knowledge created at York University. I sincerely believe in our potential to be the centre of a new innovation hub in Ontario.

Today's challenges to the post-secondary education sector

As with all universities today, there are challenges within the post-secondary education sector. The first has to do with fiscal sustainability – ensuring that we have the revenue to achieve our overall goals, and that our expenses do not exceed our revenue. Universities today are facing a serious challenge related to funding and the way we are funded – namely, that currently the only way to access new money is to grow. With that in mind, we must ask how we can be more efficient. Second, we must continually assess the quality of our education: how do we improve quality in terms of class size and facilities, as well as the use of technology? How do we offer the quality and breadth of programs that are needed by society to attract top students? A third major challenge is the threat to institutional autonomy. The government is seeking a more differentiated system, and is currently conducting an ongoing review of the university funding model. While ultimately this may be positive, we must ask how far it will go. Will we eventually have teaching-only universities? And while universities are discussing a differentiated system, colleges continue to expand their degree-granting capacity.

In an address to a presidential symposium at New York University in 2009, where presidents from four Canadian universities and universities in fifteen other countries came together for a series of roundtable discussions, I argued that the three challenging contexts universities around the world now face are: (1) the tension between public funding and demands for accountability on the one hand, and university autonomy on the other; (2) the tension between providing social opportunity, assisting in nation-building and democratization, and contributing to local and regional development versus demands that universities serve the labour market; and (3) the challenge of embracing internationalization, mobility, transferability, and equivalence while maintaining distinctiveness and local particularity.

I believe that universities endure because they respond to society's needs and because they help to drive change. Throughout history, great universities have helped society to articulate, define, argue, and achieve the next stage of progress. Never in its history has the university been more important than it is today. Nevertheless, universities are facing multiple and sometimes contradictory demands from government, the private sector, and civil society groups.

Expansion: York University in York Region

For years now, many university and community leaders have believed that expanding the University, given its position at the doorstep of the fastest-growing region in the province, would answer the demand for undergraduate spots in the GTA. As my predecessors have acknowledged, the subway extension to Vaughan is key to the school's development. York University has always seen itself as York Region's university, and as the history of York's planning documents shows, a York Region campus has been part of our aspirations for decades, at least since the University Academic Plan of 1988.

In December 2013 the Ministry of Training, Colleges and Universities (MTCU) launched a Major Capacity Expansion Framework, and in March 2014 issued a formal call for proposals to universities wishing to establish new campuses or expand existing campuses. Once bids were submitted to the province, a multi-ministry panel reviewed the applications and made final recommendations to cabinet through MTCU. Cabinet then made the final decision about successful proposals, with the outcome announced in early 2015.

In September 2014 we submitted our proposal to the government for a York University campus in the City of Markham, with the full support of our strategic partners – York Region, the City of Markham, and Seneca College. As the only municipality in North America with one million people and no university campus, there was tremendous support for a new campus in York Region from both public and private sector partners. The Region committed up to $25 million for a new campus and the City of Markham committed five acres of land located close to amenities such as the Pan Am Stadium and the YMCA. The University and our partners believed that a new campus in Markham Centre would help to address increasing demand, as almost 60 per cent of young people in York Region go on to attend university, and they should be able to fulfil their academic aspirations close to home.

Our aim is to offer a wide range of degree programs, including diverse professional programs that encourage research and innovation at all levels. Several of the programs would be offered in collaboration with Seneca College. The York campus would be home to four thousand students within five years, growing to ten to twenty thousand in twenty years. In situating the campus in the heart of a vibrant new urban centre, our goal was to offer programs that would be responsive to the needs of York Region while furthering the University's objective of becoming more comprehensive by growing in professionally relevant disciplinary programs and enhancing its research and innovation activities. Students would have real-life learning experiences in the workplace and laboratory, including placements with employers, research opportunities that connect students with outstanding faculty and innovative organizations, and opportunities for business incubation and entrepreneurship.

In May 2015 we were delighted to learn that the government of Ontario had selected the York University–Markham Centre campus project as the sole proposal among nineteen to receive government funding through the Major Capacity Expansion Policy Framework. In his announcement, Minister Reza Moridi referenced the unprecedented period of growth in the province's education system over the past decades, with demographic projections showing that there will be a strong demand for post-secondary opportunities in areas of the province such as York Region that are experiencing strong population growth, but that are currently underserved. The new campus in Markham Centre solidifies York's reputation as one of the country's leading multi-campus universities, prepared to meet the increasing demand for high-quality education and workplace-based learning opportunities, and well-positioned to spur economic growth in one of the fastest-growing major urban areas in the province. The University is now at work on the detailed planning and implementation phases, with a strategy being developed that will be responsive to educational and research needs as evident in emerging labour market requirements, in order to contribute to the creative economy of York Region and the province.

York Today

This brings me to today. Over the years, York University has transformed into a leading interdisciplinary research and teaching university, all while staying true to its original values of commitment to accessibility, social responsibility, and academic excellence. Today, we have a student population of over fifty-five thousand, nearly three hundred thousand alumni worldwide who are excelling in their fields, and a total budget of one billion dollars – making us the second-largest university in Ontario and the third-largest in Canada.

We have much to be proud of. We have leading departments in the Humanities and Social Sciences, the leading Business and Law schools, a new Engineering school, and strong and evolving Fine Arts programs. We have excellent Faculties of Science and Environmental Studies, and the largest Faculty of Health in the country. We also have the only French and bilingual post-secondary programs in southern Ontario.

We remain committed to augmenting the University's global vision and strong research networks. As mentioned, Schulich recently opened a new campus in Hyderabad, India, in partnership with the GMR Foundation to launch its new MBA in India Program. Our Faculty of Health has introduced its new Global Health degree program, the first of its kind in Canada to combine core courses in global health with specialized electives across the disciplines. Graduates of this program will go on to fulfil leadership and advocacy positions in education, research, health systems, and business locally, nationally, and internationally. Our more than 288 international partnerships are helping our students to think bigger, broader, and more globally than ever before.

In addition to our global outlook, we have adopted a multidisciplinary approach to post-secondary education that fosters entrepreneurship with the private sector and opportunities for experiential education for our students. Among our many research achievements, between 2006 and 2012 York researchers received more Social Sciences and Humanities Research Council (SSHRC) awards valued at $1 million or more than any other institution in Canada. In 2013–14, the University was awarded four State-of-the-Art Facilities-Scale SSHRC partnership grants valued at more than $18.6 million in total project funding, and we continue to increase our share of Natural Sciences and Engineering Research Council (NSERC) grants for collaborative research and development with industry partners, including receiving two of the fifteen NSERC Collaborative Research & Training Experience Program (CREATE) grants awarded nationally that year. Our faculty continue to be recognized with prestigious awards, including the Order of Canada, the Royal Society of Canada, and many others. We continue to be recognized as a campus sustainability leader.

To ensure that York's future evolution is guided by a clearly articulated plan, we have invested a great deal of effort in strategic planning for the future. The White Paper and the UAP, developed through an extensive consultative process, reflect the University's aspirations and outline our road map for the future. From a broad perspective, our planning documents reflect a commitment to three strategic objectives: academic excellence, student success, and community engagement. Within these objectives are several clearly defined priorities, including:

- intensifying research;
- increasing the scope of our programs to be aligned with the needs of society and to be more comprehensive – that is, expanding Engineering, Health, and Life Sciences;
- enhancing the first-year experience;
- introducing more experiential learning and international engagement opportunities for students;
- building a stronger community through valuing people and community engagement; and
- enhancing our financial sustainability through integrated resource alignments.

For the University to continue to succeed, we need to be efficient, and that is why operational efficiency has been one of my priorities. In 2010 we introduced PRASE, the Process Re-engineering and Service Enhancement initiative, which was led first by our provost and VP academic, Patrick Monahan, and today by Provost Rhonda Lenton and VP Finance and Administration Gary Brewer. The aim of PRASE is to develop more effective services and use of resources, as a more efficient organization also leads to a more engaged and happier workforce – a key element if we are to implement our goals. We are also working with MTCU on our Strategic Mandate Agreement to ensure that York's strategic objectives are substantially aligned with the government's policy objectives, and to realize the vision articulated in our 2010 White Paper, including the physical transformation of our Keele campus.

We are well on our way to becoming a world-class teaching and research institution, with a strong academic foundation and a strategic, integrated approach to planning. But our success will depend on our ability to change and to respond nimbly to the challenges facing post-secondary education in general, and the University in particular.

In this sense the York University of today is at an inflection point. We are one of the most ethnically diverse universities in the world, with enormous potential for future development given our location in the centre of a region experiencing the fastest growth in population and innovation. In just a few years we will be connected to the GTA by subway. In the summer of 2015 we hosted the Pan Am/Parapan Am Games in our new, state-of-the-art athletics stadium on our Keele campus, and in September 2015 our thriving new Lassonde School of Engineering moved into its iconic new facility. In a few years our new Markham Centre campus will be established in the Region, and we will have advanced our reputation as a leading comprehensive, research-intensive university that is blazing trails in social innovation – and has been since we opened our doors.

In the 2014 World University Rankings by *Times Higher Education*, York was one of only four Canadian institutions to improve its position in the rankings. Of eighteen Canadian institutions, York's was the largest improvement, with an increase of fifty-seven places. We have the land, the locations, the people, the programs, and we are fortunate that we can build upon them by expanding in areas of need.

Raising the profile of research at York will also help to attract leading academics, but we need to continue to be socially responsive. Whatever business practices we engage in should be done to serve the academic mission of the University. The core mission cannot be lost, which is that whatever we do is done to serve those who are teaching in the classroom, those who are receiving knowledge in the classroom, and those who are working in our labs and libraries.

Along with the need to be socially responsive, I believe that a progressive, twenty-first-century university must also be linked to the social and economic development of the area in which it is located. To be truly progressive, a university must be a driver of development. We also need to be a university that values life-long learning. For any society to be competitive, it will need to continuously train people and prepare them for evolving and changing roles. If there is a university that is suited for that, it is York.

One of York's biggest challenges over the years has been a lack of direct connection with the centre of the city. This will be addressed by the extension of the subway to York and the 905 region, which will help to alleviate many of the perceived disadvantages of York's location. As part of a very strong and prosperous metropolitan area with the most diverse population one can imagine, the subway extension will help us to eliminate most – if not all – of the disadvantages of our location, and start enjoying the advantages.

Our students are our highest priority, and the reason we are here. Our focus on academic excellence, student success, and community engagement is about creating a better learning environment for students, with new programs and new opportunities that are relevant to their future careers and their development as global citizens. As they prepare to leave the University and embark on the next stage of their lives, the greatest advantage we can give them is the ability to think broadly, to imagine new things, and to build networks.

Conclusion

The past is to be respected and acknowledged, but not to be worshipped.
It is our future in which we will find our greatness.
– statement attributed to Pierre Trudeau, 1970

Today, after only fifty-six years, the founding vision of York University to become one of the country's leading teaching and research universities continues to become a reality. We have a vibrant culture of student success, academic excellence, and community engagement, and a distinctive York spirit.

As York's seventh president, I am fortunate to be surrounded by so many talented students, faculty, and staff. Each member of the York community plays an integral part in our plans for the future. Together we are building a York that is a leader among Canadian post-secondary institutions and around the world. As I said in my installation speech, this is an exciting time in York's history.

I am honoured and humbled to be a part of it. Most important, I continue to see York's incredible potential to build on its heritage of academic excellence and commitment to community engagement and to evolve as one of the leading universities of the twenty-first century.

As I look out from the windows of my office in Kaneff Tower, I can see the new subway station nearing completion on our Keele campus. This is a time of dramatic change at the University, and I look forward to continuing to explore our strengths and aims, engaging our global community of alumni, friends, and partners, and reaffirming our deep commitment to academic and social innovation. This truly is our time – our time to let the world know that York has arrived, and that the best is yet to come.

NOTES

I would like to acknowledge Dr Liisa Stephenson, Director, Communications for the Office of the President, for her contributions to this chapter.

1 Greg MacDonald, "York's new president vows to be inclusive," *National Post*, 8 February 2007, A10.
2 William J. Clinton, "The President's News Conference with Prime Minister Jean Chrétien of Canada in Ottawa, February 24, 1995," in Gerhard Peters and John T. Woolley, *The American Presidency Project*; available online at http://www. presidency.ucsb.edu/ws/index.php?pid=51022&st=&st1=.
3 Richard L Alfred, *Managing the Big Picture in Colleges and Universities: From Tactics to Strategy* (Westport, CT: Praeger, 2006).
4 We also received $25 million for the Osgoode Renovation and Expansion Project under the KIP program, a project that permitted us to accommodate more graduate students, faculty, and staff; improve teaching facilities and student community space; and house six legal and interdisciplinary research centres.
5 See York University Organizational Charts 2007 and 2009.
6 See York University, President's Task Force on Community Engagement, "Towards an Engaged University: Final Report and Recommendations" (Toronto, 5 February 2010); available online at http://www.yorku.ca/commeng/documents/finalreport.pdf.

7 York's Crises Resolved: The Future Is Secure

LORNA R. MARSDEN

The crises of the early 1970s are now over forty years in the past. No one is asking now if York University should continue to exist. There are strong academic and organizational features of York seen as models in Canadian post-secondary education. Now, as then, government is asking York University to expand its enrolment and be more efficient, a continuing feature of Ontario's educational history.

The early 1970s, when these defining organizational crises occurred at York, was a period of massive change for Ontario universities, as described in detail in Edward Monahan's study of the Council of Ontario Universities.[1] A whole series of reports was commissioned by the government of Ontario to provide guidance on "system planning," including the Wright Commission on Post-Secondary Education in Ontario, the Lapp Commission on engineering, entitled *Ring of Fire*, and several others. As Monahan points out,[2] in 1968 the treasurer of Ontario informed the legislature that education was the "principal tool for increasing the productive capacity of our economy, for creating a better society, and for providing the opportunity for every citizen to develop his fullest potential"; in the following year the minister of university affairs told the legislature that government could no longer afford to increase expenditures on universities. The provincial government began both to cut spending over the years that followed and to increase its grip on university autonomy. In the 1970s all universities in Ontario were affected by cuts and changes, but the new universities, such as York, having never had full funding per capita or planning security, felt it most keenly. The message those events conveyed to the public also affected their faith in the importance and role of universities.

The three major crises at York identified in Chapter 1 – the crises of succession, of financial support, and of government policy – have been resolved or routinized over time, but in rather different ways. To capture the candid views of the presidents who served in these years, no attempt was made to direct the content of their chapters. The differences in approach to their presidential work are clearly seen in these individual chapters. Some presidents were more focused on building on the plans of their predecessors; some faced compelling problems that required immediate attention, sidelining other plans; those with a longer time in office were able to take on new priorities in a second term. This chapter, by comparing the approaches of each of the presidents to the major issues of those crises, shows that, despite very different styles of leadership, the problems have been addressed and many changes brought about to prevent their repetition.

Not surprisingly, in many cases it has taken more than one president's initiative or term of office to resolve the difficulty. The relief of per capita underfunding is a central theme in several of these chapters. Rebuilding the morale and spirit of the York community took several presidential terms. Crises of succession might still occur, but they will be quickly dispelled. In a period when presidential terms have shortened considerably across the country, during the forty years studied here the Board of Governors has appointed only five individuals to lead the University.[3]

A more fundamental crisis underlying the woes of 1973 was the sudden need to change academic plans and priorities to accommodate the demanded rapid enrolment growth. This was in and of itself a shock, but to be required to do so without being provided the resources needed to support it in faculty complement and infrastructure such as buildings, technology, and library resources was daunting. Perhaps the most important change at York since 1973 has been the successful evolution towards widely accepted and consistent academic planning. Examining this transformation over the five presidential periods illustrates how the doubts and fears described in accounts by Saywell and others were gradually resolved. Today's clear confidence in the Senate and Faculty planning processes has emerged over the years. One can see the stages of resolution, institutionalization, and now expansion of academic planning. President Shoukri's chapter shows the emergence of renewed vigour in York's academic planning. I document this evolution below.

The financial crisis that beset President Slater in 1970 was serious in its implications for York's future but it was doubly serious because the University had not yet developed financial planning strengths, a cushion of scholarships and other endowments, or allies among other universities and government members to help cope with changing government policies. The financial squeeze on York has varied over the forty-year period, but it remains serious. Over time the University has developed analysis and forward planning of capital accumulation. It has multiyear budgets for operating, capital, and special projects.

There has been considerable innovation and discipline in securing additional sources of funding.

The crisis of morale among the faculty and staff members that built up in the 1968–74 period took some years to resolve. When resolution came, it was in a style particular to York. Some excellent faculty and staff left, but many excellent faculty and staff joined the University. Personal relationships among faculty, staff, and administrators helped restore trust among many, although not all, members of the community. Customs developed in relationships among faculty members, staff, and students to enable all to work together outside the formal organizational structures. Unionization helped to routinize processes. Policies and procedures guiding human resources were developed. Successes in research and honours received by faculty members have built pride and self-confidence in each of the Faculties. A lively, disputatious, but collegial culture characteristic of an egalitarian atmosphere began to prevail in the Senate and in campus meetings. Governance was strengthened, creating the resilience required to move the University forward.

These myriad changes focused by public presidential priorities involved virtually everyone connected with York at some point. Communicating these changes has been helped by the growth of several alumni associations and activities, by students' success in academic and sports competitions, and by campus developments and University publications. York's international and national reputation has grown stronger, boosting enrolments, exchanges, and faculty recruitment. Strong governors have lifted York's standing in the local and wider communities. Finding loyal donors has become easier.

There have been some intensely difficult and painful moments in the lives of each president, as described in previous chapters, but there is no evidence that any of our five presidents felt that the University would founder at these times. No president has been terminated in mid-term. No one has raised questions about York's long-term future. Collectively, these presidents resolved each of the serious problems of 1972–74 while carrying on the routines of the presidential position, including many new challenges and opportunities.

Academic Plans Are Resolved

Not surprisingly each new president has focused on the academic enterprise and strengths, but they have approached it in different ways. President Macdonald knew he had a lot of rebuilding to do, and the organizational changes he made in 1974 and thereafter illustrate his method of achieving the goal of restoring the focus on the academy. The chronology, however, is significant. First, he became his own academic vice-president, signalling that academic plans were his number-one priority. Second, by the fall of 1974, academic planning was beginning, and by May 1975 – less than a year after President Macdonald came into office – the Senate Academic Planning and Priorities Committee was asked to "prepare a draft statement of the University's priorities and academic goals and the process by which they could be realized" (see Chapter 2). The Committee, in turn, proposed a smaller group that would nest the academic priorities and plans into a wider university planning context. By September 1975 the President's Commission on Goals and Objectives was approved by the Senate and its members elected. The work of the Commission was wide ranging and involved very large numbers of people in its consultations and committees. It reported finally in 1977, taking three years from start to finish, followed by implementation stretching out several more years.

While all this was going forward, the president was busy with other projects. For example, the status of women at York had been an issue during the earlier crisis. It was an issue in the entire country following the December 1970 Report of the Royal Commission on the Status of Women. President Macdonald arrived already familiar with those issues, and welcomed the Senate report tabled early in 1975. He subsequently created the position of advisor to the president on the status of women.[4] This bold move caught the attention of women faculty and staff all across the country. York University took the lead in this issue in academic ways – in courses and eventually in degree studies, in library acquisitions, and in consideration of tenure and promotion. All this helped to focus minds away from the crisis and towards the possibilities for action and success. There were other similar projects, such as new research centres, described in Chapter 2.

President Arthurs observed all this from his decanal position in the Osgoode Hall Law School, and saw that to achieve academic excellence more resources – fewer "secret police" as he puts it – were required. He also saw the need to rebalance the academic programs among the Humanities, the Sciences, and the professions. The organizational question was how to do this. The founding Ross regime had talked about Engineering, Medicine, and more Science programs, but had made beginnings only in Science.[5] As he points out, President Arthurs saw the need for a new framework for academic planning to overcome some of the earlier problems, and created APAY – Academic Planning at York. As he says in Chapter 3, "the planning process was at least as useful as the plan itself," incorporating self-study, a three-to-five-year rolling academic plan, consultation and clear responsibilities for the plan, and budgeting to achieve it. By the late fall of 1985, about a year after President Arthurs' arrival, APAY was approved by the Senate and the Board. The following year, the first University Academic Plan was approved. In short, academic planning at York was not narrowly focused on scholarly and scientific content, but on the broad issues of the University as a community in the context of the society around it, or on "how knowledge in Western civilization is organized."[6] At the end of his terms as president, Harry Arthurs saw the *2020 Vision: The Future Development of York University* plan approved by the Senate and the Board. In the meantime he made strides in securing resources and developing the Keele campus.

At that point, in 1992, eighteen years of very hard work on academic matters had passed, and two of the post-crisis presidents had completed their terms. Now York University had academic priorities, plans, and processes so very well established and accepted that they are referred to in this volume by all subsequent presidents. There was no further crisis of academic focus. Changes in academic plans and organization have been complex and continuous, but by no means as crippling as they were in 1970–74. Orderly change in academic planning has become institutionalized in York's procedures and culture.

The resolution of this crisis allowed subsequent presidents to build in new ways. Drawing on these documents, President Mann decided to raise the game, to explore "the frontiers of scholarship," to ensure "scholarly vitality and innovation" (see Chapter 4). Working hard to keep up academic goals and priorities, President Mann was met by a tsunami of budget cuts and enrolment demands. Yet she led in building academic strengths by winning donations for student support, attracting international graduate students, and in general expanding and building the Faculty of Graduate Studies programs. Two further academic gains were the successful agreement with Seymour Schulich for a historic gift to the then School of Administrative Studies, and another agreement with Seneca College for academic and geographic cooperation. The latter put York in the forefront of the move to help students and employers by combining academic studies and skills training. As President Mann reports, "[t]he existence of an academic plan for the University and the process of establishing and updating it made it much easier to determine ... that ... academic endeavours remain paramount."

These three post-crisis presidents – Macdonald, Arthurs, and Mann – had all faced up to the financial squeeze of those years that came to a head in the 1990s during the "social contract" of the Rae government followed by the Harris government's "common sense" cuts. The faculty strike that burst out at the end of President Mann's term of office (and after President Marsden had been named her successor) had been developing since the crises of 1973 – a one-day faculty strike in the Arthurs years was a symptom – and, as President Mann says, "what really fuelled the strike ... was the perception of my faculty members that their status was declining and their working conditions were worsening."

So when President Marsden arrived just weeks after the settlement of that strike, the mood was tense. It was not tense because of academic visions and plans, but because of an atmosphere in the province, highlighted through budget cuts, which carried the message that academics and their knowledge and practice were not valued – that the public had lost faith in the role of academic authority. It was a populist message that "elites" had to be controlled and that technology could replace much of what academics did. Reactions to those messages came through in the rhetoric during that strike. In the post-strike period, the York community clung to the academic plan and the long-term vision. Those strong plans carried the work of the Senate forward.

A looming problem was the declining situation at the Glendon Faculty, described in Chapter 5. Would we have to close one of our Faculties? Work on the Glendon problems was the initial impetus to demonstrate that the academic plan would be kept intact during the Marsden years. At the same time, creating improved working conditions by building more or improved space for several Faculties and their members was a priority. Because of the successes of President Mann's administration, the resources were there to build a new Science building. Retaining a focus on academic priorities in the Senate and its committees led to some considerable rethinking of how the Senate operated, as Chapter 5 illustrates. Bringing the Board of Governors into closer contact with the academic priorities made resource allocations clearer and easier to achieve. While reported as changes in governance, these were really underpinnings to the success of the academic plans through the closer engagement of the wider York community. Later during the Marsden years, the creation of a new Faculty of Health, several new programs, and the rethinking of the Atkinson Faculty furthered the realization of the standing academic and strategic plans.

President Shoukri, still in the process of fulfilling his vision for York, brought a new concept of academic leadership in the position of provost. At the universities of Toronto and McMaster, the position of provost[7] is where academic and budget plans come together. The provost, with the president and vice-president finance, provides the leadership of a complete and integrated vision and the means to implement that vision. In the creation of this version of the position at York, academic planning and the implementation of those plans were lodged with the provost.

So, as President Shoukri points out in Chapter 6, as part of his vision of encouraging and supporting the region's economic development, a strong Engineering Faculty at York was necessary. The time was ripe: the provincial ban on additional engineering schools in Ontario was no longer in place, the small Engineering program at York had excellent faculty and leadership, and a very generous benefactor contributed the means to create the Lassonde School of Engineering. This was only one step in the new strategic academic planning President Shoukri brought to York.

All five presidents put academic issues first in their thinking, but achieving their goals was often more a matter of mobilizing the required resources. To mobilize resources usually required some reorganization of people, departments, and procedures, as I show below.

The Financial Crises Are Mitigated, if Not Resolved

At this point, patient reader, you have worked through six accounts of the financial challenges York has faced – one from each president and the historic context of this issue in Chapter 1. All academic ambitions, which led these five presidents to take up the appointment in the first place, were stymied or shaped by the challenge of resources. The resource limitations were in large part a result of the decisions of governments, including their power to determine most tuition fees and operating grants. But those decisions were aggravated by the problems of inflation, recession, competition with other universities' salary levels and pension arrangements, and union negotiating positions. The time scale of universities is much longer than that of governments, and so is the planning cycle.

President Macdonald is an economist, and arrived highly knowledgeable about provincial finances, but even he was jolted by a freeze on capital funding and the requirement to take more students for less money. As he points out in his chapter, inflation exceeded revenue increases in every one of his ten years. The lesson learned from the problems faced by his predecessor, President Slater, was that analysis, forecasting, and careful budgeting were crucial aspects of survival.

The professional backgrounds of the other presidents were neither in economics nor financial management, but all of them were committed to keeping resources as strong and orderly as possible. They were supported by splendid senior financial officers and analysts – William Farr and Sheldon Levy for presidents Arthurs and Mann, Phyllis Clark for presidents Mann and Marsden, and Gary Brewer for presidents Marsden and Shoukri. Without them who knows what might have happened? They – the VPs finance – would no doubt say that, without their own staff, who supported them in their jobs, they know quite well what would have happened, and it would not have been pretty. Of course, York always had governors who were knowledgeable advisors and sophisticated about financial matters. Two former deputy ministers of finance in the government of Canada served on our Board: Governor and then Chair of the Board Marshall Cohen, and Governor Fred Gorbet. From the start we were fortunate to have leading business people from investment firms and accounting firms and many who sat on audit, investment, and finance committees of public companies. Their oversight of budgets, pensions, audits, and fundraising was always a key to keeping the University in sound financial shape.

Budgeting was a complex exercise involving the need for support from both the Senate, with its great academic ambitions, and the Board, with its need for budget constraint. Although the division of labour between the two governing bodies was clear, in practice both senators and governors had opinions on the issues in the other jurisdiction. Presidents played various roles in this depending upon their expertise and interest, but all were called upon to make final decisions and then to convince senators and governors that those decisions were wise. Through the Ontario Council on University Affairs and the Council of Ontario Universities, all presidents were party to constant discussions among colleagues and with government about funding, tuition and other student fees, and every other financial matter. We studied the provincial and federal budgets closely and usually presented briefs to the relevant legislative committees. Sometimes York was in agreement with other institutions' presidents and sometimes we disagreed. Occasionally, as you saw in earlier chapters, we stood alone.

The funding of universities is complicated and constantly changing, as outlined in the previous chapters. President Macdonald explains the ravages of inflation in an unfair funding system. President Arthurs explains the funding system and its many complexities and inequities, including discounting. President Mann describes the series of cuts to university budgets, and President Marsden examines several particular sources of new funding from government special programs and new methods of building capital funds. President Shoukri, still in office, has opportunities ahead, but focuses on the impact of donations and government grants in acquiring needed resources.

At the end of the day, however, three results are evident. As revenue sources, tuition and student ancillary fees are higher than ever; government grants per full-time equivalent student are lower than ever; and endowments have grown. Two governments over the forty-year period put in programs to recognize inequities in per student funding – the Fair Funding program of 1998, described in Chapter 5, and the Reaching Higher program of 2005. No government has recognized the real inflationary pressures, but modest increases in per student funding have occurred, most recently in 1999. Although, for the most part, governments have kept increases in tuition no higher than inflation, in the 1990s tuition fees and ancillary fees were allowed to rise by as much as 10 per cent annually to offset cuts in grants. Furthermore, between 1998 and 2002, tuition fees for professional programs and graduate programs were deregulated and allowed to rise by what the market would bear. In 2006 international fees for students were fully deregulated.

The changes in tuition, grant, and special programs affected overall enrolment growth during most presidential terms. Particular programs were affected by the enrolment implications of these changes. Enrolment at York grew in each president's terms, but, depending on cuts, increases, deregulation, and programs, balancing enrolment became extremely complex. Over the forty years, the student body rose from about twenty-three thousand to more than fifty-five thousand full-time equivalent students. With a gradual increase in graduate enrolments over more recent years, York has complied fully with the demands the government made of President Ross in 1968. He was told to abandon the idea that York would remain a university of about twelve thousand students[8] and instead become a very large institution absorbing much of the increased demand for accessibility for Ontario students. However, as the temper of the province shifts towards ensuring the high quality of post-secondary education, enrolment planning may focus increasingly on the program balance, the quality of student applicants, and the standard of the education they receive.

An emphasis on a balance between access and quality in government policy would be a welcome development. In his account of the work of the association of presidents of Ontario universities, known as COU, Monahan describes the period from 1962 to 2000 as one of rapidly accumulating despair. It is not only that successive governments focused their policies on increasing access to universities, but that they also had not made good-quality education a high priority. There have been some excellent and helpful government programs and grants, as this study shows, but for Ontario universities as a whole the result has been the deterioration of faculty-student ratios, larger classes, a higher proportion of part-time faculty members, and therefore fewer hours of mentoring of undergraduates, newer faculty members, and even doctoral candidates by eminent tenured faculty. In fact, it is impressive to see how deans and faculty members manage to carry on their scholarship and research at an internationally competitive level.

Endowments, reflecting the generosity of individuals, corporations, and alumni, sometimes with matching grants from government, are a happier story. The slow and steady growth of the endowment funds – from $364,000 when Ian Macdonald began his presidency to $415 million in 2014 – is important evidence of the confidence donors have in the University and its long-term future. It also shows commitment to the values, programs, and students of the University. Since many generous gifts to York University have been directed to capital programs for buildings – such as those in matching gifts through the period of the Harris government's programs – rather than endowments, the size of the endowment fund is quite remarkable. It will take the endowment funds many years to catch up with those of longer-established institutions, of course. Increasingly, however, planned giving through the estates of graduates and benefactors of York will build that fund. In the 2013 ranking of university endowment funds in Canada, prepared by the Canadian Association of University Business Officers and published annually in its journal, *University Manager*, York ranked twelfth among sixty-six Canadian universities. Considering York's youth and its rapid intake of students this is impressive.

Organization and Governance

By 1974 the revised legislation creating York University had long passed and the basic structure of governance has remained: the chancellor as titular head of the University, the Board of Governors, the president as chief executive officer.[9] As the previous chapters have illustrated, however, governance has continued to evolve and adjust both in process and organization. New bodies such as the York University Development Corporation and the York Foundation were created with specific powers and duties in the University community. As government has intruded further and further into the governance of universities, compliance with law and regulation has taken more of the attention of the Board of Governors and administration, and requires specific knowledge in staff. Human rights legislation and programs at both the federal and provincial levels of government, privacy and transparency issues, and reporting requirements all have steadily increased.

Outwardly the organization of the University might remain little changed. Deans are still the academic leaders of Faculties, the University librarian still commands the libraries and archives, and there is still a principal of Glendon College. There are still masters of the residential colleges. However, the administrative organization changes frequently, as different views of how to achieve the strategic plans for the University come into effect. It is to be expected that each new president selects his or her immediate office staff and influences the selection of senior officers. By written requirements in the York University Act, 1965, collective agreements, and custom, however, the selection of those who fill the vice-presidential and decanal positions emerges from a committee search. The formal appointments are made by the Board of Governors on the recommendation of the president. It is not customary at York for the vice-presidents to submit their resignations to an incoming president as a matter of courtesy, as it would be in many other organizations.

During the Arthurs years, as described in Chapter 3, there was continuity in the administrative organization in the vice-president administration, but also new senior administrators in the vice-president academic position, and a variety of working groups. In addition, President Arthurs appointed Ian Lithgow as vice-president advancement, the first professional in that position. This reflected the growing need during the 1970s for fundraising by universities.

Between 1992 and 1997, faced with dramatic budget cuts, President Mann had the unhappy task of reorganizing her team to achieve savings. A vice-presidential position was cut and the York University Development Corporation became smaller, as did all possible administrative bodies in order to save the academic faculty and staff. Sheldon Levy moved into the vice-president administration position, and Michael Stevenson was selected as vice-president academic.

In the Marsden years the position of vice-president research was created, reporting directly to the president; the advancement functions were divided to focus specialized talent on moving briskly forward the objectives in alumni affairs and records, fundraising, and marketing and identity. Internal audit was reorganized to comply with contemporary governance standards, and the vice-presidents became attached to Board committees. The Office of Institutional Research and Analysis (now the Office of Institutional Planning) was centralized, and overlapping offices in human rights were amalgamated into a single office.

President Shoukri has rearranged the senior officers, as he describes in Chapter 6. To build the revised academic and strategic plans, he has moved several offices under that of the vice-president academic and provost, so that the work of academic planning and budgeting is now the province of the provost. And he has merged the York University Foundation back into the general advancement services of the University.

The fact that all presidents writing here discuss their organizational changes illustrates the key point that, to achieve the agreed-upon academic objectives and strategic plans for the University, there must be flexibility for the president in the number and functions of administrative officers. Governance at York, while legally found in the York University Act, 1965, is clear but sufficiently broad so that the changing not only of senators and governors, but also of the administration can effectively ensure that the University thrives under ever-changing external conditions. This is a point of contention, because the provincial and federal governments view higher education as a "system," while the universities recognize the major differences among institutions. Governments want to pass "system" laws and regulations affecting universities, whereas universities strive for differentiation with varying goals and commitments. Governments of any political stripe and their vertical bureaucracies have a very different worldview than do universities, with their relatively flat and distributed governance structures.

Building Reputation

As President Macdonald illustrates in Chapter 2, overcoming public discussion of the crises at York in the early 1970s was a serious matter. He undertook to do this by calming and reassuring the community internally and speaking to as many community groups as possible. The third element of his program was to enhance the international links of the University. The reputational problem was a local one in Toronto, and he worked hard to ensure that it was not transferred elsewhere.

By the time the Arthurs years began in 1985, it was possible to move on to another issue in York's reputation: the Keele campus. Students of the very early years revel in stories about the distant parking lots and windswept acres. President Arthurs commissioned new campus plans drawing on studies of how to block winds, make pleasurable sitting and walking conditions, and develop rational relationships among buildings for various programs.

There have been changes to the Arthurs plan, but the main elements remain. The development of the campus plans by all later presidents includes parking garages with easy access to the inner core of the University, good stormwater drainage, signage, lighting, and many safety and environmental improvements. The subway stations on campus follow in general the flow of foot traffic on campus. The Glendon campus has always been extraordinarily beautiful, and the Keele campus has – bar many construction projects – reached that level. Several buildings at York have won architectural prizes, and the environmental sustainability projects have been widely acknowledged in "green" recognition.

President Macdonald spent many days directly promoting York's values and strengths wherever he was invited to speak. He enhanced York's reputation both locally and internationally, and every later president has followed that lead. All presidents seek out York's friends and potential friends in order to raise funds for scholarships, bursaries, and many other important projects. President Arthurs emphasized that "friend-raising" was not only for funding, but also for acquiring allies among other universities. In this, York had an advantage. The COU has offices and meets in downtown Toronto. This means that universities outside Toronto, which is most of them, can be represented only after expensive and time-consuming travel. Senior administrators at York began circulating information from meetings that other presidents had to miss, including analyses of policy and funding alternatives. For these other universities, this was of great benefit, and York's analyses and worldview began to build.

President Mann, as the first woman and bilingual president of York University and one of the first five women presidents of a Canadian university that admitted both men and women, enjoyed wide attention, and she built exchanges and relationships internationally as well.[10]

By the turn of the twenty-first century, it became possible to respond to the aggressive competition for students in Ontario through branding of various kinds. In her chapter, President Marsden describes a number of steps taken to sharpen up York's identity locally and across the country both as to the University's purpose and in terms of visual images such as consistent red and white colours.

President Shoukri brought with him the attention of the engineering community, important to the future of York's programs, and has carried on a determined campaign with our now well-established alumni, 270,000 strong.

The ranking of universities in Canada began in 1991 with *Maclean's* magazine's efforts to guide students entering undergraduate studies. It continues as one point of reference for students, now supplemented by a major university fair every fall at which all universities in Ontario have booths where students and their parents can engage in comparative shopping, although guidance counsellors, family tradition, and Web information have more influence on their decisions. From the academic point of view, the rankings of any significance are those in their field of specialization. Faculty members study the ranking of departments within their discipline and, increasingly, subdiscipline. Professional school rankings began many years ago, and there are many of them. From a presidential point of view it is helpful to look at how universities compare in local, national, and international rankings, because the general reader is interested in them and they influence alumni, donors, and student recruitment.

The "media spotlight" referred to by President Macdonald in connection with the crisis of succession in 1973 is now less focused on York University. Since those years, York gradually has found its geographic footing and its academic strengths in the community. Now the challenge for the president is less and less "what is York about and should it exist?" than dealing with particular incidents and occasional attacks on the institution. As the academic and community strengths of York have become better known, presidents spend less time on the general criticisms and attacks on the entire University and more promoting the strengths and resolving particular problems – just as other established universities do. When one considers that York University is only fifty-five years old, that the first class graduated only fifty-one years ago, that the founding president remained in an honorary position at York until his death in 2000, and that the first university buildings on both the Glendon and the Keele campuses are only recently being renovated, it is astonishing how much has happened and how established York University has become.

Conclusion

In this volume we have studied a relatively short period in what will be a long history of York University. It was, however, a crucial period, a turning point for the University. We have examined it exclusively from the presidential viewpoint, and there are many other viewpoints that would deepen the analysis. Indeed, others, such as Dean John Saywell, Dean James Gillies, and Professor Michiel Horn, have preceded us in writing their own accounts. University people have myriad layers of experience and understanding of their workplace. Each point of view adds to the understanding of the institution as it develops.

As presidents, we have worked with remarkable individuals whose devotion is to the institution – chancellors, Board chairs, senators, administrators, faculty, staff members, alumni, and colleagues from other spheres – and with our predecessors and successors, all for the strengthening of York. We have found an understanding of the importance and value of a university that expresses modern values and combines them with the traditional values of higher learning. We have found the support of the communities around us: the municipalities, the cultural communities, the business communities that helped in times of crisis. We have worked with politicians and public servants, sometimes together and sometimes on opposite sides of an issue. We have attempted to understand their priorities and to get them to understand ours. Above all we have worked with generations of students and their families to understand their ambitions, concerns, and pleasures while at York and as alumni.

York University is a tough taskmaster, but it has been a privilege for all of us to contribute to its continuation. It will be fascinating to watch York's future development. We see brilliant faculty members and students making their mark on the country and around the world, devoted alumni, beautiful buildings fully maintained, first-rate athletic teams, a splendid endowment fund capable of supporting the brightest students in every field, and all of it on a verdant, sustainable campus.

NOTES

1 Monahan, *History of the Council of Ontario Universities*, chap. 2.
2 Ibid., 59.
3 Several presidents of other universities in Canada were dismissed during the years covered in this study for a variety of reasons, but the governors of York have always managed to avoid such a situation by their close attention to the campus climate, oversight of finances and legal matters, and sensitivity to looming problems.

4 The position of advisor to the president on the status of women changed over time as other human rights such as sexual orientation, sexual harassment, employment equity, race and ethnic relations, disabilities, and Aboriginal rights were added to the organizational bodies at York. See Teiman, *Idealism and Accommodation.*

5 As a result of the report of the Council of Presidents of the Universities of Ontario, *Ring of Fire: A Study of Engineering Education in Ontario* (Toronto, 1970), known as the Lapp Report, no new Engineering programs were permitted in Ontario universities, thus preventing York from developing in that direction.

6 This is a quotation from Professor Thelma McCormack's minority report to the Macdonald President's Commission.

7 Until this point, the term "provost" at York referred to the military origins of that term as someone who kept discipline, and was applied to the title of the vice-president students.

8 Depending upon the source, the size that Murray Ross planned for York's capacity was somewhere between twelve thousand and twenty-five thousand students.

9 For details and a copy of the York University Act 1965, see http://secretariat.info.yorku.ca/governance-documents/york-university-act-1965/.

10 Mount Saint Vincent, in Halifax, a women's religious college for most of its history, always had women presidents. Apart from that unique situation, Pauline Jewett was the first woman president, at Simon Fraser University in 1974; Roseann Runte became president at Collège Ste-Anne in 1983, Marsha Hannen at the University of Winnipeg followed in 1989, Geraldine Kenney-Wallace at McMaster in 1990, and Susan Mann at York and Lorna Marsden at Wilfrid Laurier, both in 1992.

Appendix

Tuition, Government Grant Revenue, and Endowments, York University, 1971–2014

| | Revenue Source | | |
	Tuition	Government Grants	Endowments
		. ($)	
1971	7,692,681	29,087,135	285,142
1972	8,853,801	31,055,408	293,610
1973	10,163,000	37,864,000	346,000
1974	10,928,000	40,675,000	364,000
1975	11,742,000	45,969,000	498,000
1976	12,510,000	51,084,000	648,000
1977	13,127,000	61,076,000	787,000
1978	14,249,000	65,172,000	905,000
1979	14,608,000	64,554,000	907,000
1980	15,537,000	66,861,000	984,000
1981	18,324,000	70,357,000	1,287,000
1982	22,858,000	77,059,000	1,413,000
1983	30,579,000	86,882,000	1,476,000
1984	36,793,000	96,393,000	2,291,000
1985	40,898,000	104,271,000	3,822,000
1986	43,086,000	113,395,000	3,972,000
1987	45,815,000	117,344,000	4,287,000
1988	48,359,000	132,520,000	6,014,000
1989	53,572,000	146,527,000	15,183,000
1990	58,502,000	160,658,000	17,868,000
1991	68,212,000	181,844,000	21,455,000
1992	80,982,000	194,233,000	22,796,000

(continued)

Tuition, Government Grant Revenue, and Endowments,York University, 1971–2014
(Continued)

	Revenue Source		
	Tuition	Government Grants	Endowments
		($)	
1993	89,541,000	205,237,000	27,173,000
1994	87,867,000	190,310,000	29,618,000
1995	94,050,000	188,613,000	33,317,000
1996	102,526,000	182,727,000	38,895,000
1997	124,104,000	154,446,000	54,606,000
1998	136,991,000	155,933,000	67,573,000
1999	157,074,000	159,146,000	118,000,000
2000	178,680,000	173,392,000	118,000,000
2001	191,287,000	179,896,000	146,100,000
2002	205,581,000	181,069,000	150,900,000
2003	236,955,000	198,253,000	145,200,000
2004	267,375,000	228,481,000	161,100,000
2005	287,629,000	248,303,000	219,000,000
2006	301,306,000	283,659,000	263,200,000
2007	316,327,000	314,441,000	302,900,000
2008	331,738,000	314,776,000	300,900,000
2009	339,017,000	303,282,000	251,500,000
2010	370,042,000	310,932,000	292,900,000
2011	404,376,000	316,447,000	335,900,000
2012	433,611,000	319,377,000	331,700,000
2013	453,140,000	314,589,000	371,800,000
2014	476,691,000	308,584,000	414,901,000

Notes: Tuition revenues, grant revenues, and gifts to endowment changed in every financial reporting period, making it extremely difficult to sort out whether or not, taking into account enrolment growth and inflation, the University was better off in the long run. Because of those complications, only the unadjusted numbers in those variables are shown here. The University changed its year-end from June 30 to April 30 in 1972, so figures for 1972 are for ten months. Tuition revenue includes both credit and noncredit tuition revenue, as well as referenda and ancillary fees. Grant revenue includes operating grants only.

Sources: Grant revenue: York University, Financial Statements, 1971–97; Cofo Reports and other internal data from 1998 onwards. Endowments: York University, Financial statements, 1971–2001; internal reports from 2002 onwards.

Works Cited

Alfred, Richard L. *Managing the Big Picture in Colleges and Universities: From Tactics to Strategy*. Westport, CT: Praeger, 2006.

Arthurs, Harry. "Why Businesses Should Be More University-like." *Canadian Speeches* 4, no. 5 (2 March 1990).

Axelrod, Paul Douglas. *Values in Conflict: The University, the Marketplace, and the Trials of Liberal Education*. Montreal; Kingston, ON: McGill-Queen's University Press, 2002.

Berdahl, Robert O., and James Duff. *University Governance in Canada*. Toronto: University of Toronto Press, 1966.

Bladen, Vincent. *Bladen on Bladen: Memoirs of a Political Economist*. Toronto: University of Toronto, Scarborough College, 1978.

Brown, Robert Craig. *Arts & Science at Toronto, A History, 1827–1990*. Toronto: University of Toronto Press, 2013.

Burnside, Sharon. "Did story treat York fairly?" *Toronto Star*, 4 June 2005.

Cave, Martin, Stephen Hanney, and Maurice Kogan. *The Use of Performance Indicators in Higher Education: The Challenge of the Quality Movement*. London: Jessica Kingsley, 1997.

Conway, Jill K., *True North, A Memoir*. Toronto: Alfred A. Knopf, 1994.

Council of Presidents of the Universities of Ontario. *Ring of Fire: A Study of Engineering Education in Ontario*. Toronto, 1970.

Demerath, Nicholas J., Richard W. Stephens, and R. Robb Taylor. *Power, Presidents, and Professors*. New York: Basic Books, 1967.

Donovan, Kevin. "Report clears York U in housing deal." *Toronto Star*, 21 June 2005.

Fallis, George. *Multiversities, Ideas, and Democracy*. Toronto: University of Toronto Press, 2007.

Fallis, George. *Rethinking Higher Education: Participation, Research, and Differentiation*. Montreal; Kingston, ON: McGill-Queen's University Press, 2013.

Friedland, Martin L. *The University of Toronto: A History*. Toronto: University of Toronto Press, 2002.

Frum, David. "Something's seriously wrong at York University." *National Post*, 20 February 2014.

Gillies, James M. *From Vision to Reality: The Founding of the Faculty of Administrative Studies at York University, 1965–1972, A Memoir of One of the Most Interesting times in My Career.* Toronto: Schulich School of Business, 2010.

Gross, Edward, and Paul V. Grambsch. *Changes in University Organization, 1964–1971.* New York: McGraw-Hill, 1974.

Hamilton, Roberta. *Setting the Agenda: Jean Royce and the Shaping of Queen's University.* Toronto: University of Toronto Press, 2002.

Harvey, Edward. *Industrial Society: Structures, Roles, and Relations.* Homewood, IL: Dorsey Press, 1975.

Horn, Michiel. *York University: The Way Must Be Tried.* Montreal; Kingston, ON: McGill-Queen's University Press, 2009.

Hume, Christopher. "Vari Hall gives York University a new image." *Toronto Star*, 19 September 1992.

Lombardi, John V. *How Universities Work.* Baltimore: Johns Hopkins University Press, 2013.

MacDonald, Greg. "York's new president vows to be inclusive." *National Post*, 8 February 2007.

McKenzie, Judith. *Pauline Jewett: A Passion for Canada.* Montreal; Kingston, ON: McGill-Queen's University Press, 1999.

McKillop, A.B. *Matters of Mind: The University in Ontario, 1791–1951.* Toronto: University of Toronto Press, 1994.

Monahan, Edward. *A History of the Council of Ontario Universities, 1962–2000.* Waterloo, ON: Wilfrid Laurier University Press, 2004.

Moore, Kathryn M., Ann M. Salimbene, Joyce D. Marlier, and Stephen M. Bragg. "The Structure of Presidents' and Deans' Careers." *Journal of Higher Education* 544, no. 5 (1983): 500–15.

Muzzin, Linda J., and George S. Tracz. "Characteristics and Careers of Canadian University Presidents." *Higher Education* 10, no. 3 (1981): 335–51.

Ontario. Ministry of Training, Colleges and Universities. *The Ontario Operating Funds Distribution Manual.* Toronto, October 2009. Available online at http://www.uoguelph.ca/analysis_planning/images/pdfs/2009-10-Operating-Manual-Sept09.pdf.

Ontario Council on University Affairs. *Sustaining Quality in Changing Times: Funding Ontario Universities.* Toronto, 1994.

Ontario Federation of University Faculty Associations. "Making Sense of the Funding Formula for Ontario Universities." *OCUFA Report* 9, no. 8 (2015). Available online at http://us1.campaign-archive2.com/?u=ca9b5c14da55e36f1328eb0f1&id=03222d971f&e=.

Paul, Ross. *Leadership Under Fire: The Challenging Role of the Canadian University President.* Montreal; Kingston, ON: McGill-Queen's University Press, 2011.

Ross, Murray G. "The Dilution of Academic Power in Canada: The University of Toronto Act." *Minerva* 10, no 2 (1972): 242–58.

Ross, Murray G. *The New University*. Toronto: University of Toronto Press, 1961.

Ross, Murray G. *The Way Must Be Tried: Memoirs of a University Man*. Toronto: Stoddart, 1992.

Ross, Murray G., et al. *These Five Years 1960–65: The President's Report, York University*. North York, ON: York University, 1965.

Ross, Murray G. *Those Ten Years 1960–70: The President's Report on the First Ten Years of York University*. North York, ON: York University, 1970.

Royce, Diana M. "University System Coordination and Planning in Ontario 1945 to 1996." PhD diss., University of Toronto, Ontario Institute for Studies in Education, 1998. Available online at http://www.collectionscanada.gc.ca/obj/s4/f2/dsk2/ftp02/NQ35418.pdf.

Sandberg, L. Anders. "Vari Hall: A public or private space?" *Alternative Campus Tour*. Available online at http://alternativecampustoiur.info.yorku.ca/sites/vari-hall, accessed 18 June 2014.

Saywell, John. *Someone to Teach Them: York and the Great University Explosion, 1960–1973*. Toronto: University of Toronto Press, 2008.

Sloper, D.W. "The Work Patterns of Australian Vice-Chancellors." *Higher Education* 31, no. 2 (1996): 205–31.

Spence, Edward. "The Spadina Subway Extension through York University: Reflections on the Struggle for Approvals." *Contour Lines* (York Geography Alumni Association), March 2013.

Spence, Edward, and Robert Everett. *Glendon College & Academic Planning: The Context for a Consideration of Options*, Background Report Submitted to the Academic Policy and Planning Committee of Senate. Toronto: York University, 1999.

Stenton, J. Paul. "The Ontario University Operating Grants Formula: Its Development to 1986." PhD diss., University of Toronto, 1992.

Tamburri, Rosanna. "The Evolving Role of President Takes Its Toll." *University Affairs*, 12 February 2007. Available online at http://www.universityaffairs.ca/news/news-article/the-evolving-role-of-president-takes-its-toll/.

Teiman, Gillian. *Idealism and Accommodation: A History of Human Rights and Employment Equity at York University, 1959–2005*. Toronto: York University, 2007.

Tennyson, Alfred Lord. "Ulysses." In *An Anthology of Verse*, ed. Roberta A. Charlesworth and Dennis Lee. Toronto: Oxford University Press, 1964.

Veysey, Laurence R. *The Emergence of the American University*. Chicago: University of Chicago Press, 1965.

Wickens, Christine W. "The Organizational Impact of University Labor Unions." *Higher Education* 56, no. 5 (2008): 545–64.

York University. *Fact Book, 2012–13*. Toronto: York University, 2013.

York University. *York's Appeal to OCUA and MCU concerning Advisory Memorandum 86-VII, Modifications in the Operating Grants Formula*. North York, ON: York University, 30 March 1987.

York University. Department of Campus Planning. "York University Campus – 1980." In University Planners, Architects and Consulting Engineers, *Master Plan for the York University Campus*. Toronto: UPACE, 1963.

York University. Management Information Infomart. "York University Factbook: York University's Enrolment History as of November 1st 1960 through 2012." Toronto: York University, Office of Institutional Planning and Analysis, 2013. Available online at http://www.yorku.ca/factbook/factbook/index.php?year=2012%20-%202013.

York University. Office of the President. *Impact: President's Impact Report, 2014.* Toronto: York University, 2015. Available online at http://president.yorku. ca/2015/04/annualreport2014/, accessed 24 June 2015.

York University. President's Task Force on Community Engagement. "Towards an Engaged University: Final Report and Recommendations." Toronto: York University, 5 February 2010. Available online at http://www.yorku.ca/commeng/documents/ finalreport.pdf.

York University. Task Force on the Colleges. "Strengthening York's Neighbourhoods." Toronto: York University, November 2006. Available online at http://www.yorku.ca/ vpstdnts/pdfs/TFOC_execsummary.pdf, accessed 18 June 2014.

York University. University Secretariat. "Doing Less Better: The Context of 1995 Academic Planning." Report to the Community from the Academic Policy and Planning Committee. North York, ON: York University, 20 July 1995.

Zinni, Deborah, Parbudyal Singh, and Anne F. MacLennan. "An Exploratory Study of Graduate Student Unions in Canada." *Industrial Relations* 60, no. 1 (2005): 145–76.

Index

Note: Page numbers indicating photographs are in **bold**. Those indicating charts or tables are in *italic*.